THE WOMEN'S REVOLUTION

THE WOMEN'S REVOLUTION

How We Changed Your Life

MURIEL FOX

New Village Press • New York

Published in the United States by New Village Press
bookorders@newvillagepress.net
www.newvillagepress.org
New Village Press is a public-benefit, nonprofit publisher
Distributed by NYU Press

Paperback ISBN 978-1-61332-243-7
Hardcover ISBN 978-1-61332-244-4
eBook Trade ISBN 978-1-61332-245-1
eBook Institutional ISBN 978-1-61332-246-8

Library of Congress Control Number: 2024931342

Dedicated to My Dear Family
And to the Hundreds of Thousands of Feminists
Who Fought to Make Our Revolution Successful

CONTENTS

INTRODUCTION

THIS BOOK IS ABOUT THE PEOPLE who changed women's lives. Everywhere. Forever. History should not forget their achievements.

"That's how it's always been." Women heard those words for thousands of years, as the excuse for all the injustices that oppressed and humiliated and ridiculed us. How did we finally overturn the tyranny of those five words?

The feminist fight for women's freedom has advanced intersectionally well beyond the revolution we started in 1966, but we should not forget how very much the lives of women needed to change at the beginning. And what we did to make it happen. I hope you'll find this story engrossing. Better still, I hope you'll be inspired to create additional chapters in years ahead.

I believe this book is different from others about modern feminism. It focuses on the *people* in my side of the movement, which addressed specific laws and injustices. We called our organization NOW, the National Organization for Women. Our movement is known as the Second Wave, building on the struggle of first-wave suffragists who finally won women the right to vote.

Academics and journalists have written dispassionately about our feminist achievements. Here, I'm writing passionately about my personal recollections. We'll look at feminist leaders who must be remembered.

I'll concentrate on twenty-nine women (and one man) you may not know about. Most of them have received little or no recognition in history books.

Many quotations you'll read here come from my personal recollection. (People often remarked on my retentive memory.) Many facts are based on my feminism files. The files contain hundreds of letters, clippings, and pieces of paper with information about our revolution. Through the years, numerous writers have visited those files and made notes for books and articles. I wasn't planning to write a reportorial book of my own. I sent my early papers to the Schlesinger Library of the Radcliffe Institute, Harvard University, where they are archived under "Papers of NOW officer Muriel Fox, 1966–1971."

I filled five file drawers in my home with materials retained for sentimental reasons, or for reference in my speeches and feminist activities. Pieces of paper reveal brief facts I'd gathered, such as "Catherine East chose and invited most of guests for BF hotel room."

Because this book has relied so much on those informal sources, it contains fewer than 120 references to secondary documents—far fewer citations than you'd find in books by academics. Although I don't provide a host of scholarly references, I hope readers will learn lots of feminist history through my inside information from primary sources.

In the following pages I'll confess to the times when we messed up and treated one another horribly. But despite our foul-ups, we "changed the world." That was the expression we always used. We transformed hiring practices. And language. And the image of what it means to be a woman. And jokes in the media. And women's health care. If an injustice made your grandmother furious, we probably fought to change it.

Why do I, Muriel Fox, deserve to tell this story? I was there when it began, and I remain involved in actions that are still, alas, urgently necessary.

Our movement taught women not to be modest, so here are my credentials for telling this story: As a cofounder of NOW in 1966, I was the communications specialist who helped make the second-wave revolution visible and successful. As lieutenant to Betty Friedan, the mother of our movement, I helped to implement her vision. (This book presents new information on that maddening, astounding woman.) As national chair of NOW at a crucial time, I prevented warring factions from tearing the movement apart. Until they did. As cofounder and president of the NOW Legal Defense and Education Fund, I helped to empower Title IX for education equality, and the Violence Against Women Act for women's personal safety.

Following through on our fight against employment discrimination, I helped feminists build a new bridge to the business world. Thanks to feminist encouragement, employers began to do the right thing for women because they finally realized it was good for business.

There's a chapter here on my own adventures, but this book really belongs to all the women and men who made our revolution possible. And to *you*, whom we urgently need to carry on our work.

1

UNTIL THE REVOLUTION

I JOINED THE WOMEN'S MOVEMENT because I kept thinking about my mother, Anna Rubenstein Fox. Anna's life was a failure. She grew up in New York City in the early twentieth century. Although she earned top grades in school, her parents made her drop out at the age of fourteen to work in the family grocery store. Her younger brother was supported through a law school education and became one of America's most influential jurists. Once, when I brought home a good report card, my tactless aunt remarked, "She takes after her uncle." This compounded my mother's sense that her own intelligence was irrelevant.

My mother hated housekeeping and cooking and was terrible at it. She also resented having to care for her two children. She was stuck in the wrong job. Growing up, I resolved that my life would be different. Later, I was able to help other women seize control of their lives. I was in the right place at the right time for our Women's Revolution.

Today I'm distressed when critics call the early work of our movement "bourgeois" and "conservative" because we did not address the complete list of intersectional problems that still need attention today. In 1966 and the years that followed, we did not accomplish 100 percent of women's needs. But what we did accomplish was a real, earthshaking revolution. Although women have not achieved NOW's goal of "*equal* partnership" with men, we're partners. Not just possessions. Or outsiders.

What was it like in the old days? We were barred from most good jobs, and the ads specified "Help Wanted Male" and "Help Wanted Female." Women couldn't have credit cards or mortgages in their own name. It was legal to say "We don't admit women" in order to exclude women from jobs and labor unions and law schools and medical schools and business schools and restaurants and certain airline flights. We earned fifty-nine cents for every dollar earned by men. Hardly any organizations, or governments, promoted any women to positions of authority. Some states gave longer prison sentences to women because they "took longer to rehabilitate." Husbands could beat or rape their wives with little fear of police action. And many frustrated women like my mother ended up with serious mental illness.

How did the feminist movement change all that? In your lifetime (or the lifetime of parents and grandparents), we helped half of the world's population achieve a new destiny, a new reason for living. Before our time, for many thousands of years, males held overpowering mastery over females. They expected us to dedicate our lives primarily to bearing and raising new offspring, and to find meaning and satisfaction from doing this. My mother and I, and millions of women like us, were unhappy with that destiny. We wanted to be valued as human beings, not as the second-class other half of Earth's population.

Today our world is governed by new beliefs and practices that women never dared to imagine in previous centuries. We've changed our name from mankind to humankind. In most countries, we've completely transformed the long-standing contract between men and women. Women have begun to participate in the full range of human experiences.

As a result of our revolution, human beings have been raising new questions about what is meant by concepts of "man" or "woman." The gap between those identities continues to grow smaller and smaller, with varying degrees of fluidity in between. Age-old definitions are evolving—radically.

Before 1966, the old system did not change after Aristotle described it in 350 B.C.E. In *Politics* he announced, "Between the sexes, the male is by nature superior and the female inferior, the male ruler and the female subject." William Blackstone, who laid out the legal system for England and the United States, wrote in 1765: "the very being or legal existence of the woman is suspended during the marriage, or at least is incorporated . . . into that of the husband." (Blackstone 1765, pp. 93–98) In my mother's lifetime, women were discouraged from asserting themselves (a practice called "penis envy") by followers of Sigmund Freud, whose granddaughter said he believed that "women were secondary and were not the norm." (Roberts 2022) In the late twentieth century, our Women's Revolution rejected the doctrines of Aristotle, Blackstone, and Freud. Treat women like human beings!

Our revolution comprised millions of small battles and dozens of large ones. We're still very, very far from complete victory. Many women are still left behind. But amazing progress has been made.

First, of course, we had to help women believe it might be possible— and urgently desirable—to change their lives. Then, we needed a strong national organization to represent us in demands that powerful men could not ignore. We needed generals and lieutenants and millions of foot soldiers. We needed heroes. We needed Consciousness Raising, which made women eager for change.

To pave the way for our revolution, we thanked the courageous suffragists who won women the vote. And educators who prepared women for new lives. And the admission of female workers into nontraditional occupations, a trend that accelerated during World War II. And most especially, the long-overdue civil rights movement, which fought for equality for *all* human beings. And the Pill (God bless it), approved by the Food and Drug Administration in 1960. All made a crucial difference.

But change was still slow. Despite some progress after women won the vote in 1920, mankind was still saying, with no legal restrictions: "We don't hire women." "We don't rent to women." "We don't admit women," "We don't give credit cards to women." "Men are the head of the household." "Women don't have the mind for that." "We're excluding women for their own protection." "We're excluding women because they interfere with how we do things." "We won't promote her because women can't be bosses." "We won't promote her because she's bossy and unfeminine." "We hired a woman once, and it didn't work out." "Women are too emotional to handle that." "A woman would be taking a man's place in that job [or school or business or union seniority list]." Every day of our lives, women and girls were reminded of our second-class existence.

I maintain that today's new era for women and men began on October 29, 1966, when we founded the National Organization for Women (NOW). After that date, the wheels of progress began to turn everywhere. Though they've slowed down in recent years, they're still turning, and far faster than we'd expected. Our revolution in the United States started a movement for "women's rights" throughout the world, all the way from Abu Dhabi to Zambia, from bedrooms to boardrooms. Roles and behaviors evolved rapidly. We began to insist, once and for all, that female human beings would never again be the subsidiaries of males.

I was privileged to play a role in this revolution. I'll share with you, truthfully, the good and bad things we did. At our founding conference of NOW, we knew we were "changing the world" forever. (To the best of my knowledge, only two of us who were active in that conference are alive today.)

Today we bemoan our losses in abortion protection, the Equal Rights Amendment, universal child care, and electoral politics. But our world will never be the same as it was before October 29, 1966.

If our revolution began with the founding of NOW, it was previewed three years earlier, in 1963, when Betty Friedan published her eye-opening book *The Feminine Mystique*. Millions—yes, millions—of women throughout the world said it changed their lives. Betty Friedan taught them to challenge the millennia-old premise that a woman exists primarily to raise offspring and to support her male mate while he runs the world. That old tenet was frustrating and unsatisfying for many women, especially those with an extensive education. Many women thought their personal frustration was their own personal problem, not recognizing it as an ailment of society.

Betty Friedan implored the world to make fuller use of women's talents and energies. She urged women and men to join together as

"Congratulations. You just spent twelve thousand dollars so she could join the
typing pool." This caption headed NOW LDEF ads that concluded with the
slogan "WOMANPOWER. It's much too good to waste."

"equal partners" to overcome sex discrimination in all phases of society. The U.S. civil rights movement, targeting racial discrimination, was
gaining momentum. Women began to wonder, less and less politely,
Shouldn't it be our time, too?

A number of us had succeeded in overcoming some of the barriers.
We managed to attain fairly good jobs, somewhere in the middle of
the system. But we still faced obstacles. Other women, like my mother,
were left behind. My mother's life was a failure because the feminist
movement arrived too late to rescue her.

THE STORY OF A PREVIOUS WOMAN

My mother's story was atypical because she had severe psychological
problems. Let's look at the life of a woman who had all the privileges

that would allow for success (white, middle-class, educated, able-bodied, etc.) except for her gender. We'll call her P.W., or Previous Woman.

It's the year 1956. With the help of her parents, student loans, and after-school jobs, she graduates cum laude from a good university. She'd never felt confident with math or science subjects, but she's a good writer.

Before graduation, she studies the employment ads. She dares to apply for jobs listed under "Help Wanted Male," though she feels like an impostor. No employers reply to her carefully crafted résumé.

Finally, she hears from one company's personnel director. (The term *Human Resources director* has not yet emerged.) He advises her that her education failed to include two necessary subjects—typing and shorthand. She needs to start out as a secretary. Would this lead to better jobs in the future? Well, we'll see.

P.W. spends the summer taking a commercial course in secretarial skills. In September, she's hired as a secretary in a large corporation.

Her boss is just a few years older than she is. He takes it for granted that she'll bring him coffee from the office kitchen every morning. It's annoying when he refers to her as "my girl," as in "I'll tell my girl to send you two copies." He occasionally assigns her a personal errand, such as ordering baseball tickets or buying a birthday gift for his wife or picking up a jacket from the dry cleaner.

Two years later, her boss is promoted. There's no formal job-posting process, but she applies to the Personnel Department for her boss's position. She updates her résumé to include her varied experience in the department. Nothing happens. A week later, she learns that a young man recently graduated from college has been hired as her new boss. She's asked to train him for the job. In the years that follow, she trains other young men to be her boss.

Two bosses make passes at her. They seem surprised when she says, "No, please." She worries that they might punish her. Men in the office sometimes comment about the body parts of other secretaries. None of the comments is as rude as the widely quoted true story of a vice president in the NBC publicity department at 30 Rockefeller Plaza. He proclaimed loudly to his department's twelve-woman secretarial pool: "You've been taking too much time for lunch. Long lunch hours are no longer allowed here. By two P.M. I want to see twenty-four tits at those typewriters." That executive was not disciplined for that remark.

P.W. cannot obtain a credit card. Banks explain that they don't extend credit to single women. "Just wait until you're married." She finds a nice apartment, after numerous tries. Several landlords had explained, knowing she'd understand: "We don't rent to unaccompanied women."

She notices that several men are less articulate when they return from a "three-martini lunch." This happens often. The men like to gather at a local bar after work. Women almost never join them. The bar might refuse to serve women unless they're accompanied by a man. Certain restaurants refuse them even if no drinks are involved.

By the age of twenty-six, P.W. begins to feel like an undesirable old maid. She meets and dates a pleasant man, and they get married. After some discussion, he agrees to "let his wife work" until children arrive. When their daughter is born, she dutifully quits work. The bank grants her a second credit card, in her husband's name. If she uses the card to buy a new dress, he joins his friends in jokes about their wives spending their money.

He spends two nights a week bowling and/or drinking with friends. If he's had too much to drink, and she doesn't respond warmly to his amorous advances, he occasionally slaps her. He apologizes the next morning. He does not apologize for the times he raped her against her will—that's a husband's legal prerogative. Their marriage doesn't work out. They try couple therapy, but it doesn't succeed.

They agree to a fairly amicable divorce. The bank cancels her credit card. He hires an expensive lawyer, who threatens her with a child custody battle. To avoid this risk, she agrees to settle for modest child support and no alimony. Some months he pays the child support, but some months he doesn't. As for custody visits, that isn't a problem. Her concern is how to cajole him to visit their daughter more often.

P.W.'s former employer takes her back as a secretary. In the late spring of 1967, she learns about a local chapter of the new National

Organization for Women. She joins immediately, and volunteers to work on the chapter's Employment Committee. Several members of the committee, like her, are dissatisfied secretaries with college degrees.

NOW's arrival doesn't transform her employment world overnight. But at least, beginning in early 1969, she can seek a new job advertised in a column labeled "Help Wanted Male and Female." Her longtime employer would never hire a former secretary for a staff position, so she switches to a smaller firm that welcomes her experience. After the Equal Credit Opportunity Act has been passed, in 1974, she has no trouble opening credit accounts at several stores.

She'll never feel comfortable trying to ask for a promotion, a higher salary, or better benefits. Her daughter, when she grows up, will be more assertive. Her daughter will know how to file a complaint if a man makes an unwanted pass.

Thanks to reading a book by Sheila Tobias called *Overcoming Math Anxiety,* P.W. gains confidence and skill in managing her family finances. Why had she considered math so difficult?

Life has changed for women in so many ways!

WHO DID IT?

Who are the people to thank for this revolution? Okay, young students and established business executives, here's a question: What do you know about Mary Eastwood, Catherine East, Ann Scott, or Holly Knox? Little or nothing? I'll do my best to change that. I aim to show why our Women's Revolution is crucial to history—and to all people's lives. Our feminist heroes should be as widely celebrated as Patrick Henry, Paul Revere, and Betsy Ross.

As you read the inside story of our revolution, I hope you'll feel special appreciation for the thirty people who played transformative roles in making it happen. With a few exceptions, our champions are not as well known as they deserve to be. They follow in the footsteps of Susan B. Anthony, Elizabeth Cady Stanton, and other leaders of the first wave—most of whom did not live long enough to see women win the vote in 1920.

My list begins, of course, with Betty Friedan, who belongs in a feminist Valhalla all by herself. Then, please remember Bella Abzug, Kathy Bonk, Heather Booth, Kay Clarenbach, Mary Jean Collins, Catherine East, Mary Eastwood, Muriel Fox, Ruth Bader Ginsburg, Edith Green, Martha Griffiths, Dorothy Haener, Aileen Hernandez, Shere Hite, Phineas Indritz, Holly Knox, Barbara Love, Kate Millett, Pauli Murray, Alice Paul, Marguerite Rawalt, Pat Reuss, Sylvia Roberts, Bernice Sandler, Ann Scott, Barbara Seaman, Eleanor Smeal, Tish Sommers, Gloria Steinem. When you see their stories in this book, please join me in saying a silent "Thank you." We'll mention other influential activists in the chapters ahead, but I consider those thirty the *most* influential.

Let's express gratitude to all the other women and men whose labors made it happen *so quickly*. Betty Friedan had envisioned "an elite cadre" of professionals who'd work as a small team to transform public opinion and get the necessary laws passed and enforced. Instead, our little revolution exploded almost overnight into a mass movement. Each one of our fighters attacked the specific injustices that made her (him) especially angry. We met in one another's apartments and in church basements. We trespassed impolitely into stockholder meetings and academic conferences, into government hearings where all the "experts" on female issues were men.

I serve as chair of Veteran Feminists of America (VFA), a group of Second Wave pioneers and supporters dedicated to documenting our history for the public. We try to inspire future generations to carry on our work. Through the University of Illinois Press, VFA has published a book called *Feminists Who Changed America 1963–1975*, edited by Barbara Love. I served as senior editor on the book. The book, which is available on Kindle, celebrates more than 2,200 women and men who made an important feminist difference in their community, their company, their school, their labor union, their religion, their profession, their art world, their sport, their social group, their country, and in their home and personal relationships—every entity that was treating women unfairly. Those 2,200 feminists were all leaders. All confronted the injustices of the patriarchy with their own special skills.

Chapter 18 of this book will discuss radical feminists (aka women's liberation, or by other names in various parts of the country). Fortunately, several of those women wrote about what they did to change public and private consciousness. They focused on helping society understand the power of the patriarchy. They vivisected male-female relationships, and reminded the world that "the personal is political." They originated the phenomenon of Consciousness Raising. They empowered the fight for abortion rights with true stories by women who'd undergone abortions.

Some radicals may question this book's lopsided emphasis on my sisters and brothers in NOW. All I can say is, *we did it all together.* My book emphasizes NOW more than other groups because I experienced NOW personally.

Frankly, I believe that NOW's law-centered actions created the most meaningful results. I believe we needed to change laws before we changed personal attitudes. A man needed to work alongside a woman in a factory, after Title VII had mandated her to be there, before he could realize she was a deserving coworker. Men having a "business lunch" needed to be joined by female executives, after the Human Rights Commission had forced restaurants to admit women, before they could feel comfortable in a coed social environment. This is the same logic used successfully by Black civil rights leaders who insisted, "We don't need to wait till we've changed hearts; let's change the laws first."

Without doubt, the driving force behind our revolution was Betty Friedan. I said this at Betty's funeral, in 2006: "First, she wrote the book that awakened the world to the need for change. Then she led the organization most responsible for winning that change. It's as if Harriet Beecher Stowe, following the publication of *Uncle Tom's Cabin,* then organized the forces of the abolition movement." I'll devote a full chapter to the life of Betty Friedan.

2

HOW IT STARTED

IN THE SAME YEAR as *The Feminine Mystique* was published, 1963, Congress passed the Equal Pay Act, which mandated equal pay for men and women performing equal work. (Executives and professionals were excluded.) Employers failed to take this law seriously. Why should they, when the government was not pressuring them to obey the regulations?

In 1964, when Congress was debating President Lyndon Johnson's Civil Rights bill, Congresswoman Martha Griffiths of Michigan spearheaded a group of feminists who proposed a groundbreaking addition to the bill's Title VII, outlawing job discrimination. They pressured Congress to prohibit discrimination based not only on "race, color, religion, and national origin" but also on sex. Representative Howard Smith of Virginia, chairman of the House Rules Committee, agreed to add the word *sex* to Title VII because as a southerner he hoped this one word would kill the entire Civil Rights bill. His introduction of the word in Congress was greeted with widespread laughter and assorted jokes. (I'm told that years later Smith told Griffiths, "Martha, I'll tell you the truth. I offered it as a joke.") Griffiths and other feminists, led by lawyer Marguerite Rawalt, lobbied aggressively to keep women in Title VII. The bill passed narrowly through Congress on July 2, 1964.

However, people in power considered the inclusion of sex in Title VII to be a trivial distraction from the important target of race discrimination. *The Washington Star* called inclusion of that three-letter word "a nuisance . . . and nonsensical outrage." *The New York Times* decried what they called "the Bunny Law."

The Equal Employment Opportunity Commission (EEOC), the federal agency mandated to enforce Title VII, refused to pay serious attention to complaints they received about sex discrimination. Franklin D. Roosevelt, Jr., chair of the EEOC, said publicly that efforts to enforce gender equality should proceed "gradually." EEOC executive director Herman Edelsberg called the inclusion of sex in Title VII "a fluke . . . conceived out of wedlock." (*Congressional Record—House*, June 20, 1966, p. 13689) An article in *The Wall Street Journal* predicted that the government would insist upon installing "a shapeless, knobby-kneed male 'bunny' serving drinks to a group of stunned businessmen in a Playboy Club." (*Wall Street Journal*, June 22, 1965)

Opposition at the EEOC wasn't limited to its top administrators. According to Sonia Pressman, the EEOC lawyer who surreptitiously provided material to NOW's Legal Committee, hardly any EEOC employees wanted to deal with sex discrimination, even though it engendered 37 percent of all complaints the first year. Sonny told me that EEOC employees "had all come there to do something about race discrimination in the United States. They didn't want the agency's resources, time, and money diverted in this sex discrimination thing." In EEOC's first five years, fifty thousand women filed complaints. Many were ignored completely. Feminists were furious. We needed an "NAACP for women."

BETTY'S LETTER

Since my name was on Betty Friedan's huge Rolodex, I received the following letter, dated August 31, 1966.

Dear Muriel,

Some of us have finally decided to do something about organizing a kind of N.A.A.C.P. for women, a Civil Rights for Women organization, as you will see from the enclosure.

> The idea, for the moment, is not to set up a big bureaucratic organization with lots of members, but rather to get together women and men who share our purpose, and who can work effectively to stimulate the action that is needed now on a number of problems. There is no organization that now exists to do this. One is very much needed if we are ever to change the stereotyped image of women in America, create some of the new social institutions that are needed, and break through the silken curtain of prejudice and discrimination that now exists.
>
> I am pretty sure you share my thinking on many of these questions, as do the others with whom I've been working to get it started. I hope that you will join right away, and send your $5.00 right in to Kay Clarenbach so that you may still be counted as a Charter Member. I hope also that you will attend the organizing meeting, to be held probably in Washington in late September, because it will be important to have your thinking as we formulate program policies, organizational structure, techniques of action, and elect officers.
>
> I hope to see you there.
>
> Sincerely,
> Betty

That form letter capped a yearlong courtship of Betty by Pauli Murray, Mary Eastwood, and Catherine East (you'll see those names here often). Betty responded, "I'm not an organizing type of person." No, she wasn't. But she had the talent to inspire *other* organizers. Here's how they finally stepped into action.

THE JUNE 30 SIGN-UPS

Presidents Kennedy and Johnson had established state commissions on the status of women. During the last week of June in 1966, the Third Annual Conference of the Commissions on the Status of Women met in the Washington Hilton hotel in D.C. Feminists failed to persuade the conference to adopt two resolutions. The first asked the EEOC to reappoint commissioner Richard Graham, an outspoken friend of sex equality, whose one-year term was expiring. The second called for the EEOC to outlaw advertising columns of "Help Wanted Male" and "Help Wanted Female," as violations of Title VII. Betty Friedan attended the conference as a journalist. Some fifteen to twenty angry women met in her hotel room on the final evening of the conference and resolved to start a militant organization for women if SCSW chair Esther Peterson continued to reject their two proposals. The next morning, June 30, Peterson refused to allow a vote on either resolution, insisting the SCSW was purely advisory and not permitted to consider resolutions. NOW was born that day at the final SCSW luncheon.

At one of two feminist tables near the front of the International Ballroom, Betty Friedan—in an act that is now legendary—wrote on a napkin "National Organization for Women, NOW . . . full equality for women, in fully equal partnership with men." After lunch, the women met for another hour to discuss details. They chipped in five dollars apiece for dues. Altogether, there were twenty-eight who signed up. NOW's records list them as Betty Friedan, Mary Eastwood, Kathryn Clarenbach, Caroline Davis, Dorothy Haener, Catherine Conroy, Pauli Murray, Gene Boyer, Inka O'Hanrahan, Anna Roosevelt Halsted (daughter of FDR and Eleanor Roosevelt), Caroline Ware, Aida Allness, Gretchen Squires, Nancy Knaak, Mary Evelyn Benbow, Lorene Harrington, Esther Johnson, Helen Moreland, Pauline Parish, Edna Schwartz, Betty Talkington, Analoyce Clapp, Edith Finlayson, Mary Lou Hill, Min Matheson, Ruth Murray, Eve Purvis and Mary-Jane Ryan Snyder. The first nine listed here became key leaders of the new organization.

Members were recruited over the summer. Like many recipients of Betty's form letter, I responded immediately. I forwarded membership applications to friends in American Women in Radio and Television (AWRT). Some colleagues, mid-level executives, turned me down. One replied, "There's no need for such an organization." (That woman later walked through the door that NOW had opened and became the first female manager of NBC's TV station in D.C.)

After my energetic response to her letter, Betty invited me to her apartment. She asked if I'd do the publicity to introduce our movement to the world. "I have a more-than-full-time job and two small children," I replied, "but I'll do what I can." In later speeches, Betty cited my response as typical of her recruits. "They say they'll help just a little bit, and they end up working for NOW like demons."

OUR FOUNDING CONFERENCE

Mary Eastwood made all arrangements for the founding conference of NOW to take place exactly four months after the June 30 luncheon, on the weekend of October 29 and 30, 1966. (It was Halloween weekend, but that's irrelevant.) We gathered in the basement of *The Washington Post*. The *Post* did not charge for nonprofits in its John Philip Sousa Community Room. Some thirty-two members met in Washington, D.C., and officially launched our movement. We represented some 350 women and men who had signed up since June 30.

The number of participants can't be given precisely because some people attended for only a few hours, and the roster included two men with differing stories. One was Bob Gray, husband of Patricia Perry. Pat was my co-employee in the worldwide public relations agency of Carl Byoir & Associates. She worked in our D.C. office and became an early member of NOW. Bob Gray sat next to me in our famous photograph of the occasion, but he never got involved in our movement. The other man was my husband, Dr. Shepard Aronson. Shep was an active NOW member and very much involved. Shep failed to participate in most of the conference because he was escorting our small son and daughter around Washington. He did not show up for the photograph.

I, too, was in and out as a participant. I set up a chair and a type-writer on a small metal table on the left side of the room and throughout the meeting worked on a press release to announce our new organization—feeling sorry for myself because I was too busy typing to do much speaking. I did lots of listening. Pat Perry had "liberated" (the word we used in those days for stealing employer materials for NOW) a batch of stencils from our D.C. office. I'd never typed a stencil before, but I carefully pecked out the press release for later mimeographing and distribution.

On the first day of the conference, we approved an inspiring "Statement of Purpose" written by Betty Friedan, with input from Murray, Eastwood, East, and several others, including me.

Pauli Murray, early on the first day, pointed to the unusual medallion she was wearing. "Do you see this medallion? It's a jail door with a lock and chain. In 1917 the great Alice Paul presented this to women who'd been jailed for picketing the White House for woman suffrage. It's up to all of us in this room to follow the lead of our courageous suffragist foremothers. This may take years of sacrifices, but we must not give up." (I learned later that Pauli had received the medallion from her suffragist friend Betsy Graves Reyneau.) (Rosenberg 2017, p. 131)

Alice Rossi, a University of Chicago sociology professor whom we elected to our board, recalled that exactly one hundred years earlier two British women had taken the first petition for woman suffrage to the British Parliament. To smuggle it inside, they hid it in the bottom of a cart of apples being delivered for the (male) members.

On the second day, Pauli presented us with a "Target for Action of Equal Rights and Responsibilities as Citizens." Her task force on government proposed abolition of ladies' auxiliaries in political parties, abolition of laws that kept women off most juries, and election of many more women to political office. We set up other task forces covering Employment, Education, New Image of Women, War for Women in Poverty, and Social Innovations for Equal Partnerships Between the Sexes.

Another speaker at the meeting was Sister Joel Read, then a history professor at Alverno College, a progressive women's college in Milwaukee. She'd somehow heard about our meeting, and walked in without an invitation. When we each stood up and introduced ourselves, Joel said, "I am Sister Joel Read of Alverno College in Wisconsin. I am one of fifty thousand American nuns. We are workingwomen, and we are oppressed!" (Three decades later, when Joel was president of the college, I spoke at a feminist reunion there. I mentioned her 1966 declaration. Joel smiled. "Did I really say 'oppressed'? Well, we're still oppressed.")

Betty Friedan, pleased with the optics possibilities of a nun in full habit, appointed Joel to NOW's first board of directors. At Joel's suggestion, we also added psychologist Sister Austin Doherty to our board. Both nuns abandoned their photogenic habits a year later. Austin once urged me to stop describing NOW as a "militant" organization because the word sounded too warlike.

Anna Roosevelt Halsted, who'd signed up for NOW at the June 30 luncheon, also signed our register for the October 29 meeting. I don't recall her ever speaking out, even when speakers criticized her brother, FDR, Jr., chair of the EEOC.

In a letter Betty later wrote to charter members, she recollected: "We wasted no time on ceremonials or speeches, gave ourselves barely an hour for lunch and dinner . . . kept going until we had to vacate our meeting room . . . met in Task Forces over breakfast . . . At times we got very tired and impatient, but there was always a sense that what we were deciding was not just for now but for a century."

At Pat Perry's recommendation, I'd hired photographer Vincent Graas to take pictures of the meeting. I still have his contact sheets. His historic October 30 group photograph of founding members appears frequently in publications around the world. We're sitting with legs primly together, some of us wearing hats and nobody wearing

Founding Conference of NOW, October 29, 1966
Photographer Vincent Graas, courtesy of the photographer

slacks. Those in the photo are listed as Inez Casiano, of New York; Clara Wells, of New York; Inka O'Hanrahan, of California; Alice Rossi, of Chicago; Lucille Kapplinger, of Michigan; Ruth Gober, of Wisconsin; Caruthers Berger, of Washington, D. C.; Sonia Pressman, of Washington, D.C.; Amy Robinson, of Indiana; Betty Friedan, of New York; Morag Simchak, of Washington, D.C.; Mary Esther Gaulden, of Texas; Pauli Murray, of Washington, D.C.; Mary Eastwood of Washington, D.C.; Caroline Ware, of Virginia; Sister Joel Read, of Wisconsin; Dorothy Haener, of Detroit; Anna Arnold Hedgeman, of New York; Bob Gray, of Washington, D.C.; Muriel Fox, of New York; Patricia Perry, of Washington, D.C.; Colleen Boland, of Chicago; and Charlotte Roe, of New York.

On Pauli Murray's urging, many of the small-group photos I set up with Vince Graas featured a prominent civil rights leader, Anna Arnold Hedgeman of the Commission on Religion and Race of the National Council of Churches. I also included Inez Casiano, an attractive Latina from the U.S. Department of Labor, an advocate for Puerto Rican rights.

I phoned Vince Graas in the early 1980s. He was no longer working. Pleased that his founding photo had achieved worldwide fame, he gave me permission to use his photographs.

When our meeting ended, shortly after 1:00 P.M. on Sunday, October 30, Mary Eastwood helped me get the press release mimeographed. With the stencils gingerly cradled in my arms, we took a taxi to the Senate Office Building and the suite of Senator William Proxmire of Wisconsin. Mary had made an arrangement with one of Proxmire's secretaries, but we couldn't get the mimeograph machine to work. Luckily, Mary had also contacted the office of Senator Philip Hart of Michigan. His wife, Janey, was a member of our board. We mimeographed my five-page release on Senator Hart's machine. Then Mary and I delivered it to D.C. news outlets, using a press list from Pat Perry. I took taxis, and Mary borrowed Pauli Murray's Volkswagen.

The press release appears in the appendix at the end of this book. It began: "More than 300 men and women have formed a new action organization called National Organization for Women (NOW), to work for 'true equality for all women in America' and 'a fully equal partnership of the sexes, as part of the world-wide revolution of human rights.'"

Some history books say my release was ignored by the press. Betty Friedan's biographer Rachel Shteir claimed "the media did not take NOW seriously." (Shteir 2023, p. 115) But this is far from the truth. Newspapers throughout the country displayed the story prominently. Some reprinted, often word for word, the article written by Joy Miller of the Associated Press. My scrapbook includes the AP story, with big headlines, in the *New York Post, Philadelphia Bulletin, Baltimore Sun, Washington Star, Minneapolis Star, Miami Herald, Oakland Tribune,* and numerous other papers. (We could not afford a clipping service, and I relied on NOW members to send me clippings.) *The Washington Post* carried its own story. *The Milwaukee Journal* ran two lengthy features. AP Wirephoto ran a picture of Richard Graham.

Betty Friedan had recruited twenty-one prominent women and five men for our board of directors, including Richard Graham, former director of the National Teacher Corps, as vice president. (The EEOC had not reappointed him as commissioner because they considered him overly attentive to sex discrimination.) Former union leader Aileen Hernandez had resigned from her post as EEOC commissioner, but her resignation would not become effective until November 10. Therefore, we named Anna Arnold Hedgeman as temporary acting executive vice president. Aileen would step into this position after her EEOC term ended.

We maintained the fiction that our secretary-treasurer was Caroline Davis, director of the Women's Department of the United Auto Workers. In truth, Caroline was seriously ill; all her tasks were performed by her capable assistant, Dorothy Haener. I never did meet Caroline. With approval of UAW president Walter Reuther, one of America's most enlightened union leaders, the UAW was responsible for all of NOW's mailings, finances, registrations, and literature in our first year of existence. Dorothy Haener managed it all.

The early operations of NOW were divided among three locations: Detroit for clerical work, D.C. for actions related to the U.S. government, and New York for the organizing work led by Betty and me. In addition, Kay Clarenbach spearheaded activities in the Midwest out of her office in Madison, Wisconsin.

Other recruits for our first board of directors included professor Carl Degler, chairman of the Department of History at Vassar College; CBS network commentator Betty Furness; and Dean Lewis, official of the United Presbyterian Church in the U.S.A. My press release mentioned that board member Jane Hart, wife of Senator Philip Hart, was a professional pilot who campaigned for admitting women into the NASA astronauts program and was the mother of eight children. (To make it clear that we supported families, I mentioned children often in press releases.)

Altogether, the board comprising Betty's "elite cadre" of professionals included seven university professors or administrators, five labor union officials, four government officials, four business executives (including me), two nuns, and one doctor. Seven held Ph.Ds. The five union officials could also be categorized as working-class women.

On the morning of the second day, we received a visit from Colleen Boland, head of the Air Line Stewards and Stewardesses Association. Colleen asked for support against airline requirements that women must retire at age thirty-two or thirty-five (depending on the airline) or when they married. The NOW board immediately passed a resolution condemning the airline policy as a violation of Title VII. We added Colleen to our board of directors.

WE MEET THE PRESS

A month later, we held our first board meeting, Sunday, November 20, in Betty Friedan's dramatically decorated "Victorian parlor" in the legendary Dakota building at 1 West Seventy-second Street, Manhattan (John Lennon would be assassinated there in 1980. Incidentally, John and Yoko Ono both joined NOW.) I arranged our first NOW press conference for Monday morning at 10:30 A.M.

My invitation to the press appears in this book's appendix. It began: "Through the years I've used a lot of adjectives to describe press conferences, but this is the first time I'd presume to use the word 'historic.'" My last sentence: "We hope you'll have reason to tell your grandchildren one day, 'Yes, I was there when it all started.'" The result was a good turnout of reporters and TV cameras.

That morning I was so excited that in parking my car on Central Park West, I left my key in the ignition. When I returned afterward, the car was gone. My husband, Shep, contacted the police. The car showed up the following morning, unharmed, in Brooklyn. Probably someone had stolen it for a joyride.

The New York Times had disappointed us by not carrying my announcement of NOW's founding conference. I wrote to the *Times* managing editor, Clifton Daniel, who was married to Harry Truman's daughter, Margaret. She was a patient of Shep's. My letter to Daniel said, "If a story hasn't appeared in the New York Times, it isn't really news yet." Daniel responded by assigning a top reporter, Lisa Hammel, to interview Betty Friedan. Hammel wrote a long, informative article about the birth of the modern women's movement. It appeared on the *Times* women's page on November 22, above a story on "How to Carve Your Thanksgiving Turkey."

In NOW's first decade, we persuaded newspapers to abolish their separate women's sections. Women, we insisted, should be covered as news throughout the paper. Be careful what you wish for. That victory worked against us. Many women's page writers lost their jobs. The lucky ones were reassigned to news sections. Much of our most knowledge-able coverage had appeared on women's pages, written by outstanding journalists like Lisa Hammel or the world-class Enid Nemy. We received less press coverage after news editors (predominantly male) became the ones to decide whether or not our feminist stories were newsworthy.

The National Organization for Women's 1966 Statement of Purpose

We, men and women who hereby constitute ourselves as the National Organization for Women, believe that the time has come for a new movement toward true equality for all women in America, and toward a fully equal partnership of the sexes, as part of the world-wide revolution of human rights now taking place within and beyond our national borders.

The purpose of NOW is to take action to bring women into full participation in the mainstream of American society now, exercising all the privileges and responsibilities thereof in truly equal partnership with men.

We believe the time has come to move beyond the abstract argument, discussion and symposia over the status and special nature of women which has raged in America in recent years; the time has come to confront, with concrete action, the conditions that now prevent women from enjoying the equality of opportunity and freedom of choice which is their right, as individual Americans, and as human beings.

NOW is dedicated to the proposition that women, first and foremost, are human beings, who, like all other people in our society, must have the chance to develop their fullest human potential. We believe that women can achieve such equality only by accepting to the full the challenges and responsibilities they share with all other people in our society, as part of the decision-making mainstream of American political, economic and social life.

We organize to initiate or support action, nationally, or in any part of this nation, by individuals or organizations, to break through the silken curtain of prejudice and discrimination against women in government, industry, the professions, the churches, the political parties, the judiciary, the labor unions, in education, science, medicine, law, religion and every other field of importance in American society.

Enormous changes taking place in our society make it both possible and urgently necessary to advance the unfinished revolution of women toward true equality, now. With a life span lengthened to nearly 75 years it is no longer either necessary or possible for women to devote the greater part of their lives to child- rearing; yet childbearing and rearing which continues to be a most important part of most women's lives—still is used to justify barring women from equal professional and economic participation and advance.

Today's technology has reduced most of the productive chores which women once performed in the home and in mass-production industries based upon routine unskilled labor. This same technology has virtually eliminated the quality of muscular strength as a criterion for filling most jobs, while intensifying American industry's need for creative intelligence. In view of this new industrial revolution created by automation in the mid-twentieth century, women can and must participate in old and new fields of society in full equality—or become permanent outsiders.

Despite all the talk about the status of American women in recent years, the actual position of women in the United States has declined, and is declining, to an alarming degree throughout the 1950's and 60's. Although 46.4% of all American women between the ages of 18 and 65 now work outside the home, the overwhelming majority— 75%—are in routine clerical, sales, or factory jobs, or they are household workers, cleaning women, hospital attendants. About two-thirds of Negro women workers are in the lowest paid service occupations. Working women are becoming increasingly—not less—concentrated on the bottom of the job ladder. As a consequence, full-time women workers today earn on the average only 60% of what men earn, and that wage gap has been increasing over the past twenty-five years in every major industry group. In 1964, of all women with a yearly income, 89% earned under $5,000 a year; half of all full-time year round women workers earned less than $3,690; only 1.4% of full-time year round women workers had an annual income of $10,000 or more.

Further, with higher education increasingly essential in today's society, too few women are entering and finishing college or going on to graduate or professional school. Today, women earn only one in three of the B.A.'s and M.A.'s granted, and one in ten of the Ph.D.'s.

In all the professions considered of importance to society, and in the executive ranks of industry and government, women are losing ground. Where they are present it is only a token handful. Women comprise less than 1% of federal judges; less than 4% of all lawyers; 7% of doctors. Yet women represent 51% of the U.S. population. And, increasingly, men are replacing women in the top positions in secondary and elementary schools, in social work, and in libraries—once thought to be women's fields.

Official pronouncements of the advance in the status of women hide not only the reality of this dangerous decline, but the fact that nothing is being done to stop it. The excellent reports of the President's Commission on the Status of Women and of the State Commissions have not been fully implemented. Such Commissions have power only to advise. They have no power to enforce their recommendation; nor have they the freedom to organize American women and men to press for action on them. The reports of these commissions have, however, created a basis upon which it is now possible to build. Discrimination in employment on the basis of sex is now prohibited by federal law, in Title VII of the Civil Rights Act of 1964. But although nearly one-third of the cases brought before the Equal Employment Opportunity Commission during the first year dealt with sex discrimination and the proportion is increasing dramatically, the Commission has not made clear its intention to enforce the law with the same seriousness on behalf of women as of other victims of discrimination. Many of these cases were Negro women, who are the victims of double discrimination of race and sex. Until now, too few women's organizations and official spokesmen have been willing to speak out against these dangers facing women. Too many women have been restrained by the fear of being called "feminist." There is no civil rights movement to speak for women, as there has been for Negroes and other victims of discrimination. The National Organization for Women must therefore begin to speak.

WE BELIEVE that the power of American law, and the protection guaranteed by the U.S. Constitution to the civil rights of all individuals, must be effectively applied and enforced to isolate and remove patterns of sex discrimination, to ensure equality of opportunity in employment and education, and equality of civil and political rights and responsibilities on behalf of women, as well as for Negroes and other deprived groups.

We realize that women's problems are linked to many broader questions of social justice; their solution will require concerted action by many groups. Therefore, convinced that human rights for all are indivisible, we expect to give active support to the common cause of equal rights for all those who suffer discrimination and deprivation, and we call upon other organizations committed to such goals to support our efforts toward equality for women.

WE DO NOT ACCEPT the token appointment of a few women to high-level positions in government and industry as a substitute for serious continuing effort to recruit and advance women according to their individual abilities. To this end, we urge American government and industry to mobilize the same resources of ingenuity and command with which they have solved problems of far greater difficulty than those now impeding the progress of women.

WE BELIEVE that this nation has a capacity at least as great as other nations, to innovate new social institutions which will enable women to enjoy the true equality of opportunity and responsibility in society, without conflict with their responsibilities as mothers and homemakers. In such innovations, America does not lead the Western world, but lags by decades behind many European countries. We do not accept the traditional assumption that a woman has to choose between marriage and motherhood, on the one hand, and serious participation in industry or the professions on the other. We question the present expectation that all normal women will retire from job or profession for 10 or 15 years, to devote their full time to raising children, only to reenter the job market at a relatively minor level. This, in itself, is a deterrent to the aspirations of women, to their acceptance into management or professional training courses, and to the very possibility of equality of opportunity or real choice, for all but a few women. Above all, we reject the assumption that these problems are the unique responsibility of each individual woman, rather than a basic social dilemma which society must solve. True equality of opportunity and freedom of choice for women requires such practical, and possible innovations as a nationwide network of child-care centers, which will make it unnecessary for women to retire completely from society until their children are grown, and national programs to provide retraining for women who have chosen to care for their children full-time.

WE BELIEVE that it is as essential for every girl to be educated to her full potential of human ability as it is for every boy—with the knowledge that such education is the key to effective participation in today's economy and that, for a girl as for a boy, education can only be serious where there is expectation that it will be used in society. We believe that American educators are capable of devising means of imparting such expectations to girl students. Moreover, we consider the decline in the proportion of women receiving higher and professional education to be evidence of discrimination. This discrimination may take the form of quotas against the admission of women to colleges, and professional schools; lack of encouragement by parents, counselors and educators; denial of loans or fellowships; or the traditional or arbitrary procedures in graduate and professional training geared in terms of men, which inadvertently discriminate against women. We believe that the same serious attention must be given to high school dropouts who are girls as to boys.

WE REJECT the current assumptions that a man must carry the sole burden of supporting himself, his wife, and family, and that a woman is automatically entitled to lifelong support by a man upon her marriage, or that marriage, home and family are primarily woman's world and responsibility—hers, to dominate—his to support. We believe that a true partnership between the sexes demands a different concept of marriage, an equitable sharing of the responsibilities of home and children and of the economic burdens of their support. We believe that proper recognition should be given to the economic and social value of homemaking and child-care. To these ends, we will seek to open a reexamination of laws and mores governing marriage and divorce, for we believe that the current state of "half-equity" between the sexes discriminates against both men and women, and is the cause of much unnecessary hostility between the sexes.

WE BELIEVE that women must now exercise their political rights and responsibilities as American citizens. They must refuse to be segregated on the basis of sex into separate-and-not-equal ladies'auxiliaries in the political parties, and they must demand representation according to their numbers in the regularly constituted party committees—at local, state, and national levels—and in the informal power structure, participating fully in the selection of candidates and political decision-making, and running for office themselves.

IN THE INTERESTS OF THE HUMAN DIGNITY OF WOMEN, we will protest, and endeavor to change, the false image of women now prevalent in the mass media, and in the texts, ceremonies, laws, and practices of our major social institutions. Such images perpetuate contempt for women by society and by women for themselves. We are similarly opposed to all policies and practices—in church, state, college, factory, or office—which, in the guise of protectiveness, not only deny opportunities but also foster in women self-denigration, dependence, and evasion of responsibility, undermine their confidence in their own abilities and foster contempt for women.

NOW WILL HOLD ITSELF INDEPENDENT OF ANY POLITICAL PARTY in order to mobilize the political power of all women and men intent on our goals. We will strive to ensure that no party, candidate, president, senator, governor, congressman, or any public official who betrays or ignores the principle of full equality between the sexes is elected or appointed to office. If it is necessary to mobilize the votes of men and women who believe in our cause, in order to win for women the final right to be fully free and equal human beings, we so commit ourselves.

WE BELIEVE THAT women will do most to create a new image of women by acting now, and by speaking out in behalf of their own equality, freedom, and human dignity—not in pleas for special privilege, nor in enmity toward men, who are also victims of the current, half-equality between the sexes—but in an active, self-respecting partnership with men. By so doing, women will develop confidence in their own ability to determine actively, in partnership with men, the conditions of their life, their choices, their future and their society.

3

FOUR GREAT LEADERS

PAULI MURRAY, CATHERINE EAST, MARY EASTWOOD, AND MARGUERITE RAWALT should appear in all histories as major founders of our movement, together with Betty Friedan. Our feminist revolution might not have happened without them.

Pauli Murray, a Black lawyer and educator, showed how and why to eradicate discrimination, with special attention to the needs of Black women. She brought NOW's first leaders together. Catherine East, a Labor Department insider devoted to women's issues, educated our movement on the facts of our oppression. She organized the gathering in Betty Friedan's hotel room in June 1966. Mary Eastwood, a Justice Department attorney, made arrangements for the official birth of our movement and its early actions. She facilitated NOW's early lawsuits. Marguerite Rawalt, Internal Revenue Service attorney and leader of influential women's organizations, headed NOW's Lawyers Committee. She helped make sex discrimination illegal in Title VII and guided NOW's lawsuits through the first decade.

PAULI MURRAY

Pauli Murray established the links between race and sex discrimination in the early battles of our revolution. She and Mary Eastwood published

Mary Eastwood (left) and Pauli Murray (right) with Jo Freeman (standing)
Photographer Jo Freeman, courtesy of the photographer

the groundbreaking essay, "Jane Crow and the Law," in *The George Washington Law Review* in December 1965, outlining ways to combat both forms of injustice. "We are entering the age of human rights," they declared. "Hopefully, our economy will outgrow concepts of class competition, such as Negro v. white, youth v. age, or male v. female, . . . and individual quality will control rather than prejudice." (Murray & Eastwood 1965, p. 256) Their recommendations, especially the use of the Equal Protection Clause of the Fourteenth Amendment, influenced dozens of lawsuits against sex discrimination. They set a foundation for the gender-equality cases won in the 1970s by Ruth Bader Ginsburg of the American Civil Liberties Union's Women's Rights Project. (Lithwick 2022, p. 4)

Pauli added the following words to Betty Friedan's original version of NOW's "Statement of Purpose": "We realize that women's problems are linked to many broader questions of social justice; their solution will require concerted action by many groups. Therefore, convinced that human rights for all are indivisible, we expect to give active support to the common cause of equal rights for all those who suffer discrimination and deprivation, and we call upon other organizations committed to such goals to support our efforts toward equality for women." Pauli was especially adamant about including the word *deprivation,* since most people in poverty are women.

Where does one start when describing Pauli Murray? She was a lawyer, educator, activist, poet, author, theologian. Her mixed-race ancestry included enslaved people, antislavery white Quakers, and Cherokee Indians. Her mother died when Pauli was three years old, and her father spent much of his life as a violent inmate of mental institutions.

Pauli endured what is now called gender dysphoria. Long before the days of the trans movement, Pauli privately called herself a "pseudo-hermaphrodite." Unsuccessfully, she kept begging doctors for hormone treatments that might transition her to malehood. She suffered from several nervous breakdowns. In February 1940, she was confined overnight to New York's Bellevue Hospital by a psychiatrist who posited, "Schizophrenia . . . suffers from the delusion that she's a man." (In the years I worked with Pauli, I had no idea of the ordeals she had suffered.) Pauli often declared she was not a lesbian, though she had two long relationships with "straight" women. She said she was playing the man's role, rather than a lesbian role.

Pauli's life is celebrated in an excellent 2017 book, *Jane Crow: The Life of Pauli Murray,* by Professor Rosalind Rosenberg. (Dr. Rosenberg's name will appear again later with regard to her testimony against NOW in the Sears lawsuit.) The book states, "Murray insisted to the end of her life that nontraditional gender identity and sexual orientation were private matters . . . She never joined the Daughters of Bilitis, worried with Betty Friedan that radical lesbians within NOW might destroy the nascent organization . . ." (Rosenberg 2017, p. 131)

Pauli compiled and edited a 746-page book in 1952 entitled *States' Laws on Race and Color*. Thurgood Marshall referred to this book as "the bible" in helping the NAACP win the landmark case of *Brown v. Board of Education* in 1954. (Lithwick 2022, p. 5) Pauli's book proposed that school segregation is illegal under the Equal Protection Clause of the Fourteenth Amendment.

In 1960, Pauli moved to the newly independent nation of Ghana as a senior lecturer in the Ghana School of Law. She became disillusioned with President Nkrumah's dictatorial ways, and returned to the United States less than two years later to practice civil rights law. Eleanor Roosevelt became her "mother surrogate." In 1962, Ms. Roosevelt sent Pauli a telegram inviting her to serve on Kennedy's Presidential Commission on the Status of Women (PCSW). For the PCSW, Pauli wrote a memo urging the government to combat sex discrimination by expanding the Equal Protection Clause of the Fourteenth Amendment to include gender as well as race.

Pauli worked behind the scenes for the famous March on Washington of August 28, 1963. But she objected that not a single woman was invited as a featured speaker in the three-hour program. (Singer Josephine Baker did make a brief appearance.) Martin Luther King, Jr.'s "I Have a Dream" speech made no mention of Black women.

In 1965, Pauli spoke out forcefully against Daniel Moynihan's famous (or infamous) report, which proposed a return to male-headed families and male-only job programs. Pauli reminded the public that Black women needed support as well as men. Moynihan's treatise claimed that female dominance was destroying Black families because it prevented Black men from strutting. "The very essence of the male animal, from the bantam rooster to the four-star general, is to strut." NOW was not yet born to contradict him. Betty Friedan has referred to this as "a special African American version of the feminine mystique, which held that black men were hurt by the excessive strength of black women." (Friedan 2000, p. 117)

When feminists were fighting to get sex discrimination included in Title VII of the Civil Rights Act of 1964, Pauli saved the day for us. Everett Dirksen and several other senators were pressing President Johnson to eliminate sex from Title VII. For a while, LBJ agreed with them. Then Pauli wrote a memorandum in support of retaining the sex amendment, explaining the parallels between racial and sexual justice. She said Title VII would help only half the Black workforce unless sex discrimination was outlawed. President Johnson praised her memo publicly, and agreed to keep sex in Title VII. Feminists distributed Pauli's memorandum to the entire Senate.

Pauli came to Betty Friedan's attention in October 1965. Speaking on the same program as EEOC chair Franklin D. Roosevelt, Jr., she attacked his claim that the EEOC should continue to permit sex-segregated "Help Wanted" ads as a "convenience" for readers. Pauli declared, "If it becomes necessary to march on Washington to assure equal job opportunities for all, I hope women will not flinch from the thought." Newspaper reports of this call to action prompted Betty to contact Pauli and initiate a friendship. Pauli introduced Betty in Washington to Mary Eastwood and Catherine East. The three women spent the winter urging Betty to start a militant feminist organization, an "NAACP for women."

There was discussion of electing Pauli as the first chair of NOW. But the founding conference elected Kay Clarenbach, a prominent (white) professor from Wisconsin. Planners felt that Kay would offer a dignified midwestern balance to the flamboyant Betty Friedan of New York City. Betty and Kay had probably reached this agreement over the summer, as a compromise to Midwesterners who wanted Kay as president. (Turk 2023, pp. 74–75) The original Steering Committee mailing had listed Kay as NOW's chair and failed to mention Betty. Once Betty made it clear that she was in charge, her recruiting letter of August 31 told people to send their dues to Kay Clarenbach.

In the weeks after the founding conference, I held several phone conversations with Pauli, and her manner was frosty. Mary Eastwood shared my opinion that Pauli was unhappy. Pauli could not possibly have served as NOW chair, or even a board member, because she'd been retained as a consultant to the EEOC in September. But Pauli might have liked to be invited anyway.

In one phone call in November, I urged Pauli to remain in the loop. "You're essential to our movement. We need your advice. We need your civil rights perspective and your contacts." Pauli replied coolly, "I don't think so. Don't count on me."

"You're important to Betty," I implored.

"She'll manage." Could Pauli and Betty have had an unpleasant discussion? With Betty, that was always a possibility.

A year later, in November 1967, at the conclusion of NOW's second national conference, we were disappointed when Pauli announced that she would not remain active in our organization. She objected to the conference vote supporting the ERA. She said we should instead fight for equality by expanding the Equal Protection Clause of the Fourteenth Amendment. (Mary Eastwood wanted us to pursue *both* pathways.) Pauli then diverted her attentions to the ACLU.

In the years that followed, Pauli published several books and held a chaired professorship in law at Brandeis University. While at Brandeis, she publicly applied to President Nixon to appoint her to the Supreme Court "to forestall the popular misconception that no qualified women applied or were available."

In August 1973, she embarked on a new career—feminist theology. She studied divinity at General Theological Seminary in New York City. On January 8, 1977, Pauli was ordained as America's first Black female Episcopal priest. She led one parish briefly, but had to retire at age seventy-two. She served various other churches as a minister without portfolio. Her lectures and college seminars were widely popular. She wrote extensively on the values of "Womanist Theology."

Pauli's family home is now a national monument. In 2012, the Episcopal Church declared her a saint. (Lithwick 2022, p. 6)

CATHERINE EAST

Catherine East earned two descriptions from Betty Friedan. One was "midwife to the birth of the women's movement." The other was "our Deep Throat." For years, Betty concealed Catherine's identity as our source of invaluable information.

Catherine was the right hand for Esther Peterson, assistant secretary of labor under President Kennedy and Special Assistant for

Catherine East and Kathy Bonk
Photograph courtesy of Kathy Bonk

Consumer Affairs under President Johnson. Peterson also served as head of the Women's Bureau in the Department of Labor during the administrations of both these presidents. Catherine fed NOW statistics compiled by the Women's Bureau of the Labor Department. Using those statistics, Catherine taught us strategies for victory.

Catherine never joined NOW. She didn't want her employers to find out who was providing us with all that sensitive information on the sorry status of women in America. Many of Catherine's statistics appear in NOW's "Statement of Purpose." She remained a precious strategist and informant for our movement until she retired from government in 1977.

In late 1965 and early 1966, Betty Friedan visited Washington, D.C., on a monthly basis, seeking material for a sequel to her *Feminine Mystique*. Catherine, Mary, and Pauli would arrive at her hotel room after dinner with specifics for building a new organization. Betty recalled, "They'd somehow start me making hypothetical lists of women I had met." (Davis 1991, p. 53)

In the last week of June 1966, at the conference of Commissions on the Status of Women, a legendary group of twelve to fifteen women crowded into Betty's hotel room to brainstorm on next steps. The meeting was hardly spontaneous. Catherine East had chosen and invited most of the women who attended.

Even before NOW became official, Catherine worked with Mary Eastwood and Marguerite Rawalt to combat EEOC's refusal to outlaw sex-segregated "Help Wanted" ads. In Catherine's basement, they printed flyers urging women to lobby the EEOC. Marguerite distributed these to her contacts in women's organizations.

Catherine held a B.A. in history. Her mother had suffered from a nervous breakdown when Catherine was eleven years old, and her father committed suicide four years later. (Several of us in feminist leadership—Gloria Steinem, Pauli Murray, I, and others—had parents who suffered from mental illness.) Catherine's marriage ended in divorce. (Again, many feminist leaders were divorced. I was a fortunate exception.)

Catherine held influential government jobs for thirty-eight years. In 1975, she served as the main staff executive for International Women's Year. In 1979, I recruited her for the board of the NOW Legal Defense and Education Fund.

THE LEGAL COMMITTEE

The members of NOW's hardworking Legal Committee were Margarite Rawalt, Mary Eastwood, Phineas Indritz, and Caruthers Berger.

Months before NOW became an official organization, the committee met every night in the summer of 1966 in Mary's apartment to select lawsuits and prepare preliminary briefs. They turned out world-changing material. After a quick sandwich supper, they worked through the night before returning to their government jobs. They typed all the motions themselves, struggling with carbon paper in the days before Xeroxing became widespread. Commercial firms printed the final briefs.

NOW's Legal Committee was sometimes joined by EEOC attorney Sonia Pressman. When the EEOC did something egregious, Sonny gave us confidential information that led to a rebuke from NOW. (Sonny and I, to the best of my knowledge, are the only two cofounders of

NOW still alive today. She married and divorced and is known now as Sonia Pressman Fuentes.)

These were our foremost lawsuits:

- *Mengelkoch v. Industrial Welfare Commission* was our first lawsuit. It earned wide publicity as a symbol of women's exploitation by state "protective laws." Velma Mengelkoch sued North American Aviation because the company denied promotions and overtime pay to women under state laws restricting the number of hours they could work. When Mengelkoch finally won her lawsuit, the court ruled that all jobs should be open to women, and it's a violation of Title VII for a state to limit their working hours.

- *Bowe v. Colgate-Palmolive Company* overturned a pernicious "protective" barrier to workingwomen. In collaboration with its labor union, Colgate had maintained separate seniority lists for men and women on the premise that women should not lift weights over thirty-five pounds. Thelma Bowe and several other women sued to unify those seniority lists and give women the same promotion opportunities as men. It took years to win this lawsuit. NOW chapters demonstrated against Colgate in local supermarkets across the country. As you'll see later, New York City NOW staged a highly publicized demonstration outside Colgate headquarters, dumping Colgate products down a toilet bowl. In September 1969, under Title VII of the Civil Rights Act, the women plaintiffs finally won promotions, compensation for back pay, and the abolition of separate seniority lists. The company's weight-lifting limit of thirty-five pounds was extended to men as well as women.

- *Commonwealth v. Daniel* righted an old wrong that blows people's minds today. Under the Muncy Act in the state of Pennsylvania, convicted women were given longer sentences than men because "women took longer to rehabilitate than men." Marguerite Rawalt and Phineas Indritz, on behalf of NOW, won this lawsuit for Jane Daniel. In July 1968, the Pennsylvania Supreme Court ruled that harsher sentences for women violated the Equal Protection Clause of the Fourteenth Amendment to the Constitution.

- *Weeks v. Southern Bell* was another case of companies deciding what is a "man's job." Lorena Weeks sued Southern Bell Telephone Company for the right to be promoted to a higher-paying job as switchman, which was denied to women because the work required lifting more than thirty pounds. Thanks to the NOW Legal Defense and Education Fund, Lorena Weeks won the switchman's job plus $31,000 in back pay. More on this later.

- *Phillips v. Martin Marietta Corp.* was a case of a corporation dictating their idea of family policy. In 1966, Ida Phillips sued Martin Marietta Corporation because they refused to accept job applications from women with very young children. On January 25, 1971, the U.S. Supreme Court ruled: "Under Title VII of the Civil Rights Act of 1964, an employer may not, in the absence of business necessity, refuse to hire women with pre-school-age children while hiring men with such children."

- *Pittsburgh Press Co. v. Pittsburgh Commission on Human Relations* marked the culmination of NOW's strenuous battle against ad columns saying "Help Wanted Male" and "Help Wanted Female." Through heavy pressure, NOW chapters forced influential newspapers to comply with Title VII. However, some newspapers still held out. The Pittsburgh chapter of NOW filed a mandamus action against *The Pittsburgh Press*. Finally, on June 21, 1973, the court ruled that "the Pittsburgh Press will be required to abandon its press policy of proved sex-designated columns." This case went up to the U.S. Supreme Court, and we won by a 5-4 decision.

MARY EASTWOOD

Mary Eastwood is the person I credit as the number-two influence, after Betty Friedan, in the formation and early victories of NOW. With Pauli Murray and Catherine East, Mary pressured Betty throughout 1965 and early 1966 to launch a women's rights organization. With Pauli she wrote "Jane Crow and the Law," showing how to end sex discrimination by private employers and the government. Mary was the main organizer for the birth of NOW.

Mary was born on a farm and, as one of eight children, spent her early years doing farm work. After law school, she joined the Department of Justice's Office of Legal Counsel. She was slender, with bright red hair and delicate features. (She once wore a black wig while marching in a NOW demonstration, so her bosses wouldn't learn about her participation.)

Many of the meetings that created our movement and our lawsuits took place in Mary's Washington apartment. Often, visitors from outside D.C. slept on Mary's couch. Betty Friedan phoned Mary several times a week for advice. Mary arranged our founding conference. She was NOW's most valuable organizer and legal strategist (until the sad moment in the fall of 1968 when she betrayed us).

At the legendary SCSW luncheon on June 30, 1966, Mary and Catherine East assembled the two tables where Betty Friedan wrote on a napkin "NOW, National Organization for Women." Mary later told me that the organizers considered it an unexciting name. But they accepted the "temporary working title" until a better name could be proposed.

At that luncheon, a group of union women led by Catherine Conroy of the Communications Workers of America—seeking control so they could preserve the protective labor laws—came well prepared. They omitted the name of Betty Friedan in their Steering Committee. They decreed that the new organization's founding conference should take place in Chicago under the presidency of Professor Kay Clarenbach. Mary Eastwood and Betty Friedan fought back successfully over the next few weeks. Betty would lead the Steering Committee as our president. And Mary would arrange for our founding conference in D.C.

The Steering Committee for NOW met over the summer in Mary Eastwood's apartment. Mary handled all details for our founding conference, October 29–30 in the basement of *The Washington Post* building. Mary attended nearly all future board meetings but could not join our board of directors officially because she was a government law employee. When Betty Friedan, touring the country with feminist speeches, was approached by women asking for legal advice, she gave them Mary Eastwood's phone number.

On New Year's Day, 1967, Betty decided we should petition the EEOC to outlaw sex-segregated "Help Wanted" ads. She phoned Mary for advice, and Mary suggested a writ of mandamus. Mary drew up the writ, and I wrote a January 2 press release about NOW's legal action.

Mary's close relationship with Betty began to erode in 1968 after Ti-Grace Atkinson was elected president of our New York City chapter. In late June of that year, Ti-Grace publicly hailed as a "feminist hero" a young woman named Valeria Solanas, who had shot artist Andy Warhol on June 3 in the name of her Society for Cutting Up Men (SCUM). To our surprise, Mary mused, "Maybe Solanas presents a feminist issue."

I shouted, "Mary, you've gotta be kidding!" Mary insisted, "Ti-Grace is my good friend, and all of you are stepping on her too hard."

Ti-Grace led a group who proposed new chapter bylaws with "a more democratic formula." Instead of vesting responsibility with elected leaders for a one-year term, we should choose chapter officers and committee chairs by lottery and rotate them every month. Again to my surprise, Mary Eastwood praised what Betty Friedan called "this cockamamie bylaws proposal."

Our controversy with Ti-Grace came to a boil at the New York chapter meeting of October 17, 1968. Members overwhelmingly rejected the proposed bylaws, and Ti-Grace led her followers out of the organization.

Still another argument with Mary: She tried to persuade our national NOW board to publish a letter urging that women should be drafted for the Vietnam War, equally with men. We voted down her suggestion. I explained: "Sure, we believe in equal treatment. But this would lose us potential members. And as you know, many NOW members oppose the war altogether."

Dissension in our Legal Committee came to a head at the NOW board meeting of September 14–15, 1968, at the Holiday Inn in Louisville. Oh, that meeting! Throughout the two-day session, Marguerite Rawalt and Caruthers Berger bickered angrily over the conduct of our lawsuits, especially the *Colgate* case. The fight became so vitriolic that Marguerite withdrew from the *Colgate* case as attorney of record.

(Caruthers had written the final brief but could not affix her name because she worked for the government.) Marguerite said she'd remain chair of our Legal Committee, and she offered to remain on the *Mengelkoch* and *Weeks* cases. The day after our Louisville debacle, Caruthers phoned the Colgate plaintiffs and also Velma Mengelkoch and persuaded them all to remove their cases from NOW in favor of a brandnew organization that she and Mary would be forming.

In the following weeks, we tried to make peace between the warring factions. We didn't succeed.

Years later, Mary explained her actions to me: "Marguerite left us in the lurch, and we needed support quickly. The cases had expenses to meet." Mary and Caruthers turned to National Woman's Party icon Alice Paul, who promptly made out a $350 check to Caruthers. They opened a bank account in the name of "Civil Rights for Women" and later changed it to "Human Rights for Women." The directors were Mary, Caruthers, Alice Paul, Sylvia Ellison, and Ti-Grace. By December, Mary had incorporated HRW, with full ownership of the *Colgate* and *Mengelkoch* cases that NOW had initiated.

We all felt deep gratitude to Mary for her heroic role in the birth of NOW, but we were heartsick at her abandonment. Although Betty Friedan regularly hung up the phone on all of us, she'd never done so to Mary. However, when Mary refused to budge on removing our lawsuits, Betty hung up on Mary with a rain of furious expletives.

Mary's memo to the Executive Committee on October 21 declared, "I am quitting as NOW's 'main volunteer' in running the national office." The memo ended with her saying, "I tried to stop the 'revolution' but events since the Louisville Board meeting have proven I was wrong." In my opinion, that was not the complete story.

NOW did retain the *Weeks* case. Marguerite Rawalt and Phineas Indritz later led us to other legal victories.

In Human Rights for Women, Mary and Ti-Grace experimented with the unorthodox rotation system that New York NOW had rejected. As Mary described it to me, "We have everybody's name for secretary, for treasurer and president in separate envelopes. And at each meeting we draw. Then after you've served your term, it goes into another envelope and you start all over." Perhaps it might have worked for a small organization like HRW, but for NOW it would have been a disaster.

Although Mary resigned from NOW in late 1968, she did rejoin when Wilma Heide was president in 1971–1972. She agreed to chair the Resolutions Committee at our annual conference.

In 1967, Mary joined the National Woman's Party, working to pass the Equal Rights Amendment. They later elected Mary president. She organized a campaign to preserve the Sewall-Belmont House, home of NWP founder Alice Paul. Betty Friedan lobbied to have this mansion donated to NOW as our permanent headquarters, but Mary had other ideas. Today the house is a historic museum known as the Belmont-Paul Women's Equality National Monument. It's a popular tourist attraction in D.C.

In her later years, Mary was crippled by arthritis and could no longer travel. When Veteran Feminists of America voted to present her with an Achievement Award in June 2008, I tried to persuade Mary to make the journey to New York, so we could thank her publicly for all she'd done for feminism. Mary said to me, "Sorry, the arthritis has me conquered." Mary's two nieces came to New York to accept on her behalf.

Like me, Mary avoided publicity because of her job. I'm sad that few people know of her important contributions to our revolution.

MARGUERITE RAWALT

Marguerite Rawalt exemplified the professionalism that helped NOW's founders win results. We persuaded people in power because of our expertise as lawyers, government administrators, educators, organizers, politicians, communicators.

Marguerite was a tall, handsome woman with dark hair and a slight Texas accent. She was older than the rest of us, and we turned to her for advice. She'd retired in October 1965 from the Office of Chief Counsel, Bureau of Internal Revenue but retained her impressive contacts.

Marguerite Rawalt
Photography courtesy of the Smithsonian
Institution Archives

Together with Mary Eastwood, Marguerite filed the papers that incorporated NOW in Washington, D.C., in 1966. Then she rescued us once more: After we failed for months to incorporate our tax-exempt NOW Legal Defense and Education Fund in New York State, I phoned Marguerite. "We're desperate. Grace Cox has been stringing us along for a year. Can you incorporate us in New York State?" Marguerite responded, "Not in New York, but I'll do it in D.C." Marguerite, again with help from Mary, incorporated NOW LDEF on March 16, 1970.

As chair of our Legal Committee, Marguerite brought trailblazing cases to our attention. With Mary, she wrote bylaws for NOW, and standard bylaws for the chapters. As a recent retiree, she was the only member of our Legal Committee to work for NOW full-time. Other committee members still held demanding government jobs.

Through key roles in an incredible number of women's organizations, Marguerite mobilized those groups to press Congress for inclusion of sex in Title VII of the Civil Rights Act of 1964. She also lobbied for years to pass the Equal Rights Amendment. She was a genius at letter-writing campaigns. At the height of our ERA efforts, Martha Griffiths called Marguerite every night and told her which congressmen should be targeted by her letter writers on the following day.

At NOW's board meeting in Louisville in September 1968, after Marguerite fought with Caruthers and withdrew as attorney of record in our *Colgate* case, she remained loyal to us as NOW's general counsel and head of our Legal Committee. She said to me, sighing, "We won't give up. There's lots of other cases."

You may be tempted to skim over the following, but it's amazing. This is a partial list of positions held by Marguerite Rawalt. She enlisted most of her organizations as allies for our movement: She was president of the National Federation of Business and Professional Women; president of the Federal Bar Association; president of the National Association of Women Lawyers; chair of the Civil and Political Rights Committee of the Commission on the Status of Women (Marguerite was the only pro-ERA person on this commission); chair of the Task Force on Family Law and Policy of the Citizens' Advisory Council on the Status of Women; first woman on the American Bar Association's House of Delegates (she lobbied to get women admitted). She served on NOW's early boards of directors and also the advisory board of the Women's Equity Action League (WEAL). She chaired the ERA Ratification Council. In addition to incorporating NOW and NOW LDEF, she also incorporated and obtained tax exemptions for BPW, WEAL, the Federally Employed Women's Legal Defense Fund, and the General Federation of Women's Clubs. She was a longtime friend of President Lyndon B Johnson and numerous congressional leaders.

Marguerite organized NOW's second chapter (New York was the first) in Washington, D.C., on April 27, 1967. She presided at the meeting with Jane Hart, Dick Graham, and Barbara Ireton. Barbara, whose day job was director of women's activities for the American Trucking Associations, was elected president.

Like all of us, Marguerite encountered sex discrimination throughout her career. She was denied admission to Georgetown Law School because they excluded women. And she was forced to keep her marriage to Harry Secord a secret for years, until the government repealed its Depression-era Economy Act forbidding employment of two people from the same family.

Marguerite held vivid memories of the many ways workingwomen were oppressed during the Great Depression. She reminded us that thousands of women lost their jobs to men, especially if the women were married. I have in my files an article about the Kansas City Power Company. Refusing to hire married women, they said they'd fire any woman employee who got married after July 1, 1933 ("Women Workers Get Until June to Wed . . ." *New York Times,* 1932). As late as the beginning of World War II, twenty-six states had laws prohibiting married women from working. (Clark 2020, p. 26)

Unlike some of us whose careers ultimately flourished because of changes in laws and attitudes created by the women's movement, Marguerite was one of many women who missed the boat because they were considered too old. As a candidate for the position of associate chief counsel for the IRS, she was passed over because of her age. (Paterson 1986, p. 155)

4

IT'S ABOUT JOBS

THREE LETTERS

During the summer of 1966, the Legal Committee of NOW drafted three letters for government officials. My revisions made them more persuasive and press-friendly. These letters would be sent to President Lyndon Johnson, to the EEOC Commission, and to Attorney General Ramsey Clark. All three began "We greet you on behalf of NOW, a new action organization of men and women devoted to full equality for women."

Our letter to the President urged him to give the EEOC enforcement powers, to appoint more women to judgeships and policy-making posts in the federal government, and to "include women in your Great Society program for the underprivileged and excluded." We requested a meeting in the White House—which Mary eventually arranged for January.

Our letter to the attorney general asked him to amend all antidiscrimination statutes to include women—especially Title VI, covering education and job training, and Title II, covering public accommodations. We asked that women should not be excluded from jury service in federal and state courts. And we especially requested him to assist us in the case of *Mengelkoch v. Industrial Welfare Commission.*

Our letter to the EEOC urged them to combat sex discrimination under Title VII in addressing the "Help Wanted" ads, the airlines case, the *Mengelkoch* case, retirement and pension plans, and affirmative action programs. We asked the EEOC to "issue comprehensive guidelines on the rights of women employees who are forced to leave the labor force temporarily for maternity reasons . . . with no loss of employee benefits."

After approval at our November board meeting, we revealed these three letters to the media in our first press conference. My press release reported that NOW "accused government agencies of dragging their heels in enforcement of laws against job discrimination based on sex." It added that NOW "placed main emphasis on employment; but we also declared war on separate ladies' auxiliaries in the political parties, quotas against women in universities, and exclusion of women from public restaurants." It said NOW would "organize conferences or demonstrations to protest discrimination against women."

CHILD CARE

We announced another important priority, to be repeated in NOW actions again and again: We called on the government to fund a national network of child-care centers, charging that "America lags by decades behind many European countries." We demanded that income tax laws should be amended "to permit deduction of full child care expenses for working parents."

"HELP WANTED"

Today's young people tell me they cannot believe that American newspapers until very recently listed job ads under "Help Wanted Male" and "Help Wanted Female." Such blatant bigotry! In those days, ambitious women looked for good jobs in the "Male" columns, but we knew that some employers might disregard our applications.

Title VII of the Civil Rights Act of 1964 declared it unlawful "for an employer . . . to cause to be published any notice . . . indicating any preference ... based on race, color, religion, sex or national origin." (*Congressional Record—House*, June 20, 1966, p. 13691) But the EEOC deliberately refused to enforce this rule, saying sex-segregated job ads were helpful to job seekers, and the separation was a response to bona fide occupational qualifications (BFOQs). NOW countered this by insisting that the only legitimate BFOQ jobs were wet nurse and semen donor.

Martha Griffiths sent a letter of protest to the EEOC on May 19, 1966. She insisted that "sexigration" of ads "is most pernicious because it reinforces prejudicial attitudes limiting women to the less rewarded and less rewarding types of work."

Martha gave a riveting speech on the want ads in Congress on June 20. Her speech played a role in the birth of NOW. She proclaimed, "I charge that the officials of the Equal Employment Opportunity Commission have displayed a wholly negative attitude toward the sex provisions of title VII. I would remind them that they took an oath to uphold the law—not just the part of it they are interested in ... What is this sickness that causes an official to ridicule the law he swore to uphold and enforce?"

EEOC Commissioner Luther Holcomb claimed the "Help Wanted Male" columns were a "convenience" for readers that could be ignored. Then Martha Griffiths replied, "If even a single employer uses sex-segregated ads for the purpose of discrimination, that is prohibited by law. . . . I have never entered a door labeled 'men' and I doubt that Mr. Holcomb has frequently entered the women's room." (*Congressional Record—House*, June 20, 1966, p. 13690)

Mary Eastwood and Catherine East arranged for the entire Griffiths speech to be distributed to attendees at the State Commissions on the Status of Women conference. At the final SCSW luncheon on June 30, Martha Griffiths gave an address that was loudly applauded. Women in the room were conspiring to establish the National Organization for Women.

In the early years of NOW, we held meetings and demonstrations, filed lawsuits, and lobbied politically to pressure the EEOC and the most egregious newspapers to change their (clearly illegal) policy. At

Betty Friedan's request, I wrote a letter under her signature to her personal friend, *Washington Post* editor Katharine Graham, explaining the inequity of job ad sexigration. Graham's reply rejected our appeal. She claimed the columns were a service to readers. In truth, the publishers were making money from this practice because many employers posted the same job ad twice, in both gender columns.

The New York chapter of NOW held a meeting with executives of *The New York Times*. I attended with other NOW officers, including my brother, attorney Jerry Fox, a chapter vice president. The *Times* representatives refused our request for desexigration. To our amusement, their behavior was exaggeratedly polite—holding chairs for the women, lighting our cigarettes, and otherwise demonstrating their chivalry.

Our chapter picketed the *Times* regularly. Mimicking a *Times* ad of that year, one of our male members carried a signboard saying I GOT MY JOB THROUGH THE NEW YORK TIMES while the sign of the woman next to him said I DIDN'T.

NOW's first big nationwide demonstration addressed this issue on December 14, 1967. Chapters throughout the country picketed their newspapers and local EEOC offices. In D.C., they dumped bushels of red tape at the EEOC's doorstep. Marguerite Rawalt told us this was "the first big national demonstration since suffrage."

Our pressure finally paid off. I still have a copy of the want ads section of *The New York Times* for December 1, 1968, with a unified column saying "Help Wanted Male and Female." I found this especially gratifying because we were concluding a year of angry scuffles within our chapter. When the new *Times* want ads appeared, I sighed and said, "It was worth it!"

OUR MEETINGS IN WASHINGTON

Soon after our first press conference, Mary Eastwood set up meetings for us in D.C. These were follow-ups to the three letters we'd sent to LBJ, Attorney General Ramsey Clark, and commissioners of the EEOC. Our first two meetings took place on January 12 and 13. Betty Friedan and I were joined by Marguerite Rawalt, Dorothy Haener, Jane Hart, and Anna Arnold Hedgeman, who was still serving as acting executive vice president while we waited for Aileen Hernandez to take office.

On behalf of President Johnson, a cordial John Macy met with us in the White House. Macy was LBJ's special adviser on employment matters; he was also the chairman of the U.S. Civil Service Commission. Macy expressed surprise that we asked to be treated the same as other groups who were suffering from discrimination. "Don't you want special consideration because you're women?" I replied, "No, we're the same as all the others. It's a matter of civil rights."

We asked John Macy to use his influence to see that more women were appointed to key government posts. He nodded his head affirmatively. And he agreed to the importance of our demand for "a nationwide network of child care centers to aid working mothers."

Our meeting with Attorney General Ramsey Clark did not go that well. Clark had a reputation as a liberal. But to us, his manner seemed cool and unfriendly, and he never smiled. We asked Clark to intervene in our *Mengelkoch* lawsuit, and to press for new civil rights laws to put teeth in Title VII by withholding federal funds from uncooperative companies. Despite Clark's unwelcoming demeanor, my follow-up letter, over Betty Friedan's signature, thanked him for his hospitality. I lied: "We were encouraged by your courteous attention to our discussion of today's 'new woman' and her striving toward . . . full partnership with men."

We held a press conference for the D.C. media after our Clark meeting on January 13. Betty Friedan opened by saying, "NOW will fight for stronger enforcement of the Civil Rights Act of 1964 against *all* employment discrimination."

We were delighted when Congresswoman Martha Griffiths showed up to support our demands. She disclosed that she had just introduced H.R. 643 to give women the same rights as men employed by the federal civil service. It took a long time for that bill to pass.

Betty and I had argued about the lede I'd written for the release for our press conference. I finally relented and used her lede. The next afternoon, when we were back in New York, Betty surprised me. She suddenly said, out of the blue, "You were right. Your lede would have been better."

We couldn't obtain a meeting with EEOC officials during our January 12–13 visit, but Mary Eastwood arranged an appointment for January 22. We flew back to Washington again and met with top EEOC officials, led by Stephen Shulman, who'd succeeded Luther Holcomb as chairman. That meeting was unproductive. All I remember now is that Schulman complimented me on a multicolor turban I was wearing. Not very rewarding for our special trip to Washington. (We were paying our own travel expenses.) In retrospect, our most successful January meeting in D.C. was our visit to John Macy in the White House. More on that below.

AFFIRMATIVE ACTION FOR US, TOO

Active enforcement of Title VII was the first big step in our employment crusade. Another major goal was getting women included in affirmative action, which is defined as "the practice of favoring individuals belonging to groups known to have been discriminated against previously." This would open up the pipeline of job openings and promotions for millions of American women of all races and classes.

(We faced opposition on affirmative action from the American Civil Liberties Union, which called it "reverse discrimination." We reminded them that white males had received affirmative action for thousands of years. The ACLU finally came around in the mid-1970s; they're active supporters now.)

At our meeting with John Macy in the White House on January 13, we pressed him to persuade President Johnson to add women to affirmative action policies. I'm especially proud of the follow-up letter I wrote to Macy, over Betty Friedan's signature, on January 24, 1967, explaining why this directive was essential. The president did what we requested!

On October, 13, 1967, LBJ signed Executive Order 11375. This decision added women to Executive Order 11246, which he had originally signed in 1965, prohibiting discrimination and establishing affirmative action in the federal government and all organizations with federal contracts.

Jobs for women—many millions of jobs—were at the heart of our revolution. When I revel in our success, I give special thought to two numbers: First, Executive Order 11375 and second, Revised Order No. 4. Here's how No. 4 changed the job world forever:

To enforce affirmative action, a strong government agency was needed. That was the Office of Federal Contract Compliance in the Department of Labor, which could force compliance by denying federal contracts or subcontracts to delinquent employers. The department's Order No. 4 decreed that companies must submit numerical goals for improving their affirmative action programs, with timetable dates to get it done. The important words there are *goals* and *timetables*. Originally, women were not included.

Ann Scott
Photograph courtesy of the Schlesinger Library,
Harvard University

ANN SCOTT MAKES A DIFFERENCE

Ann Scott, NOW's vice president of legislation, should be honored in history as the activist most responsible for putting teeth into affirmative action for women. Affirmative action was not enforced effectively for women until NOW pressured the government to threaten companies with loss of business if they failed to comply. Ann Scott is the one who did it. On December 2, 1971, the Labor Department issued the directive now known as Revised Order No. 4 with this pronouncement: "Contractors and subcontractors will be required to make good-faith efforts to correct any deficiencies in the utilization of women at all levels and in all segments of their work force."

Businesses were required to prove compliance by listing the percentages of women they hired and promoted. John Bryan, CEO of Sara Lee Corporation (coincidentally, a Byoir client whose account I supervised) summarized the new environment: "What gets measured gets done." If a business did not comply with Revised Order No. 4, its contracts could be canceled and it would be barred from future government contracts or subcontracts.

Ann Scott had been a professor of English literature at the State University of New York at Buffalo. She chaired our national Campus Coordinating Committee. In 1970, she wrote a model affirmative action plan for colleges and universities and submitted it to the Labor Department. That same year, she published a report in her university newsletter called "The Half-Eaten Apple," an attack on academic discrimination. Ann failed to receive tenure; that article was probably a reason.

Ann resigned from UB in 1972 to move to Washington, D.C., and work full-time (unpaid) as a lobbyist for NOW and other organizations. She led our legislative office in D.C. until her untimely death from breast cancer in 1975, at the age of forty-five.

A beautiful woman with strong classical features and a resonant voice, Ann was a tenacious persuader. NOW treasurer Gene Boyer once recalled "watching Ann grab a government official by the lapels, sticking her face right into his and shouting. It looked like he withered under her grasp, and he did support our position." (Love 2006, p. 413)

I was intrigued to learn that Ann's first husband, whom she divorced, was a musician, her second husband a poet, her third an artist. The third, final husband, Tom Scott (prematurely gray-haired and exceptionally handsome) often accompanied her to NOW meetings.

After we'd successfully pressured the EEOC to take sex discrimination seriously, the EEOC became a strong ally. But at first it had no enforcement powers. Then Ann Scott, on behalf of NOW, lobbied successfully for the Equal Opportunity Act of 1972, which amended Title VII to give the EEOC authority to conduct its own enforcement litigation. From then on, EEOC frequently advised judges to interpret civil rights laws in our favor.

Ann Scott led NOW's campaign that persuaded Congress in 1972 to pass the Equal Rights Amendment. Also in 1972, when the still recalcitrant AT&T held a press conference to announce a weak "sweetheart deal" on sex discrimination, Ann interrupted the press conference by reading aloud her entire NOW press release denouncing the deal. Nobody dared to interrupt Ann's interruption.

With journalist Lucy Komisar of NOW's New York chapter, Ann published in 1971 a pamphlet entitled "Business and Industry Discrimination Kit," as well as "And Justice for All," an exposé of the government's failures to enforce laws against sex discrimination.

Ann gave me hell one day, after I'd supported a cut in the budget of her legislative office. NOW was struggling through financial difficulties. But later, when I realized how much Ann was accomplishing, I apologized. We hugged, and agreed to search elsewhere for the necessary budget amounts. At the end of my term as NOW national chair, Ann recruited Tom to create for me an elegant red glass pendant in the shape of a feminist equality sign. (In the early days of our movement we settled disagreements amicably. Beginning in the year 1973, as you 'll learn, our conflicts grew increasingly irreconcilable.)

WE BOMBARD THE AIRLINES

In the old days, people considered the job of airline stewardess to be especially glamorous and desirable. But there was a catch: If you worked as a stewardess, you'd be fired if you got married, or if you reached the unglamorous age of thirty-two (for some airlines, the age was thirty-five). This was an obvious violation of Title VII, but the airlines fought us tooth and nail. Although they claimed the reason was sex appeal, their real motive was money. The airlines saved millions of dollars by not vesting stewardesses for pensions. The "out at thirty-two" policy had been in effect since November 1953. The airlines had persuaded their unions to consent by exempting women who were employed at that time. Also, the flight unions were completely dominated by men—which is why Colleen Boland and her sisters formed the Air Line Stewards and Stewardesses Association.

NOW became involved in this battle when Colleen paid a visit to our founding conference on the morning of October 30. We voted unanimously to support the stewardesses in their lawsuit.

Colleen, who was thirty-seven years old when she appealed to us, insisted that stewardesses should be hired not for their sex appeal but, rather, for their competence in preparing and serving food, attending to sick passengers, or giving critical direction in case of an emergency. Instead, airlines promoted themselves deliberately as "flying bunny clubs." (Hathaway 1965) She quoted one airline executive: "If we put a dog on a plane, 20 businessmen are sore for a month."

Our savvy board member Alice Rossi countered to the press: "They'd be better off with older stewardesses, who'd project a motherly image and make the passengers feel safe."

On Christmas Eve, 1966, Betty Friedan and I became embroiled in this battle. We were subpoenaed to appear in a downtown Wall Street office, from late afternoon into evening, at a deposition organized by Jesse Friedin, fiery attorney for the Air Transport Association. The EEOC had issued a preliminary ruling against the airline firing practices on November 9, 1966. But Friedin sued to nullify the ruling on the ground that EEOC commissioner Aileen Hernandez was guilty of a conflict of interest when she voted against the airlines, in view of Aileen's "imminent employment in an executive capacity" in NOW. (All NOW positions, of course, were unpaid.) Aileen had resigned from the EEOC on October 10, but her resignation would not become effective until

November 10. My October 30 press release had said we'd elected Aileen as our executive vice president "subject to her consent." Betty was deposed as president of NOW; I was deposed as author of the press release.

On February 27, 1967, a judge ruled against us, siding with Friedin's complaint about Aileen's so-called conflict of interest. He ordered the EEOC not to release its previous decision against the airline firings.

Justice did not prevail until more than a year later, on August 10, 1968, when the EEOC finally ruled officially that the airline hiring practices violated Title VII. "Sex is not a bona fide occupational qualification for the position of flight cabin attendant." The wording for this overdue decision was written by EEOC attorney Sonia Pressman, who had surreptitiously advised NOW's Legal Committee.

We also attacked the airline practice of firing married stewardesses—many of whom were forced to conceal their marital status for years in order to keep their jobs. The year 1968 brought resolution to two lawsuits that ended this practice. They were *Neal v. American Airlines* and *Calvin v. Piedmont Aviation.* Courts did not buy the contention of American Airlines that female employees must remain unmarried "to avoid the stress on home and family life which would be caused by married stewardesses." In addition to their contention about stress, the airlines justified their rules by saying that "married women would miss work too often and would gain weight." (Davis 1991, p. 23) Those were the days of stereotypes.

Still another airline conflict involved me personally. Beginning in 1953, United Air Lines operated flights called "The Chicago Executive" between New York and Chicago at 5:00 P.M., going in either direction, six days a week, excluding Saturdays. Advertisements boasted that its "Club in the Sky for Men Only" offered a relaxing atmosphere in "congenial company." No women or children could take these flights. A mailroom boy could board as an entitled male passenger, but not a female executive. Flight attendants provided the men with slippers, free cigars (which they lit for them), closing market quotations, cocktails, and steak dinners.

I have a copy of the letter I wrote to United Air Lines on April 2, 1968, protesting this practice. United had sent a sales solicitation to

American Women in Radio and Television, of which I was a director, asking us to fly their airline to our annual convention in Los Angeles. My letter pointed out that United's male-only flights were a violation of the Civil Rights Act of 1964. Unfortunately, in order to impress the airline, I made the mistake of writing my protest on my official letterhead as a vice president of Carl Byoir & Associates, then one of the top three public relations firms in the world.

The CEO of United Air Lines personally phoned the CEO of Carl Byoir at his home over the weekend, complaining about my letter. My CEO called me into his office on Monday and chewed me out. I promised never again to write anything on company stationery that might annoy a business firm.

It wasn't until 1970 that United discontinued their executive flights for men only. They'd been pressured by a lawsuit from the Chicago chapter of NOW. That chapter picketed UAL offices on Valentine's Day with signs saying UNITED DOESN'T LOVE WOMEN.

A respected historian recently wrote that "to test the policy and highlight its absurdity in the mid-1960s, the advertising executive Muriel Fox booked her young son on one such flight, unaccompanied, but she could not buy a ticket for herself." (Turk 2023, p. 15) This is completely incorrect. She based her comment on the transcript of a mistaken supposition by Karen DeCrow—I don't know how Karen got that idea—and then she must have imagined my motives. (My son was eight years old in 1968. And because of my job, I never criticized any company in public. My letter to United had been unpublicized.)

One remnant of airline sexism lasted decades longer: Emphasizing their policy of employing attractive stewardesses, the airlines forced them, on penalty of being fired, to keep their weight under certain limits. My husband, Dr. Shepard Aronson, who had served as the first board chair of the New York chapter of NOW, wrote frequent letters to airlines, complaining that this requirement was unfair to his stewardess patients. He said some women needed more weight to support their larger bone frames. "And besides, this vestige of an emphasis on a flight attendant's appearance has nothing to do with her ability to serve passengers."

Martha Griffiths
Photograph courtesy of the Library of Congress

OUR CHAMPION, MARTHA

Again and again, Martha Griffiths proved herself a feminist hero whom history must revere. During the 1960s, she was our most effective advocate for women's rights in the U.S. Congress.

A year before NOW was founded, in 1965, Martha introduced a bill in the House of Representatives to outlaw the airline firings of flight attendants. Her bill never received serious attention. Congressmen referred to it as "the Old Broads Bill." But Martha continued to pursue the injustice.

In 1967, responding to airlines insistence that male business passengers preferred stewardesses who were young and attractive, Martha called out to them in Congress: "What are you running, an airline or a whorehouse?" (Collins 2009, p. 83)

Martha Griffiths had already served our cause by helping to insert sex in Title VII of the Civil Rights Act of 1964. As the first woman to serve on the House Ways and Means Committee, Martha cajoled Representative Howard Smith into adding that magic word. She could have sponsored the addition herself, but she knew it would garner more votes from southern congressmen if Smith made the motion. Yes, Smith's main motive was to kill the entire Civil Rights bill. And yes, the *Congressional Record* states officially that his proposal was greeted with laughter. But Martha knew how to turn around that mocking mood in the House.

After Smith introduced his motion, congressmen sauntered around the chamber, exchanging sexist jokes. Humor filled the air. Would our cause be laughed out of Congress once again? Then Martha Griffiths stood up and proclaimed, "If there had been any necessity to have pointed out that women were a second-class sex, the laughter would have proved it." Martha's rebuke put an end to the hilarity. Marguerite Rawalt, who was sitting in the balcony, reported what happened next: "[T]hey quieted right down and got back into their seats, most of them, and listened." (Davis 1991, p. 42)

During the next few days, Marguerite and Alice Paul and other feminists waged a vigorous campaign for keeping sex in Title VII. Letters and phone calls poured into Congress. Pauli Murray wrote a memo to LBJ that persuaded him to support us. Then Martha Griffiths and Marguerite and their allies helped to get the entire Civil Rights Act passed by Congress. We won!

In later years, Martha also helped pass the ERA bill through Congress. *The Guardian* dubbed her "the mother of the Equal Rights Amendment." (Jackson, 2003)

Martha retired from Congress at the end of 1974 and practiced law with her husband. In 1982, Michigan elected her lieutenant governor on the ticket with Governor James Blanchard. They served together for eight years. To our outrage, Blanchard decided not to name her for his ticket in 1992. He encouraged rumors that Martha was too old. Although she'd reached the age of eighty, she was as energetic as ever.

Martha Griffiths fought hard for the feminist principle that all human rights are indivisible: "I don't know really that I have so much

Phineas Indritz and Muriel Fox at the 25th reunion of NOW, 1991
Photograph courtesy of Muriel Fox

perseverance as I do a sense of indignity at the fact that women are not justly treated. I have the same sort of feelings for Blacks, Latinos, and Asiatics. If we are America, then we ought to be what we say we are. We ought to be the land of the free and the brave. What people sought in this land was justice." (National Women's Hall of Fame)

PHINEAS INDRITZ BEHIND THE SCENES

The media often get our organization's full name wrong. We keep insisting we're the National Organization *for* Women, not *of* Women, with men serving actively in our chapters and national board. Phineas Indritz was an influential male example of this partnership. History should not forget him.

Phineas had a small law practice, but for twenty years he spent most of his time working for the U.S. Department of the Interior and also as a staffer for members of Congress and civil rights organizations. For NOW, of course, he labored without pay. Phineas researched and wrote most of Martha Griffiths's speeches in Congress, so it's hard to know which memorable bons mots were created by whom. He was also an energetic member of our Legal Committee in NOW's early days. He wrote trailblazing briefs for our feminist lawsuits. And he accomplished even more, as you'll see.

We're especially grateful to Phineas for his work in the case of *Commonwealth v. Daniel*. It addressed another outrage that people find hard to imagine today. Under the Muncy Act in the state of Pennsylvania, convicted women were given longer sentences than men because "women took longer to rehabilitate than men." *The Journal of Criminal Law and Criminology* justified this practice by saying women delinquents "belong to the class of women who lead sexually immoral lives." This injustice prevailed in several states besides Pennsylvania.

On behalf of NOW, with the help of Marguerite Rawalt, Phineas won this lawsuit for Jane Daniel, who'd been sentenced to an indeterminate term of imprisonment for a minor robbery. Thanks to Phineas, the Pennsylvania Supreme Court threw out the Muncy Act in July 1968, declaring that harsher sentences for women violated the Equal Protection Clause of the Fourteenth Amendment to the U.S. Constitution. As a result of this decision, nearly two hundred Pennsylvania women were released from prison.

Phineas Indritz also authored the Pregnancy Discrimination Act of 1978. This act amends Title VII of the Civil Rights Act of 1964 to prohibit discrimination on the basis of pregnancy, childbirth, or related medical conditions. It prevents employers from forcing a pregnant woman to take a leave from her job if she's willing and able to work. In 1972, under Phineas's guidance, NOW had persuaded the EEOC to issue new guidelines, treating pregnancy the same as other temporary disabilities. In 1978, these guidelines became an act of Congress.

At times, Congress passes a new law to right the wrong of a Supreme Court ruling. The Pregnancy Discrimination Act is one example. It was introduced in Congress because the Supreme Court had recently ruled, in the case of *General Electric Company v. Gilbert*, that pregnancy discrimination was not covered by the Civil Rights Act of 1964. After

Congress passed our pregnancy bill, this condition was definitely covered from then on.

A similar instance occurred during the presidency of Barack Obama. In 2007, in the case of *Ledbetter v. Goodyear Tire & Rubber Co.*, the Supreme Court ruled against Lilly Ledbetter's equal-pay lawsuit on the grounds that Lilly had not discovered her pay differential from male employees until she was ready to retire, and Goodyear's initial salary decisions had been made more than 180 days prior to the date she filed her suit. Congress overturned this Supreme Court interpretation with the Lilly Ledbetter Fair Pay Act of 2009—the first act Barack Obama signed when he became president. With the new act, Congress declared that discrimination might occur as a new violation every time an employee's wages, benefits, or other compensation is paid. An important victory for feminists!

Phineas was short and pudgy and wore round eyeglasses. I was amazed when he told me he'd qualified for the U.S. Olympic gymnastics team in 1936. Phineas? He'd gained a lot of weight since the old days. He did excel in another activity—as a world-class juggler. In his spare time, he amused passersby by juggling on the Capitol lawn. "I started juggling in 1944. I'd been a good gymnast in college. But . . . I began to notice I was getting hurt. So I looked around for something I could do by myself or with others, indoors or out . . . and to a very old age. The only activity that met those qualifications was juggling."

As a member of NOW's Legal Committee, Phineas enlisted Mary Eastwood and Catherine East to draft a paper critical of the EEOC's stand on the want ads. He used this in a speech he wrote for Martha Griffiths to deliver in Congress. This speech appeared in the *Congressional Record* and greatly helped our cause.

In the fall of 1968, after the blowup that led Mary Eastwood, Caruthers Berger, and Sylvia Ellison to resign from the NOW Legal Committee, we begged Phineas to remain with NOW. "Don't worry," he reassured us. "You can count on me and Marguerite. Caruthers was driving us crazy, so I won't miss her." Phineas told me that Caruthers had accused him of being "a tool of the Women's Bureau" because he kept insisting that Congress was not ready to pass the ERA yet, and we should focus our energies on winning other victories in Congress and the courts. We could always rely on Phineas for honest, practical advice.

Phineas worked for racial and gender justice all his life. He wrote briefs for America's four most important school desegregation lawsuits. The D.C. chapter of the NAACP honored him for his legal work "involving basic civil rights of minorities."

In the *Family Law Quarterly*, Phineas wrote in 1970: "There are numerous circumstances where the law . . . relegates women to inferior or disadvantaged positions . . . (and in many circumstances irrationally discriminate against men.)" (*Family Law Quarterly*, March 1970, pp. 6–12)

In addition, Phineas persuaded Congresswoman Edith Green to hold hearings on sex discrimination in education. More on those hearings in chapter 9.

5

BETTY FRIEDAN

February 4, 1921–February 4, 2006

WHY BETTY FRIEDAN?

The feminist revolution succeeded because many thousands of women and men fought to awaken the populace and change its laws. But to do this, we needed a general. Without a doubt, our general was the woman who had also been our prophet: Betty Friedan.

Other prophets in the past spoke out for women's rights and taught us to reconsider the way of life that men had foisted upon us: Sappho in seventh-century B.C. Greece, Christine de Pizan in late-fourteenth and early-fifteenth-century France, Mary Wollstonecraft and William Godwin in eighteenth-century England, Simone de Beauvoir educating the entire civilized world in the twentieth century, and other brilliant thinkers. In the nineteenth century, our suffragist foremothers awakened us to the possibility of voting rights. Their brave sacrifices finally won women the vote in 1920.

In 1963, Betty Friedan published *The Feminine Mystique* and created a new vision of equality for educated women. Then, in 1966, she became the foremost founder of NOW.

You'll see conflicting comments about her leadership: "Betty is the one who did it!" "Mother of our movement . . ." "Betty is impossible!" "The Board of NY NOW . . . unanimously decided to cease its . . . work

Betty Friedan, Muriel Fox, and Elinor Guggenheimer, 1978
Photograoh courtesy of Muriel Fox

with Betty Friedan, who has been an increasingly abusive and disruptive force." (Cohen 1988, p. 316) "Betty Friedan changed my life!" "Betty gets too much credit for the work that all of us did."

All those comments were at least partly true. But I insist on one truth above all: Betty Friedan was the undisputed leader of our overdue revolution just as surely as Martin Luther King, Jr. and George Washington were leaders of *their* overdue revolutions. Without those three leaders, the revolutions would have happened anyway. But perhaps much later, or less completely, or in a different form.

Betty Friedan sometimes acted in unkind ways. But certain things written about her were untrue. Even statements by "experts." To help understand Betty, let's review her life briefly.

Bettye Goldstein was born in Peoria, Illinois, in 1921. Her father, Harry, owned the city's preeminent jewelry store. Betty had a brother, Harry junior, and a (much prettier) younger sister, Amy. Her attractive mother, Miriam, had been society editor of the local newspaper before marriage but then resigned to become a (discontented) housewife. Says Betty, "I sure as hell didn't want to be a mommy like my mommy." (Witchel 2000) Sister Amy has complained about their mother's "complete inability to nurture." (Shteir 2023, p. 12) Miriam suffered from painful colitis. But, after Harry became ill and she successfully took over the business, her colitis disappeared. After Harry's death, Miriam married and was widowed two additional times. She became a champion bridge player. In a press interview, she told a reporter she agreed with most of Betty's feminist goals, but "I don't like things like women forcing their way into a men's bar." (Hammel 1971) Hardly a full endorsement.

In an interview when she was seventy-nine, Betty commented, "My mother had my fire, intelligence, energy. But . . . she made our lives miserable with her frustrations . . . She gave me the emotional motivation to start the women's movement." (Witchel 2000) (I used almost the same words in describing life with my own mother in a speech I gave on Mother's Day, 1980.)

Betty's parents took her to a psychiatrist at age five. Her mother later told *The New York Times* that their reason for doing this was that Betty preferred reading books to playing with dolls, which her parents considered strange. (Hammel 1971) But I wonder if she had bigger problems and was already a lonely and withdrawn child. As an adolescent, Betty was unattractive, assertive, unfriendly. She attributed her high school unpopularity to "the injustice of antisemitism" (Sanday 1993); but her personality must have played a role, too.

She attended Smith College, where she again made few friends, edited the college newspaper, and in 1942 graduated summa cum laude and Phi Beta Kappa. She then entered graduate school at the University of California, Berkeley, where she dropped the final *e* from her first name. She won a prestigious fellowship for Ph.D. study in psychology but turned it down at the insistence of her scientist boyfriend.

Betty wrote for *Federated Press* and spent six years writing for the *UE News*, the newspaper of the United Electrical, Radio, and Machine Workers of America. In 1947, she married theater producer Carl Friedman, who later deleted one letter from his last name to create the less Jewish-sounding Friedan. She was fired from her job upon becoming pregnant. She switched to freelance magazine articles.

Although there were times when Betty could be generous and compassionate, she often behaved cruelly. Sheila Tobias, a prominent academic in NOW's early history, told me, "We used to play a game. We'd go around the room, and everyone would tell a story about a time when Betty Friedan had insulted them."

As for me, Betty was so curt and unfriendly during our first year of collaboration that I was sure she disliked me. (Perhaps she resented that I was quite good-looking in those days.) Betty did respect my public relations professionalism, even if her demeanor was cold and unsociable. Germaine Greer, renowned author of *The Female Eunuch,* wrote in *The Guardian* that Betty was "pompous and egotistic, somewhat demanding and sometimes selfish." I disagree with Germaine's use of the word *pompous,* but Betty was definitely self-involved.

Despite her unkindness, I admired Betty's vision and original thinking and endless energy. Feminists were grateful to her for creating the name and slogans for NOW, the strategies, the prophetic wisdom. She's the one who recruited most of our early leaders (except for the handful who'd recruited *her*). Other trailblazers played key roles, and thousands of people made major contributions (for example, the radical feminists introduced Consciousness Raising), but I don't believe our revolution for women's rights could have won so many victories so quickly without Betty Friedan as our first commander. By the way, Betty and I often marveled at how rapidly the movement had succeeded.

THE FEMININE MYSTIQUE

In 1957, Betty and her family were living in a large old house in a suburb called Grand View-on-Hudson, in Rockland County, New York. For her Smith College fifteen-year reunion, Betty mailed a routine questionnaire to her sister alumnae. I have a copy of it. Under "YOUR MARRIAGE" her first question was "Is it truly satisfying?" There were a dozen questions on "YOUR SEX LIFE" (all caps). Betty assumed that responses to the questionnaire would help her write an article proving that education does not hamper a woman's emotional satisfaction. She wanted to refute a preliminary study by the Kinsey Report claiming that educated women enjoyed fewer orgasms, a finding that was widely quoted in the media. Later, a bigger study by Kinsey in 1953 announced the opposite result—the frequency of orgasms actually *increased* with a woman's education.

Betty received two hundred replies to her survey. Fifteen years after graduation, 89 percent of the responding Smith alumnae listed their occupation as "housewife." Most expressed deep dissatisfaction with their lives. Betty commented, "I expected to prove that education didn't prevent women from adapting to life as housewives. Instead . . ." Betty wrote an article for *McCall's* magazine about this surprising response. It was summarily rejected. Then followed rejections from *Ladies' Home Journal, Redbook,* and other women's publications. Undaunted, Betty expanded her article into a book, proclaiming that educated women suffered from "the problem that has no name" if their lives solely consisted of housework and the nurture of husband and children. She wrote that well-educated women disagreed angrily with the 28 percent of women in a recent survey who had approved of this statement: "I like to try out new things. I've just started to use a new liquid detergent— and somehow it makes me feel like a queen" (Friedan 1963, p. 216)

Women and men throughout history had called for greater equality between the sexes, but until *The Feminine Mystique* there was no call for a full-scale revolution. Most people believed that women were happy with the way we'd lived through the centuries. Betty's book told women, You're not as happy as they say you are! And you can overturn your oppression.

Betty first called her book "The Educated Woman, Her Problems and Prospects." If she had stuck with this title, she might have short-circuited complaints about her failure to address women of color and women in poverty. They were never the subjects of Betty's book.

Betty finally persuaded W.W. Norton to give her a one-thousand-dollar advance. After its publication on February 19, 1963, *The Feminine*

Mystique sold more than three million copies worldwide in its first three years. Every time I sat in a restaurant with Betty Friedan, at least one woman rushed up to her and exclaimed, "You changed my life!"

Betty wrote her book in a scribbly longhand on lined yellow pads. On a friend's recommendation, she hired Pat Aleskovsky from nearby Tappan, New York, to type the manuscript. Pat lived in an enclave called Hickory Hill. The residents, mostly families of World War II veterans, created a uniquely sharing community. They worked on the construction of one another's houses, and developed innovative ideas for living together. Work hours served as a unit of currency; these could be used for babysitting or hair cutting or other chores. Betty was so favorably impressed that she wrote an article that appeared in *Redbook* as "The Happy Families of Hickory Hill." In one of this small world's many coincidences, I moved into Hickory Hill with my family a dozen years later.

But there was another side to the Hickory Hill story. Betty discovered that apart from the joys of community life, some of the housewives were less happy than her article implied. Nearly all the women held college degrees, yet almost none held a job outside her suburban home. Most had three or four children (110 children for the thirty-two Hickory Hill families). Many suffered from hidden resentments. Betty later revealed their discontented stories, disguised, in *The Feminine Mystique.*

BETTY AND CARL

Betty and Carl had two sons and a daughter. At Betty's funeral, her son Jonathan opened his eulogy by saying, "Our family had more psychoanalysis than any family in America." The stormy marriage between Betty and Carl lasted for twenty-two years, until she obtained a divorce in Mexico on May 14, 1969. Friends who knew them in Rockland County told me they both drank too much, and embarrassed them frequently with shouting matches in public.

Carl often broke into our telephone discussions about NOW business, shouting, "Betty, hang up!" He resented our long discussions. Perhaps we obstructed his use of the phone for his own business.

My son, Eric, recently commented on those phone calls. Eric says I received "lots" of calls from Betty during dinnertime. As a child of around nine years, Eric could always tell they were from Betty because I held the receiver far from my ear in response to her loud shouting.

In her final book, *Life So Far*, Betty depicted herself as a battered wife. In truth, she and Carl battered *each other*. Betty admitted this to me several times. Once, with a wry smile, she said, "Carl was no wife beater. He was bigger than me. So even if I started it and really hurt him, I'm the one who had the bruises."

I have a theory about Betty's allegations in *Life So Far*: Her assistant in her last twelve years, Hildie Carney, tells us that Betty was frail at the end of her life and unable to finish writing the book. Linda Francke ghostwrote the remainder of the book. In writing down Betty's endless rants about Carl, Linda may not have realized that the abuse was mutual. Betty was probably accurate in accusing Carl of stalking her with obscene phone calls when she was out of town. (Friedan 1963, p. 145) He was probably drunk.

Once, during the lengthy litigation of their divorce, Carl phoned me while a NOW chapter meeting was taking place in my apartment. "I'm downstairs in your lobby. I'm gonna call a press conference right now and tell the press that Betty is no true feminist. She's demanding a fortune in our divorce. How could a feminist do that?" In truth, Betty was fighting for child support but requested no alimony. I managed to talk Carl out of his threatened press conference.

In January 1968, Carl sent me a letter saying, "I should like to join N.O.W. and be eligible to attend. Would you kindly have someone send me an application blank and some information about dues, etc.?" Carl thought this would upset us, but I called his bluff. I replied that NOW had many male members and that we'd welcome his check.

Betty told me their bellicose divorce was the hardest experience of her life. It was traumatic for their children. In later years, Betty and Carl got together amicably for occasional family events. But first, he'd married and divorced two other women, Norene and Donatella. Norene was a thirty-six-year-old blond model. Carl boasted to *The Washington*

Post on February 7, 1971, that Norene shined his shoes and never argued with him.

He sent me a copy of a rambling newsletter from his website carl-friedan.com. Distributed in May 2000, the letter contradicted press stories that he had physically abused Betty. The letter said it took "a driven, super-aggressive, egocentric, almost lunatic dynamo to rock the world the way she did. Unfortunately, she was that same person at home." The words Carl hurled against Betty were not entirely untrue. People who worked with her could have provided additional adjectives.

Their children lovingly supported both parents through the divorce struggle and in later years. Betty says Carl "never really provided child support after the divorce." She claims he told daughter, Emily, not to apply to Harvard because it was too expensive, and to attend Hunter College, near home, instead. According to her book, Betty assured Emily, "Honey, you know you don't have to do that. You know you can go to Harvard. I'll pay, if need be." (Friedan 1963, p. 299)

Betty underwent various forms of psychotherapy throughout her life. Her assistant Hildie Carney tells me she was in therapy until her death. Why did Betty behave so badly to other people? Perhaps one could blame her parents. Or her personal rejections as a youngster. Or genetics. Probably all of the above. Betty's psychotherapists may have unearthed other reasons for her habitual hostility. A newscaster once made the sexist statement, "The women's movement might have been different if Betty Friedan had had a nose job."

Hildie recalls that "Betty's mind raced ahead of other people, and she was impatient when we didn't catch up with her. She felt she was right, and she hated when people disagreed with her."

Therapists probably learned about Betty's love (perhaps *compulsion* would be a better word) of shopping. Hildie told me, "She kept buying clothes, and filled four closets. Some of the items were pretty but weren't her size." When Betty visited me in Puerto Vallarta, her first words were, "When can we go shopping?"

In her late years, Betty purchased at least three bright red dresses. She wore one of them in a portrait titled *Betty Friedan as the Prophet,* which I purchased from the esteemed painter June Blum. Betty posed in person for June's painting, rather than sending a photo for the artist to copy. Her unhappy expression could be described as "impatient." Not the usual expression for a portrait.

Betty admitted to having an abrasive personality. In 2000, on a publicity tour for *Life So Far,* she told *The New York Times*: "My mother was sort of hypocritical. . . . I err in the other direction. I'm too brutally frank. I think I don't have enough hypocritical graces." (Wichtel 2000) That was accurate.

BETTY'S COMMUNE

Betty never had a close friend in our movement. But she did maintain long-lasting, intimate friendships with successful women who were feminists. One was *Harper's Bazaar* editor Natalie Gittelson. I complained often to Natalie about Betty's actions. Natalie would smile and say, "That's how she is. Get used to it."

Betty helped establish a close-knit "commune" of women and men who rented a large house together every summer. If a suitable house could not be found, they rented separate houses within a ten-mile radius. There were six people at a time. The cast kept changing over ten years. They included journalist-authors Betty Rollin and Heidi Fiske, professors Si Goode and Cynthia Epstein, video and TV producer Martha Stuart, attorney Howard Epstein, and entrepreneur Richard Laupot, plus other highly accomplished friends. All were truly fond of Betty, though they deplored her bursts of temper.

A TURBULENT NATIONAL CONFERENCE

Two months before our second NOW national conference, to take place in D.C. in November 1967, I urged Betty to commit NOW to support the Equal Rights Amendment. Betty waved me away with her hand. "ERA, that's so old hat!" Ever since Alice Paul presented the bill to Congress in 1923, politicians of both parties had paid pious lip service to the ERA, but it never passed. To make our stand on the ERA more up-to-date, Betty came up with an eight-point NOW Bill of Rights for Women, with the ERA as number one. (NOW Bill of Rights for Women 1967)

The second point in her Bill of Rights was pressure on the EEOC to enforce Title VII. The third insisted that "women be protected by law to ensure their rights to return to their jobs within a reasonable time after childbirth without loss of seniority or other accrued benefits and be paid maternity leave." (Today, that's standard for women employees in some but not all companies. In the old days, I relied on two weeks of annual sick leave for the birth of my two children. After my daughter was born, I added two months of *un*paid leave. Nowadays, the *men* in many companies receive paid parental leave after the birth of a child.)

The fourth and fifth rights pertained to child care, a focus of NOW from the beginning. The sixth supported "the right of women to be educated to their full potential." The seventh urged "job training, housing and family allowances for women in poverty" and also honored "a parent's right to remain at home to care for his or her children."

The eighth right was as controversial as the ERA resolution—our right to contraception and abortion.

I publicized our NOW Bill of Rights for Women in advance of the November conference. In response to the ERA resolution, factions mobilized quickly on both sides. Our diligent NOW secretary-treasurer, Dorothy Haener of the United Auto Workers, needed "at least one more year, please" to persuade her union to abandon its support of protective labor laws and switch to supporting the ERA. Biochemist Inka O'Hanrahan of California, a committed campaigner for the ERA, whispered to me that the UAW had assigned a busload of women employees to sign up as voting members at the conference to vote against the ERA. Despite union pressure, our conference did vote to campaign for the ERA. Reluctantly, Dorothy had to resign from her post. Inka took her place as secretary-treasurer. (Inka died suddenly of a heart condition in January 1970.)

HISTORIANS, PLEASE GET IT RIGHT: BETTY FRIEDAN WORKED FOR ABORTION CHOICE FROM THE BEGINNING

Several historians have inaccurately claimed that Betty Friedan failed to support abortion rights. Renowned professor Carolyn Heilbrun, in her biography of Gloria Steinem, accuses Betty of "trying to keep the movement from taking up such causes as abortion, lesbian rights, and welfare, which she regarded as so much unnecessary baggage . . ." (Heilbrun 1996, p. 242) Other academics have made the same charge. The lesbian rights issue is certainly a problem, which will be discussed later. But Betty did support women's right to abortion (and also compassionate welfare) long before most other feminists got on board with those issues. While we're setting the record straight, Betty was also a fierce opponent of the Vietnam War. A leading historian claims that Betty was "incredulous when [Flo] Kennedy suggested that NOW oppose the Vietnam War." (Turk 2023, p. 97) Betty spoke and wrote and marched against the war from the beginning. She once told our chapter we should consider taking a stand on the war, but she accepted our verdict that the cause was not directly related to sex discrimination.

At our November 1967, conference, abortion was a new—very heated—issue. During the debates, Betty as NOW president sat facing us on the dais, with Marguerite Rawalt at her side as parliamentarian. I was furious at Betty for shaking her head vigorously with approval or disapproval to sway the audience on controversial issues—especially abortion. Betty spoke out passionately for completely repealing abortion laws, not just reforming them to exclude cases of rape or incest.

I was one of the 1967 delegates who opposed NOW action for repeal of abortion laws. I declared at the conference that the issue was premature, and extraneous to NOW's goals. I predicted we'd lose members if we supported this extreme position. (I was wrong! We promptly attracted thousands of new members who cared deeply about abortion.)

Attorney Elizabeth Boyer of Cleveland, a member of NOW's board of directors, shared my concerns. Immediately after the conference vote to campaign for abortion repeal, Betty Boyer stood up and resigned from NOW: "I joined NOW to work for employment and education rights. Not abortion. I'm going to form a new organization of feminists who agree with me." She soon organized the Women's Equity Action League (WEAL), which became an effective force against discrimination. NOW collaborated amicably with WEAL on causes we shared in common.

Betty Friedan cofounded the organization that's now known as NARAL Pro-Choice America in July 30, 1968, in the New York apartment of Lawrence Lader. She gave a stirring speech at NARAL's official formation meeting in Chicago in February 1968. More than 350 members from twenty-one organizations attended.

A DISTRESSING PHONE CALL

Betty served two four-year terms as NOW's president. Some historians mistakenly say we "ousted" or "dumped" her when her second term ended in March 1970. That is not true. Betty had no interest in serving a third term, and was eager to begin making money with lectures and a new book. To keep her in the loop, we created a new post for her as chair of NOW's National Advisory Council. Betty could have utilized this position as a springboard for continued power, but she never made time to do this.

Dolores Alexander, a highly respected reporter for *Newsday,* Long Island's leading newspaper, resigned from her job in 1969 to serve as NOW's national executive director for a much-reduced salary. Dolores was tall, vivacious, and highly intelligent. She and Betty became close as they collaborated on causes they cared about. During a NOW foray into California, Dolores followed Betty's lead into group psychotherapy sessions at the Esalen Institute, part of the Human Potential Movement.

But Dolores had a mind of her own and began to argue with Betty about tactics. She dared to refuse several orders that she considered unreasonable. Betty grew increasingly impatient with Dolores's lack of servility, and kept urging the NOW executive board to fire her for insubordination. Several times we refused. On the night of February 3, 1970, at 11: 00 P.M., Betty organized a conference telephone call with the NOW executive board, presenting us with a final ultimatum on Dolores. I remember the date and time well, because it was my birthday and I was just about to have sex with my husband when the phone rang. Betty threatened that if we didn't agree immediately to fire Dolores, she would publicly accuse NOW of being taken over by lesbians. A ridiculous charge. In her threatened blackmail, Betty did not claim that Dolores herself was a lesbian. (She was not at that time, but she did cross over a year later when, as Dolores later explained to me, "I fell in love.")

The disputatious conference call lasted two hours. We kept refusing Betty's demands until the last five minutes. She finally wore us down. The reason for our surrender was the impossibility of a situation where NOW's president and executive director did not get along. Betty had already made tentative plans to move NOW's national office from New York to Chicago, where the highly capable married couple, Jim and Mary Jean Collins-Robson, were willing to take over our memberships, mailings, publications, and other NOW services. A few days after that phone call, at NOW's national board meeting, there was a vote to terminate Dolores and move our physical operations to Chicago. The office move took place promptly.

Coincidentally, earlier in the day on February 3, New York NOW held its monthly board meeting. The chapter board voted to send a memo to our same national NOW Executive Committee, beginning as follows: "The board of New York NOW . . . unanimously decided to cease its individual and collective attempts to work with Betty Friedan, who has been an increasingly abusive and disruptive force in NOW." (Cohen 1988, p. 313)

The New Yorkers' memo opposed our plan to give Betty, after her presidency ended in March, the proposed post of chairman of the Advisory Committee. After listing several incidents of bad behavior on Betty's part, it ended: "We respect the work that Betty Friedan has done in the past, and we are saddened by the emotional state to which she has arrived. But neither out of respect nor out of sympathy can we allow her to destroy NOW."

THE GREAT MARCH

Two months after our decision to move to Chicago, NOW's fourth national conference took place in late March 1970, at the O'Hare Inn in Des Plaines, Illinois, just outside of Chicago. Betty had no wish to serve another term as president. As planned, we elected Aileen Hernandez, then living in California, as NOW president and Wilma Heide of Pittsburgh as chair. Despite the objections of the New York chapter board, we elected Betty chair of the National Advisory Committee.

At the end of the conference, Betty made a speech that lasted almost two hours. To the surprise of everyone there, she proclaimed a national demonstration for August 26, the fiftieth anniversary of the Nineteenth Amendment, granting women the right to vote. She hadn't consulted any of us before the announcement, which was heavily attended by the press. Aileen Hernandez, who stood next to me, said to me out loud, "Omigod! Now *we'll* have to do the work to make that happen!" Betty called it a Women's Strike for Equality, to be staged in coalition with other feminist groups. She envisioned women taking time away from work, including housework, to march in their communities. Even if Betty's decision was undemocratic (to put it mildly), it was a great idea.

The August 26 demonstration emerged as a history-making success. Some chapters adopted Ann Scott's catchy slogan, "Don't iron while the strike is hot." We soon realized the event would involve marches rather than a strike. (Because it was originally billed as a strike, I decided not to participate on August 26. My agency might consider a strike too radical. I lament this decision.)

Some 100,000 women, men, and children marched for feminism in ninety cities and towns in forty-two states, as well as in Paris, Amsterdam, and other foreign capitals. A banner at the Arc de Triomphe said in French: MORE UNKNOWN THAN THE UNKNOWN SOLDIER: HIS WIFE.

Some media carped that few women indulged in work stoppages or actual strikes, but the communication impact of a *march* for women's rights was overwhelming. Nearly all revolutions include parades and dramatic demonstrations. Our big march of August 26, 1970, was *the* event that made millions of women and men realize that feminism was here to stay.

The march in New York City was especially triumphant, claiming more than 35,000 marchers—women, men, and children. *The New York Times* carried a big photo at the top of its front page. Our chapter had publicized the march several days in advance by taking over the Statue of Liberty and unfurling a huge banner declaring WOMEN OF THE WORLD UNITE!

On August 26, New York City officials refused to close off traffic for the event. But the marchers were undaunted. Here's how Betty Friedan wrote about it later: "We came out of the park onto Fifth Avenue, and sure enough there were the police on horses, trying to shunt us off to the sidewalk. . . . I said to the women on each side, *take hands and stretch across the whole street.* And so we marched, in great swinging long lines . . ." (Davis 1991, p. 115)

Betty's daughter, Emily, who was fourteen at the time, refused to attend the March because she and her mother were squabbling. She regrets missing it (as I do).

Responding to the success of the march, Congresswoman Bella Abzug passed a motion through Congress that August 26 would be celebrated every year as Women's Equality Day.

DISSENSION AND COMPETITION

Until this time, I'd been cajoling activists who threatened to resign in response to Betty's temper tantrums: "Please don't give up. NOW is all we have." But things began to change. New feminist organizations began to spring up, and we were no longer the only game in town. While NOW railed against "sexist laws," radical feminists decried the patriarchy. They concentrated mainly on personal relations. Radicals introduced Consciousness Raising, producing the click of comprehension that turned hundreds of thousands of women into feminists. Soon nearly all NOW chapters introduced their own consciousness-raising groups. The 1970s was our decade of greatest achievement, and worst hostilities.

As for Betty Friedan, her leadership role diminished. Gloria Steinem and Bella Abzug and other "stars" emerged. Betty chewed me out, understandably, when I once remarked to a colleague that "the media dropped Betty like a hot potato after Gloria arrived." Not only was Gloria beautiful and articulate and quick to produce newsworthy aphorisms, she was also nice. Betty sometimes hung up the phone on reporters; Gloria was gracious to everyone. Gloria appeared on the cover of *Newsweek* magazine and became *McCall* magazine's Woman of the Year in 1972. Betty never received those honors.

Betty responded belligerently to the media's abrupt enthronement of Gloria. Some of her attacks were based on ideology, but they obviously reflected personal envy as well. Betty called Gloria and her allies "man-haters." She wrote a piece for *McCall's* in August 1972, accusing Gloria unjustly of unresponsiveness to the concerns of mothers. "Why does 'liberation' or 'feminism' imply . . . the elimination of husbands or fathers, the exclusion of . . . 'womanly self' as a mother?" The article attacked Bella as well as Gloria. She described Bella's race for the congressional seat of liberal William Fitts Ryan as a "cold-blooded act." Her article ended: "It's time to leave behind as dinosaurs, or isolate as lethal freaks, male chauvinist pigs and female chauvinist boors alike." Some feminists will never forgive Betty for those cruel remarks.

Betty kept busy with meaningful activities. In April 1973, she and Sarah Kovner and a group of other feminists, in response to sex discrimination by banks in employment and loans and other policies, formed the First Women's Bank and Trust Company, an all-service bank located on an elegant corner of Park Avenue and Fifty-Seventh Street in Manhattan. I wrote the press release and sent out invitations to the press conference. (I used my Byoir VP letterhead. By that time, the agency considered feminism noncontroversial and nonthreatening.) Sarah Kovner told me that my husband, Dr. Shepard Aronson, had signed on as one of their first customers. His medical office was around the corner.

The bank never succeeded financially because it was undercapitalized. But it did motivate other banks to end sex discrimination. In 1989, after fourteen years, it changed its name to the First New York Bank for

Business, stating its belief "that women are no longer discriminated against by other banks." At the time of its name change, half of the bank's senior managers were women.

THE SECOND STAGE

Betty and our movement received helpful support from Chuck Schumer, who, at the time of this writing, is now majority leader of the U.S. Senate. He attended several feminist events and supported bills that we cared about. (We always cared about gun control, and Schumer introduced the Brady Bill for mandatory checks on handguns, along with other worthwhile bills.) When I produced a VFA webinar saluting Betty Friedan's one-hundredth birthday, Schumer recorded a video tribute to Betty. I recall a luncheon where feminists presented Schumer with our Eleanor Roosevelt Legacy Award. He pointed to his parents in the audience and said, "They keep me from moving too far to the center."

Betty became increasingly interested in problems of families. She kept reminding the world that we were the National Organization *for* Women, not *of* Women, and that equal partnership is healthy for our sons as well as our daughters. She recognized that new problems were arising as women joined the workforce. Some marriages were breaking up, although others grew stronger. How were children getting along if Mommy held a full-time job outside the home and Daddy didn't take on more responsibilities?

During my presidency of the NOW Legal Defense and Education Fund, I organized the National Assembly on the Future of the Family on November 19, 1979, a full-day event with ten panels of prestigious experts addressing various problems of evolving families. One of my goals was to prove that the feminist movement was not antifamily. Betty gave a brilliant speech at this assembly. She thanked me for highlighting what she called the "Second Stage" of feminism. She'd already started work on a book by that name. Her book addressed important family issues. But Betty diluted its influence with her unfair diatribes against other feminists. The media reacted negatively to her attacks.

BETTY AND LESBIANS

In contrast to many inspiring phrases coined by Betty for our movement, one unfortunate phrase haunted her for the rest of her life: "Lavender Menace." Betty introduced this phrase in December 1969 at a NOW board meeting in New Orleans. She believed that discrimination against lesbians, while regrettable, should be addressed in separate organizations like the Daughters of Bilitis, and she said NOW would lose too many prospective members and governmental supporters if we adopted lesbianism as an issue. This viewpoint was shared in the early days by many other NOW leaders, including Pauli Murray, Kay Clarenbach, and (to my later regret) me.

Opinions began to evolve. (I use that word frequently, don't I? It's a hallmark of our revolution.) After a year of heated discussions, members at NOW's September 1971 national conference voted almost unanimously that lesbianism was indeed a feminist issue. Six years later, in 1977, at the National Women's Conference in Houston, Betty Friedan stood up and seconded a resolution for lesbian rights. On June 24, 2002, at a Veteran Feminists of America dinner honoring Kate Millett, Betty openly apologized to Kate for failing to support her in December 1970, when Kate was attacked for her lesbianism.

Betty Friedan is still a figure of scorn among many, but not all, lesbian activists and scholars. They don't acknowledge that she ultimately corrected course and reversed her regrettable "lavender menace" positions.

MANY JEWISH FEMINISTS

Betty and I took special pride in the number of Jewish feminists who worked for our movement. In addition to Betty and me, there were Bella Abzug, Sonia Pressman Fuentes, Phineas Indritz, Gerda Lerner, Heather Booth, Shulamith Firestone, Alix Kates Shulman, Letty Cottin Pogrebin, Bernice Sandler, Barbara Seaman, Sheila Tobias, Karen DeCrow, Larry Lader, Susan Brownmiller, Eleanor Pam, Andrea Dworkin, and three-quarters of the founders of The Boston Women's Health Book Collective, known as Our Bodies Ourselves. Gloria Steinem's father was Jewish, though Gloria doesn't identify with any religion. Alicia Garza, cofounder of Black Lives Matter, converted to Judaism. According to the research of NOW founder Sonia Pressman Fuentes, 12 percent of NOW's founding members were Jewish.

This high percentage may be related to our religion's often-stated mission of *Tikkun Olam*, healing the world. Betty declared that Jewish women throughout history had been "strong, energetic and supportive." On the other hand, we can't overlook extreme prejudice against women in the teachings and practices of Ultra-Orthodox Judaism. Betty criticized the Jewish daily prayer that proclaims, "I thank thee, Lord, I was not created a woman." At NOW's August 26 march, Betty's speech offered a revised version of that prayer. Betty later organized a group to discuss "What does it mean to be a Jew?" To the best of my knowledge, virtually all the women and men in Betty's "commune" were Jewish—secular, of course.

Betty traveled to Israel in 1970 "to get in touch with my Jewish roots." After returning home, she served as cochair of the American Jewish Congress's Task Force on the Jewish Woman.

Betty became an outspoken Zionist in 1975 when attending the International Women's Year World Congress in Mexico City, with its infamous resolution that "Zionism equals racism." At the IWY conference in Nairobi in July 1985, Betty and her allies succeeded in heading off hostile resolutions assaulting Zionism. Betty told me later, "The Nairobi conference made feminists feel more Jewish."

At that conference, Betty enthroned herself every day in a chair that Kathy Bonk had placed under the biggest tree in Nairobi. The tall tree provided shade for thirty people. Every day at noon, hundreds of women gathered there to share Betty's wisdom. Sybil Shainwald, a prominent attorney who participated in the conference, recently told me a story that illustrates Betty's arrogance. Sybil registered early and obtained one of the best rooms in the Hotel Nairobi. Betty registered late and found herself in a small room. Betty shouted at Sybil, "I want your room!" Sybil refused to swap. If Betty had asked nicely and explained that a larger room was needed for meetings, perhaps Sybil might have swapped.

In 1984, Betty led a delegation of American women to Israel for a dialogue titled "Women as Jews, Jews as Women." Her speech in Jerusalem helped launch the Israel Women's Network, under the inspirational (and still influential) Alice Shalvi.

Jewish feminists were delighted when Golda Meir became prime minister of Israel in 1969, even though Golda refused to declare herself a feminist and smiled proudly when Israelis referred to her as "the only man in the cabinet." A popular poster circulating in America featured Golda's face with the caption "But can she type?" I was one of six feminist leaders who met with Golda in a New York hotel room to talk about Israel, and *People* magazine published our picture in January 1976. For some reason, Golda did not take time to meet with Betty when she visited Israel in 1970. Betty, who had already met with the Pope and other world leaders, agonized over Golda's slight.

TWO MISSED OPPORTUNITIES

Not all of Betty's visionary ideas bore fruit. In 1967, she asked me to arrange a meeting with Rosemary Park, president of Barnard College, my alma mater. When we met with Park, Betty offered to help Barnard establish a new interdisciplinary curriculum on women's history, women's literature, and other women's issues. Park made no commitments. Two years later, feminists at Cornell University introduced the first women's studies course. In 1970, San Diego University initiated an interdisciplinary women's studies curriculum. Other colleges soon followed suit.

Betty had another idea that was later realized by others. In 1968, I accompanied her to a meeting with philanthropist David Rockefeller. She urged him to bankroll her to create a new feminist magazine for women. Rockefeller declined. Four years later, in 1972, Gloria Steinem led a group of pioneers in the launch of *Ms.* magazine.

LIFE AFTER NOW

Beginning in the 1980s, Betty entered a time of increasing isolation from her former colleagues. She mended fences with some lesbians, but others continued to vilify her. She embarked on intellectual activities suitable for an elder stateswoman, and received honorary doctorates from several universities. She conducted seminars on "gender politics" at the Woodrow Wilson Center. When I asked her if that term referred obliquely to Kate Millett's book *Sexual Politics*, she said, "Yes, we have to get beyond those battles between women and men."

In 1998, the Cornell University School of Industrial and Labor Relations made her a distinguished visiting professor. The Ford Foundation provided them with a million-dollar grant to establish a D.C.-based project titled "The New Paradigm: Women, Men, Work, Family, and Public Policy," with Betty as its director. The project included symposia, research, and other activities. A friend at Ford said to me, "Betty won't have to worry anymore about chasing around for lectures to earn money."

Betty continued to rail against the stereotyped portrayals of women's lives in the media, especially TV and movies. She said they depict a world "in which all you need is a pretty face and big breasts, and you can go right out and catch that lonely billionaire." (Levine 1993)

Betty always loved the company of men. I was told that after her divorce she had a ten-year affair with a married man, who then died; then a long relationship with Irving Schwartz, widower of Felice Schwartz (of Catalyst and "mommy track" fame). There were other men, too.

By the 1990s, acquaintances conceded that Betty was "mellowing." I, for one, benefited. After years of treating me coldly, Betty began to praise my role in NOW's early communications. In the old days, Betty, for some reason, behaved rudely to my husband, Shep. But now she invited Shep and me to spend an enjoyable weekend in her attractively furnished cottage in Sag Harbor, Long Island. On the front page of her last book, *Life So Far*, Betty penned this handwritten note: "For my dear, dear friend Muriel—who's been with me through it all, and without whose counsel, wisdom and support, it would not have turned out so well. Here's to our memories of the great adventure we led—that changed the world. Love always—Betty Friedan." This unprecedented display of affection moved me deeply.

OLD AGE

Betty was a visionary in many ways. We should not overlook another concept she brought to popular attention: a new way of looking at old age. In 1982, when she was sixty-one, she embarked on a fellowship at Harvard to study everything then known about aging. Her guru was Dr. Robert N. Butler, director of the National Institute on Aging at the National Institutes of Health. Butler had created the term *ageism* to describe discrimination against seniors.

After a decade of study, Betty wrote *The Fountain of Age*, published in 1993, when she was seventy-two. In this heavily researched 671-page book, Betty advanced a drastically revised vision of senior life. She deplored talk about "senility," and insisted that many people who are accused of dementia, incompetence, or "just waiting to die" can be brought back to productive life with medical treatment, hearing aids, and meaningful activities.

Betty insisted that many millions of seniors can live rewarding lives until age one hundred or beyond. She referred to "the second half" of life as time that can be energetic and joyful, and sexually satisfying. This concept was revolutionary in 1993; today it is widely recognized everywhere. It's a guiding principle of senior living residences now blossoming throughout the world. (I live happily in one, Kendal on Hudson, outside New York City. Two of my good friends, Bill Rakower and Jean MacIntosh, are over 104 and are still lively and interesting.) Once again, Betty was ahead of her time. Her arguments against ageism are especially relevant for women, since we live longer than most men.

Betty's health began to deteriorate. In the spring of 1993, she underwent open-heart surgery for a heart valve transplant. The surgeon used a pig's valve, which was not successful. (Betty joked that her Jewish heart had rejected it.) Then she had a second valve transplant that same year; this proved successful. In September 1997, she underwent a third operation for heart valve replacement.

These surgeries may have hastened Betty's loss of short-term memory. She'd repeat the same question again and again. Apart from this memory shortcoming, she never lost her intellectual facility; people who labeled her with "dementia" were mistaken. At feminist events her speeches were perceptive and inspiring. True, she sometimes ignored the topic assigned to her. But she spoke informatively on whatever topic she chose.

Despite her short-term memory loss, Betty still traveled. At the age of eighty she successfully switched plane connections to visit me in Puerto Vallarta, Mexico. Shep and I gave her a festive birthday party with a mariachi band. Before her first dinner in Puerto Vallarta, Betty took a bath at her hotel, the Camino Real, and then realized she could not get out of the bathtub. She shouted for help and was rescued by two porters. Later she laughed this off.

Betty insisted on being an energetic tourist during her stay. Once, when I reached for her arm to help her across a street, she pushed me away, shouting, "Fuck off, Muriel!" As independent as ever.

Betty let her dyed-black hair go gray, and began to look fragile and elderly. She walked with a cane but refused to use a walker. One of her problems was hearing loss. Shep and I helped her buy new hearing aids, but she often neglected to wear them. She kept forgetting to change the batteries.

Betty had moved to Washington, D.C., where she taught a course on women's history at George Mason University. She was fortunate in hiring Hildie Carney as her assistant in 1993. Hildie took care of Betty's professional and personal affairs until the day she died. She was highly efficient, and deeply devoted to Betty. Hildie told me that Betty fired her almost every day. "You're stupid! You don't do your job!" she'd say.

In her last few years, Betty moved into the Georgetown, an upscale assisted living residence in downtown D.C. She made no friends there, and kept complaining about the food. Hildie recalls, "She'd often order a five-course takeout, and eat very little." Betty hired and fired at least three caretakers, whom she found too slow to meet her demands.

Betty died on her eighty-fifth birthday. (Moses also died on his birthday.) I felt honored that Hildie chose me to be first speaker at the funeral. I opened by saying, "Betty Friedan was the greatest woman of the twentieth century. She was the greatest woman of the second millennium." That year, I was asked frequently to speak in tributes to Betty. In a memorial at Cornell University, with Betty's son Jonathan and daughter, Emily, in the audience, I reviewed not only Betty's triumphs but also her unkind behavior. "Betty Friedan was not a good woman. But she was a *great* woman!"

6

CREDIT, BELLA, AND THE NATIONAL WOMEN'S POLITICAL CAUCUS

BELLA GIVES US CREDIT

Many women of my generation say their most infuriating experience of sex discrimination was trying to get and keep a credit card. In the bad old days, banks denied credit to single women. The card of a married woman bore the name of her husband. In case of divorce or the death of her husband, she lost her card and had to struggle mightily to get another one. Single women had to prove to banks that their job was permanent. In deciding if a divorced woman was credit-worthy, banks did not count alimony as income.

I recall a maddening time during the NOW national conference in Los Angeles in 1971, where I was elected national chair. Delegates kept calling me down to the hotel's front desk. The restaurant had refused to honor the credit cards of any woman whose husband's name was not on the card. We hadn't yet won passage of the Equal Credit Opportunity Act.

History must never forget Bella Abzug. She introduced ECOA in the House of Representatives as an amendment to the Federal Deposit Insurance Act of 1950.

In most advances won by feminists, the word *sex* was added at a later date to existing laws that banned other forms of discrimination. But in the case of Bella's ECOA, this order was reversed. Women came

This woman's place is in the House...
the House of Representatives!

Bella Abzug
for Congress.

Bella Abzug
Photograph courtesy of the Library of Congress

first. ECOA first outlawed discrimination on the basis of sex or marital status. Later, Congress caught up and applied ECOA to other victims of credit injustice. The revised law, passed in March 1976, prohibited "lending discrimination based on race, color, religion, national origin, age, the receipt of public assistance income, or exercising one's rights under certain consumer protection laws."

Also, creditors could not ask the marital status of an applicant, or whether she planned to have children. Thank you, Bella Abzug!

The ECOA sailed through Congress with almost unanimous approval, in response to heavy lobbying by the NOW Task Force on Taxation and Credit, WEAL, ACLU, Parents Without Partners, and other activists. President Gerald Ford signed it.

After the ECOA, there were still financial problems for women. I recall testifying to Congress in 1974 on women's unfair treatment with regard to Social Security and pensions. Upon divorce, a woman lost all rights to her ex-husband's Social Security payments. Many wives needed this for support in their old age. Also, if a wife predeceased her husband, he could not inherit her Social Security. As we'll see later, Ruth Bader Ginsburg won a landmark Supreme Court case proving that sex discrimination victimized men as well as women.

Bella Abzug was first elected to the House in 1970, at the age of fifty. Her slogan was "This woman's place is in the House." She'd been a leader in Women Strike for Peace, and had spoken out forcefully against the House Committee on Un-American Activities. Her famous quotes included "Women have been trained to talk softly and carry a lipstick."

In the Ninety-second Congress alone, Bella and Martha Griffiths introduced more than twenty bills for women. Bella commented in 1972, "We put sex discrimination provisions into everything. There was no opposition. Who'd be against equal rights for women?" (Evans 1991, p. 291)

Bella was a founder of the Congressional Caucus on Women's Issues, which is still strong today. She introduced the first gay rights bill in May 1974. With Shirley Chisholm, she coauthored the Child Development Act, proposing universal child care. Congress passed the bill, but Richard Nixon vetoed it.

"Battling Bella" relinquished her House seat in 1976 to run for the U.S. Senate. She lost narrowly to Daniel Patrick Moynihan. In subsequent years, she lost several other elections. In 1986, she changed her residence to Westchester County, hoping to win election to the House, but she lost that race, too.

While still in Congress, Bella introduced the resolution that created the National Women's Conference, as part of International Women's Year. That memorable event took place in Houston in November 1977. A torch was carried to the Houston Conference, 2,600 miles from Seneca Falls, by a relay of twenty-one runners wearing IWY shirts. First Ladies Betty Ford, Rosalynn Carter, and Lady Bird Johnson joined hands onstage. The conference passed twenty-six policy statements on women's issues, including the ERA, abortion, and gay rights.

A competing conference was staged across town by Phyllis Schlafly's followers. One attendee at that conference carried a placard attacking the Jewish Bella with the slogan "Kikes for Dykes." (Shteir 2023, p. 208)

Bella presented President Jimmy Carter with the conference's National Plan of Action. To implement its recommendations, Carter created a National Advisory Committee on Women, with Bella as chair. But Carter gave them no budget or investigative authority. Bella complained so loudly to the press that Carter fired her abruptly in January 1979. He refused to let her resign gracefully. We were heartbroken for Bella.

Bella remained active and relevant despite her election disappointments. She wrote two influential books and cofounded, with close colleague Mim Kelber, the Women's Environment and Development Organization (WEDO). In 1991, WEDO's World Women's Congress for a Healthy Planet drew fifteen hundred women from eighty-three countries to create a Women's Action Agenda.

Bella's stockbroker husband, Martin Abzug, accompanied her to many feminist events. We all kvelled over their happy relationship.

THREE BIRTHS FOR THE NWPC

One of Bella's great achievements was her work for the National Women's Political Caucus. I recall one incident vividly: Bella and Gloria Steinem came to visit me in my apartment in 1972. Since it was dinnertime, I served them fried chicken in my living room. Their purpose: "Can't you do something about Betty Friedan?" Betty's emotional tirades were making people in the NWPC miserable. I told Bella and Gloria that I'd try to calm Betty down, but I didn't hold much hope. Betty was labeling them "man-haters" in speeches and articles.

Historians credit the three of them, and others, with founding the NWPC in Washington, D.C., in July 1971. Actually, this trailblazing organization was born three times. The official 1971 date was the third birth. Its precursor took place in 1970. Betty Friedan said we needed a new organization, other than NOW, working specifically to promote women in politics. Betty assembled a group of activists, mostly NOW members, in the Park Avenue apartment of Elinor Guggenheimer, an inspiring feminist who would later launch the Women's Forum and the Child Care Action Campaign.

I still have the group's mission statement. Betty Friedan scribbled it on the back of her personal check, lacking other paper. Betty wrote on the check, "We hope to go into the national conventions of both major parties with bargaining power to support women candidates, and work with under-represented groups. We will work in primaries and elections across party lines and outside existing parties—drawing in women who have lost faith in the electoral process, to elect women candidates committed to our goals."

After that session in Elly Guggenheimer's apartment, our new organization held several enthusiastic meetings. Someone suggested the name National Women's Political Caucus. I composed a simple flyer. The two-sided appeal on pale green paper asked for twenty-five-dollar dues. It pointed out that women held only 1 percent of the elected offices in this country. "There is only one woman Senator, 12 Congresswomen out of 435, no governors, only one per cent of federal judges."

After several months, bitter wrangling erupted among the members, similar to disputes that savaged other feminist groups at the time. I dropped out, not wanting to become embroiled in still another brouhaha among sisters. Others resigned, too.

The second birth of the National Women's Political Caucus occurred on March, 21, 1971, according to at least one history book. (Cohen 1988, p. 313) The group's flyer stated that the original concept "came from Betty Friedan, well-known author of The Feminine Mystique and a leading feminist thinker and lecturer." Betty invited Liz Carpenter, Shana Alexander, and other prominent feminists to her 93rd St. apartment to plan a national conference. Betty did not invite me or other NOW leaders—perhaps because the earlier structure from Elly Guggenheimer's apartment was still in existence. According to Betty's printed recollections, she also phoned Martha Griffiths, Shirley Chisholm, and Bella Abzug, who "screamed at me over the phone that I had no business invading her turf." (Davis 1991, p. 141)

The third, *official* founding conference of NWPC took place July 10, 1971, at the Statler Hotel in Washington, D.C. It's the birth cited by most

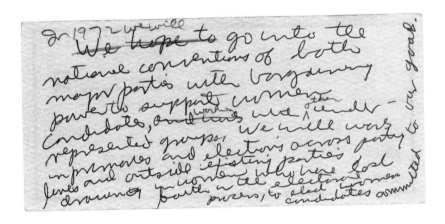

Betty Friedan wrote the mission statement for the National Women's Political Caucus
on the back of her personal check in 1970. Revisions were added by Muriel Fox.
Photograph courtesy of Muriel Fox

historians. The nearly three hundred participants encompassed a broad
spectrum of women, ranging from Republican libertarians to NOW
activists, including many women of color. Kay Clarenbach presided.
She confided to us, "I think I was drafted to chair the Caucus because I
could get along with both Betty and Bella." (Cohen 1988, p. 313).

To avoid conflict on the choice of a keynote speaker, Kay appointed
a nonpartisan panel instead of one speaker. However, the machinery
of that conference was clearly managed by Bella and Gloria (Cohen
1988, p. 116). Listed as founders were Bella, Gloria, Betty, Shirley
Chisholm, Fannie Lou Hamer, Mildred Jeffrey, and Jill Ruckelshaus.

The conference resolved "to increase the number of women in all aspects of political life—as elected and appointed officials, as judges in state and federal courts, and as delegates to national conventions." Resolutions included an absolute prohibition against any who held racist views. There were also calls to support the ERA and strengthen the EEOC, and to fight for "a woman's right to decide her own reproductive and sexual life."

Betty began to feel, rightly, that Bella and Gloria were leaving her out of NWPC decisions. This was probably because of her temper and her public attacks. They omitted her completely from the first board of directors. Betty threatened to sue for fraud, but she didn't follow through for lack of evidence. When speaking to the press, Bella and Gloria omitted Betty. There were frequent arguments as to who would be the NWPC spokeswoman. It wasn't going to be Betty. Nora Ephron, describing Gloria Steinem's role as spokeswoman at the Democratic National Convention in 1972, wrote in *Esquire Magazine* that Betty was seen "off to the side, just slightly out of the frame." (Shteir 2023, p. 178)

Despite early conflicts, NWPC began to thrive. There was a brief time in the 1990s when I joined the NWPC board of directors. Their gatherings were much more glittering than NOW events. I recall one board meeting that ended with dinner in the Georgetown house of Bob Woodward. I shared a cab from the airport with two NWPC codirectors, movie star Candace Bergen and Doonesbury cartoonist Garry Trudeau.

At one board meeting, I suggested to executive director Lael Stegall the wording for a gracious letter to notify directors who would not be renominated for another term. I said the letter should begin with "Thank you for having served on our board of the National Women's Political Caucus." Unfortunately, I was unable to help NWPC raise much money, which was their main requirement for directors at the time. After one year, I received a letter that began, "Thank you for having served on our board of the National Women's Political Caucus." Served me right.

Betty Friedan attended Bella Abzug's funeral. I saw her sitting quietly in the back.

7

GETTING THROUGH THE DOOR

ENDING INJUSTICE IN HOUSING

Many women remember, painfully, being turned away when they tried to rent an apartment. Landlords were free to say, "Sorry, I don't rent to women." Nothing illegal about that, until feminists took action.

The Fair Housing Act passed through Congress on April 10, 1968. It outlaws *all* forms of discrimination in the sale or rental of housing. Feminists joined with other civil rights leaders to pass the bill. It was controversial. Powerful opponents claimed that housing was such a personal matter, it should be decided by individual homeowners, and by individual states. The bill languished without hope in Congress until the assassination of Martin Luther King, Jr. Then, President Johnson yielded to activists' demands and hurried the bill to passage, exactly one week after King's assassination, as proof of America's commitment to human rights.

Women benefit also from the Housing and Community Development Act of 1974, which prohibits sex discrimination in mortgages. The law says that both spouses' combined income must be considered without prejudice in applying for federally related mortgage loans. Before this act, when a bank decided whether to grant a home mortgage to a married couple, only the husband's income was calculated. His wife's income was ignored. As for women without a husband, they had little chance before these bills passed. Some banks required a woman to produce a letter from her doctor certifying that she was taking birth-control pills or had been sterilized. (Davis 1991, p. 148).

PUBLIC ACCOMMODATIONS—MORE COMPLICATED

Unfortunately, gender discrimination is not prohibited in *all* sections of the 1964 Civil Rights Act. We fought hard, but unsuccessfully, to add the word *sex* to the act's Title II, which says "All persons shall be entitled to the full and equal enjoyment of the goods, services, facilities, privileges, advantages, and accommodations of any place of public accommodation, as defined in this section, without discrimination on the ground of race, color, religion, or national origin. . . . The provisions of this title shall not apply to a private club or other establishment not in fact open to the public . . ." Because *sex* is not included in Title II, we've been forced to wage our battles state by state, institution by institution.

To show how humiliating this exclusion could be: The popular Kaufman's Pharmacy in New York had a sign over its soda fountain stating that no unescorted women would be served after midnight. (*New York Times* 1993)

NOW chapters have led the way in fighting this exclusion. Thanks to heavy lobbying by New York City NOW, our city was the first to ban sex discrimination in public accommodations. But some "private" business clubs still refuse to let us in.

Today, in the 2020s, forty-four states and the District of Columbia prohibit sex discrimination in public accommodations. But four states—Georgia, Mississippi, North Carolina, and Texas—still have no statutes barring *any* form of bias in public accommodations.

Women have been routinely excluded from hundreds of restaurants, bars, and private clubs where men transact business and make valuable contacts. We've fought this injustice with lawsuits, demonstrations, boycotts, and other weapons. Our early successes in New York

State inspired other state governments to prohibit discrimination—often in response to pressure from local NOW chapters.

The NOW Legal Defense and Education Fund filed an amicus brief for a 1984 Supreme Court decision that forced the Jaycees to admit women; and in 1987, the Supreme Court also forced the Rotary Club to admit us.

Certain "private venues" still maintain the right to exclude women. The Masters Golf Tournament still rejects us. We remind the courts that important deals are initiated and consummated over lunch, or on the golf course.

Dining clubs, in excluding women, have used such outlandish arguments as "Men have a limited time to eat lunch, and women would monopolize tables, as they gossip and eat slowly." Some diehards claimed that women are unable to calculate the bill and tip correctly, and this impedes men from getting back to the office on time

I LEAD AN ATTACK ON THE PLAZA

Many of us have stories about an embarrassing exclusion from a men-only facility. My experience led me to mobilize NOW for action. In November 1968, as head of the TV-Radio Department of my public relations agency, I'd arranged for a client to be interviewed by John Aspinwall, head of Associated Press Radio. My secretary scheduled lunch, in the name of Muriel Fox, in the Plaza Hotel's elegant Oak Room, where I'd eaten dinner on several occasions. When the three of us arrived at the entrance to the Oak Room at 12:30 P.M., the maître d' stopped us at the door. "Is Muriel Fox a woman? Nobody told me that. Sorry, we don't admit women for lunch." I didn't make a fuss in front of my client. I quietly led my guests down the hall to another Plaza restaurant. It was a humiliating experience.

At the next meeting of NOW's New York City chapter, I proposed that we picket the Oak Room. The suggestion was greeted with loud cheers and an immediate resolution to call the action for February 12. This was Lincoln's Birthday, a holiday for many offices at the time.

National NOW proclaimed the week of February 9, 1969, "Public Accommodations Week." Chapters throughout the country scheduled eat-ins and drink-ins to protest women's exclusion from restaurants and bars. They were taking a page from lunch counter sit-ins of the civil rights movement.

I advised our members to dress for the protest as if they'd always belonged in the Oak Room. "If you have a fur coat, wear it." We alerted the press, which turned out in force.

At noon on February 12, fashionably attired NOW members paraded in the lobby outside the Oak Room entrance. Our signs said WAKE UP PLAZA! GET WITH IT NOW! and THE OAK ROOM IS OUTSIDE THE LAW. A group of women sneaked inside and commandeered a large round table. Four waiters promptly removed the table, leaving the women seated in a circle with nothing in between. During all the hubbub, male customers continued eating their lunch.

Betty Friedan arrived at the last minute—with a black eye! She and her husband, Carl, had been fighting. Jean Faust, past president of our chapter, was an expert on cosmetics. She applied pancake makeup on Betty's face to cover the black eye for TV interviews.

Sixty press people showed up for our protest at the Plaza. I recall that one beautiful young reporter introduced herself to me. "I'm Gloria Steinem, from New York Magazine." Gloria was not yet a publicly proclaimed feminist. She still preferred the term humanist. That night our demonstration appeared on several TV newscasts, and was covered in major newspapers.

Several months later, the Plaza backed down and opened up the Oak Room to women for lunch. Our highly publicized protest played a role, but the Plaza's surrender was due mainly to a mandate from New York City's Human Rights Commission. Eleanor Holmes Norton, a protégé of Pauli Murray, headed the HRC. Eleanor later chaired the national EEOC, and then became a distinguished congresswoman from the District of Columbia.

On the first day that women were permitted in the Oak Room at noontime, I ate lunch there with my brother, Jerry Fox. Nothing unusual happened, and none of the clientele seemed aware that history was being made.

WE OPEN UP RESTAURANTS EVERYWHERE

We soon won well-publicized restaurant admissions in cities everywhere. Among other victories, we succeeded with Heinemann's Restaurant in Milwaukee, the Polo Lounge in Beverly Hills, and the Berghoff in Chicago. During a NOW conference at the Biltmore Hotel in New York City, a group of our members stormed into the male-only Biltmore Bar and opened it up for women forever.

The Miami chapter of NOW preceded our New York chapter by opening up the Men's Grill of Burdine's department store in 1968. No picketing was required, just a series of letters and a friendly visit from chapter president Roxcy Bolton. The name Men's Grill was changed to Executive Grill, "with no restrictions as to male or female usage."

We recall Roxcy Bolton as a shining example of feminist perseverance. A year after opening up the Burdine Men's Grill to women, Roxcy made history by persuading the National Hurricane Center, which was located in Dade County, to stop designating hurricanes by women's names only. National NOW backed her campaign with a resolution demanding that hurricanes alternate between men's and women's names. (That's the practice today.) Roxcy facetiously suggested in a letter that the storms might be called "him-icanes." (Roberts 2017) An additional achievement of Roxcy and Miami NOW was the first rape crisis center in the country.

The city of Fort Lauderdale, Florida, demonstrated the value of electing a woman mayor. When its first female mayor, Virginia Shuman Young, heard about a proposed male-only Tower Club restaurant, she joined with the women's page editor of the *Fort Lauderdale News* to threaten that there would be "two grandmothers picketing on the sidewalk" if women were excluded. The Tower Club opened up quietly to women and men. (*South Florida Sun Sentinel*, December 8, 1994)

"NOT ALL PROSTITUTES"

Our fight to gain admittance in bars, where business is often transacted over friendly drinks, proved more complicated than our restaurant campaigns. Some states refused to grant a license to mixed-sex establishments, and various American cities drafted local ordinances to outlaw women in saloons and taverns.

During Prohibition, when *all* drinking was supposedly illegal, barriers against women disappeared in most saloons that stayed in business. But some bars separated the sexes with six-foot-high partitions "to prevent temperance groups from being able to damn parlours as havens for prostitutes." After repeal of Prohibition, unescorted women were again rejected by the majority of bars in the United States. Saloonists claimed to be discouraging invasion by "females of easy virtue." Sometimes women sitting at a bar were arrested without good reason and subjected to mandatory venereal disease testing by the police. Unattached women at bars were removed for "intoxication," even if they hadn't had anything to drink.

Feminists filed numerous lawsuits. Many succeeded in getting state and local ordinances amended to erase barroom barriers against women. I recall the campaign of New York City NOW to open up McSorley's Old Ale House for women. Why did we want to enter that smelly, unattractive saloon? Because it was a symbol of women's exclusion by a public accommodation.

New York Mayor John Lindsey finally signed a bill prohibiting gender discrimination in all public places. But when journalist Lucy Komisar, vice president of our NOW chapter, arrived at McSorley's, they gave her a hard time. The bartender ridiculously refused to accept Lucy's driver's license as proof that she was over the age of eighteen, and demanded that she produce a birth certificate. Lucy finally talked them into serving her, amid boos from the male customers. One man poured a glass of beer over her head. Newspapers reported the incident in detail, with irrelevant comments about Lucy's stylish white pantsuit.

In 1970, to establish a precedent, Faith Seidenberg, an attorney from NOW's Syracuse chapter, sued McSorley's in federal court, citing the

Fourteenth Amendment. The lawsuit was known as *Seidenberg v McSorley's Old Ale House.* She won an injunction.

One of Faith's colleagues in the Syracuse chapter, Karen DeCrow (later national president of NOW), demonstrated at a local bar in 1969. Karen carried a sign that read, WOMEN WHO DRINK COCKTAILS ARE NOT ALL PROSTITUTES. That wording would be considered politically incorrect nowadays, when feminists argue for the rights, safety, and respectability of sex workers.

We still face issues in public accommodations, such as the treatment of LGBTQ and disabled persons, and the right of women to nurse discreetly in public places.

8

MURIEL FOX

I FEEL HESITANT TO SPEAK ABOUT MYSELF, but feminism trained us not to be self-effacing. So here goes. These are the reasons why I believe I deserve to enter the pantheon of feminists whom history should remember: I was the communicator who made the second-wave revolution visible and therefore powerful. I produced the press conferences, press releases, and media contacts that facilitated NOW's explosive entry into public awareness. I was Betty Friedan's lieutenant and NOW's vice president for communications from 1967 to 1970. As chair of NOW's board from 1971 to 1973, I supervised chapters, chaired board meetings, and held conflicting factions together at a difficult time. I founded NOW's first chapter, in New York. With Betty Friedan, I cofounded the NOW Legal Defense and Education Fund, which I later led as president and then chair. I served as a bridge between the feminist movement and the business community for the mutual benefit of both and raised more than twelve million dollars for feminism. I was cofounder of the Women's Forum, which established professional networking among women. Today I chair Veteran Feminists of America, the foremost resource for historical information about the Second Wave. I organized groundbreaking events such as NOW LDEF's National Assembly on the Future of the Family and its Convocation for New Leadership in the Public Interest and VFA's Salute to Feminist Authors and Salute to

Muriel Fox leads Mother's Day parade for the ERA in Illinois, 1980

Feminists in the Arts. I've remained active in the movement for nearly six decades since cofounding NOW in 1966.

GROWING UP

Here's some personal information. I read somewhere that the happiest people are those who had originally been unhappy. That was true for me. Adult life brought me special fulfillment because it contrasted greatly to a sad childhood and adolescence.

I was born in a working-class neighborhood in Newark, New Jersey. My father, Morris Fox, emigrated from what was variously known as Poland or Ukraine or the remnants of Austro-Hungary to the United States at the age of eighteen. To support our family, he converted a school bus into "Fox's Traveling Grocery Market," which he drove six days a week on a daily route through several New Jersey suburbs. He'd received little high school education. To escape military service in World War I, he'd fled across Europe, doing chores for Jewish farmers. My mother, who'd been born in New York to immigrant parents, looked down on him because of his thick Central European accent and his lack of formal learning. He was handsome, quick-witted, and jovial, and might have become as successful as several affluent Fox cousins if he'd received more encouragement.

My mother, Anna Rubenstein Fox, was the main reason I became a feminist. Like most women of her day, she was stuck in the job of housewife. A highly intelligent and well-read woman, she hated housework, hated cooking, and hated the chores related to motherhood. Our apartments crawled with cockroaches and bedbugs. Our meals were tasteless. My clothes were dirty and wrinkled. Maybe it's significant that she taught us to call her "Mother" rather than the cuddly "Mommy." (We called our father "Daddy.")

The painful shame of my childhood was head lice. In those days, school nurses used to enter classrooms regularly to examine all students for lice. They didn't overtly remove me from class, but I was teased when word got out. The nurse recommended an antilice shampoo that worked, until the next time.

My parents' numerous screaming arguments, loud enough for the neighbors to hear, embarrassed me painfully. Once, when my brother and I were little, my father ran away from our apartment for several weeks. I lived in fear that he might desert us again.

When I led NOW's ERA March in Chicago on Mother's Day, 1980, I dedicated my speech to my mother, who had died from a stroke that week. (The words I used in my speech were almost identical to those used by Betty Friedan in interviews about *her* mother.)

If the women's movement had existed forty years earlier, my mother's intelligence and spunk might have led to a satisfying career. It's true that some women of her time surmounted obstacles and found callings for themselves outside the home—usually as teachers, librarians, nurses, or secretaries. But my mother couldn't cope because she suffered from depression, paranoia, and, later, other emotional problems. It's interesting that Gloria Steinem and Catherine East and I all had mothers with mental illness. (Pauli Murray's father died in a mental hospital.)

Like Betty Friedan, my mother had a younger sister who was pretty and well liked. Despite Anna's pleas (she got top marks in her classes), her father insisted on taking her out of school at age fourteen to work in their grocery store. Her younger sister, Esther, was allowed to continue her schooling and became a teacher. Their parents supported younger brother Morris through law school, and he became a well-known legal expert under the name of Maurice "Maury" Roberts. Anna ultimately earned a high school equivalency degree, and took numerous courses throughout her life, but she envied the careers of her siblings.

My mother's mental health improved greatly during World War II, when my father gave up his grocery bus and opened a fruit and vegetable store on Newark's bustling Hawthorne Avenue. My mother worked side by side with him, and they stopped squabbling. She gave up housework completely. They hired a teenage maid for three dollars a week. After we later moved to Miami Beach, my mother worked with my father in their radio and luggage shop. Again, they got along well.

My mother played the guilt card frequently. We argued incessantly, and I suffered from the self-image of a disagreeable misfit. Whenever I was sick in bed with the usual childhood ailments, my mother scolded me for causing her extra work. When she herself contracted a bad cold (never anything worse), she warned that she was dying. Throughout my childhood I was fearful of her imminent death.

As a child, I walked five blocks to the public library once or twice a week. I read books day and night. Thanks to my mother's influence, I tuned into the Metropolitan Opera on the radio every Saturday afternoon and developed a love of music. My grades were at the top of the class. All Newark students at the time were given IQ tests, and my schoolteacher aunt was informed by a friend that my IQ test score was 167. Someone told her it was the highest IQ in Newark's school system; I don't know if that was true. FYI, I've read that Betty Friedan's IQ was 180.

My tenth birthday party changed my life. My mother's sister, Esther, let us use her (less messy) apartment, and I had a great time with six boys and girls I invited from my class. (We played spin the bottle.) I vowed to stop being a disagreeable person, and to stop arguing with my mother. I'd do anything necessary to make friends. This compliant behavior continued, with rewarding results, through high school and college. I smiled a lot, made numerous friends, and sent my parents a postcard every day from college.

I daydreamed, and hoped for a bright future one day as a newspaper reporter. I worked in the family fruit and vegetable store every afternoon after classes at Weequahic High School, which later became famous through its alumnus Philip Roth (a few years younger—I never met him). Roth's books satirized and patronized the materialistic, nouveau riche Jewish families of the Weequahic area. But I idealized those girls as elegant royalty, with their cashmere sweater sets and perfect makeup.

Our family moved to Miami Beach after my brother, Jerry, contracted rheumatic fever for the third time. We settled in South Beach, then a working-class Jewish enclave. (Much later, South Beach was transformed by gay artists into high-fashion chic.)

During my two years attending Rollins College in Winter Park, Florida, on a full scholarship, I underwent one sad rejection and then many happy experiences. As a freshman, after a rush week during which I felt I'd personified wit and charm at sorority parties, I naïvely expected to receive several invitations to join sororities. I made a list of my preferences. But on the day when freshmen ritually opened up their envelopes with sorority pledge slips, my envelope was empty. Of course. I learned that Rollins sororities did not admit Jewish girls.

I ended up living in the dorm for independents, where I enjoyed warm friendships with a group of interesting, lively young women. This was during World War II; hardly any boys attended Rollins at the time. The school bused us to dances with men who were stationed at the nearby AFTAC training school for air force officers. Men from a nearby camp for conscientious objectors were also invited. I enjoyed a rewarding romance with Red Stephenson, a generous-hearted Quaker from the CO Camp. As their national service in lieu of military training, COs dug toilets for low-income families.

During a prestigious weeklong Rollins conference on the Atomic Bomb and World Government, the United Press reporter covering this event suddenly had to leave for an emergency assignment. A professor recommended me to take his place as a stringer. My UP dispatches were well written and well received. Among others, I interviewed Supreme Court Justice William O. Douglas and International Union of Electrical Workers leader James Carey, who were speakers at the conference.

I enjoyed life at Rollins and learned a lot from the school's sophisticated, affluent coeds—especially how to dress and walk and make light-hearted conversation. In other words, how to behave like a sociable WASP instead of an insecure transplant from Newark's Jewish working-class neighborhoods. But I'd used up most of that small college's most stimulating courses. I decided to transfer to Barnard College in New York City for my final two years. Barnard offered a generous scholarship.

Back in Miami, the summer before moving to Barnard, I persuaded United Press to hire me as a stringer, and filed several stories from the area. One assignment was a press conference with Eleanor Roosevelt.

In a time of postwar uncertainty, Barnard delayed confirming whether they'd found space for me as a transfer student, So I applied for a permanent job at the *Miami Daily News*. They hired me, not yet a college junior, as bridal editor and art critic. Knowing little about art, I interviewed regional artists. The city editor advised me, "Don't be too hard on the locals." When word of a Barnard slot arrived in late August, I resigned from the *News*, where my writing had been well received by editors.

During my college years, I experienced three people's suicides. At Rollins, I dated Vestal Melone, a handsome veteran just returned from the war. Vestal's wife had deserted him while he was overseas, and he spoke bitterly about women. He dropped me after a few weeks because I wouldn't sleep with him. (I remained a virgin till age twenty-four, not unusual for "nice Jewish girls" of that time.) A month later, Vestal shot himself. The second suicide was Sally, my bright but shy lab partner in chemistry class at Barnard. She overdosed on sleeping pills. I hadn't known her well.

The third encounter was more consequential to me. Because of Barnard's dormitory shortage, I had to find independent housing off campus. A friend referred me to the Bronx apartment of Bertha S., a widow whose son had been killed in the war. Mourning grievously, she welcomed a tenant to keep her company. One afternoon I returned from school and found Bertha dead (also from sleeping pills), with a photo of her son clutched to her chest. When Professor Elizabeth Reynard, a professor of English at Barnard, learned about my experience, she found me a dorm room on campus.

Was I shaken by these suicides? No. My early childhood, hardened by an unhappy home life, made me more pragmatic than most people, and less susceptible to distress after harsh experiences. In later life, I hardly cried at all after losing my husband or brother. Perhaps my range of emotions (positive as well as negative) was narrowed by early hardships. Throughout my life, I made a special effort to be in control of the situation.

This narrow range of emotion made me feel like a damaged person until I sought the benefits of psychoanalysis in my early twenties. This therapy was so very helpful to me that I wish *all* people could undergo psychotherapy in their twenties. I learned to feel affectionate toward the Muriel of my childhood, rather than accusing her of unlovable behavior. I learned to be kind to myself in the here and now. I learned to bounce back from setbacks, and not remain sad for too long when things went badly. Thanks to psychotherapy, this sense of what is and is not important has served me well in confronting life's inevitable problems.

My learning experience at Barnard was exhilarating. I was admitted into their first class majoring in American studies. My senior thesis covered "Eugene V. Debs and the Pullman Strike of 1894." I graduated summa cum laude and Phi Beta Kappa.

CAREER

After graduation I searched for newspaper work in New York City. But this was a time when several major papers were folding, and there were no openings. Through a "Help Wanted Male" ad, I found a job writing advertising copy for the Sears, Roebuck catalog. The pay was fifty-five a week. I was originally offered forty-five, but I did so well on the Sears Advertising Aptitude Test that they offered an additional ten dollars.

I wrote copy for accessories. In those days, professional women wore gloves whenever appearing in public. My boss volunteered the ad slogan "A lady never shows her hand." (Most professional women wore hats indoors, even when sitting at our desks. Photos of early NOW meetings show me and several other women with hats.)

A year into that job, I had to take a leave of absence to help my family through an emergency: My mother, after several years of getting along well with my father while they worked together in the store, suddenly became pathologically jealous. She accused him of having an affair with a seventy-year-old relative. She claimed he was flirting with women customers. She insisted he was signaling to women through the bathroom window in back.

I returned to Miami Beach to help my parents resolve this situation. The leading local psychiatrist failed to help my mother. He tried extensive electroconvulsive shock treatments, to no avail. Then came unsuccessful confinement for several weeks in a mental hospital. Finally, I sadly persuaded my father to divorce my mother, since there was no way they could live together. (Pathological jealousy seemed to be her only major problem, so she recovered when they lived apart.)

During my nine months in Florida, I took a job with Thomas Jefferson Public Relations. Tom taught me about publicity. I enjoyed doing press announcements for the Miami Opera Company and the South Florida Tennis League. Tom won a contract with the mayoral campaign of businessman William Wolfarth. I learned how to write political speeches. With our help, Wolfarth was elected mayor.

To my great joy, our firm contracted for the Dade County campaign of my idol, progressive Senator Claude Pepper. His opponent in the Democratic campaign, George Smathers, labeled him "Red Pepper" because of his liberal opinions. Smathers's red-baiting in those McCarthyite years reminded voters that Pepper had visited the Soviet Union. (He was part of a congressional delegation.)

Tom Jefferson was suddenly unable to work. He said doctors described his condition as a "nervous breakdown." I ran Pepper's Dade County campaign by myself. Alas, George Smathers's attacks on Pepper proved successful and led him to victory in the Florida Senate primary campaign. But we did carry our Dade County, thanks mainly to heavy support from labor unions.

In the spring of 1950, I returned to New York City. My mother joined me and rented an apartment on the Upper West Side. I phoned her every day and paid for her clothes. (Social Security did the rest.) She joined a wonderful city-sponsored neighborhood club for seniors and began to spend her days there with courses, bridge games, seventy-five-cent lunches, and new acquaintances. She met the nice man who became her husband. I'll always feel gratitude to that New York City senior center.

Now experienced in public relations, I carried a recommendation to Al McMillan, executive vice president of Carl Byoir & Associates, then the world's largest PR agency. When I showed McMillan my scrapbook, he announced quietly, "All impressive! But I'm sorry, we don't hire women. There's Jane Buck, head of our Women's Department. They deal with women's pages. And, of course, lots of secretaries. But Byoir doesn't hire women writers." This didn't surprise me. I walked away and found a job writing movie publicity for a small public relations agency.

I'd also applied to Jo Dine in the NBC press department. Jo was widely admired for the help he offered job seekers. No openings at NBC. But in May, Jo phoned me. "There's a job in the Radio Department at Byoir." When I told Jo that Byoir didn't hire women, he replied, "Don't worry. Bob Davis heads the department. He's a special human being. Try him." Bob hired me. He was indeed special, and certainly a unique human being. Bald, witty, and always smiling, Bob was loved by everyone in the agency. Among his many talents was a capacity for puns. When someone remarked that radio shows were recorded on acetate, Bob retorted, "He who acetates is lost."

We were still called the Radio Department because no TV stations at the time had an appreciable audience. Bob eventually changed our name to the TV-Radio Department. Our operation acquired a second staffer, a likable ex-broadcaster named Dick Rieber. I accepted that Dick earned a higher salary than I did, since he was more experienced. And, he was a man. Every afternoon Dick caught the 5:15 train home from Grand Central Station, while I usually worked till 6:00 P.M. or later.

In 1951, Bob Davis was hospitalized with a bleeding ulcer. Without being asked, I looked after the department. Dick still caught the 5:15 train. A month after Bob returned, he showed us a letter generated by public relations professionals at the White Plains Hospital. The letter thanked him for replying to a survey they'd sent out about hospital care, food, etc. It ended with "We're always happy to hear from satisfied patients. We wish you a continued recovery, and hope you'll find great joy with your new baby." So much for public relations.

The spirit of cooperation at Byoir was exhilarating. Our people were top professionals, devoted to the clients. Byoir campaigns won a large number of Silver Anvils awarded by the Public Relations Society of America. Our TV-Radio Department played a role in many successful campaigns.

Here's an example of the pride we all felt in Byoir professionalism: Our founder, Carl Byoir, had retired in the late 1940s, and Gerry Swinehart had taken over as chairman/CEO. One day in 1956, Gerry called our entire staff into the big conference room for a special meeting. He announced, "Carl Byoir has cancer. It's up to us to use our know-how and extensive contacts throughout the world to locate someone with a cure for cancer." We didn't succeed in fulfilling Gerry's naïve request, but we all tried hard to locate new information about cancer. FYI, our agency had an exceptionally large Research Department, which fortified our press materials with solid information. Today I don't know of any PR agency with a Research Department. Google and Wikipedia have taken over.

In February 1952, the agency announced that Bob Davis was being promoted to directorship of all media departments. The next day, Bob invited me to lunch. "I don't want the suspense to spoil your lunch, so I'll tell you right out: We're making you director of the TV-Radio Department." I was so surprised and intimidated by this news that I didn't tell my parents about the promotion for weeks. As a twenty-four-year-old woman, I felt like a usurper.

My anxiety was heightened when Byoir president George Hammond greeted my promotion by saying, "Well, Muriel, you've come a long way fast. We'll see if it's *too* fast." I didn't relax until ten days later, when I encountered chairman Gerry Swinehart in the elevator. I thanked Gerry for the promotion. Gerry put his arm around my shoulder. "No reason to thank me. You earned it!"

I did a good job. Our department made major placements for our clients on networks and local stations. I made many friends across the country. I frequently won Best Writer recognition in Byoir's monthly awards program.

SEX DISCRIMINATION

I didn't think about protesting the agency's sex or race discrimination, then rampant at companies everywhere. Byoir hired very few Jews among its executives, and no people of color, until the 1980s. I knew that male colleagues in comparable positions earned more money than I did. After my marriage, I felt especially timid about asking for a raise, since I couldn't say the money was necessary. It never occurred to me to say "I *deserve* more money." I didn't complain when only men were chosen for committees, client meetings, and special projects that advanced their careers. Not until the rise of the civil rights movement and NOW did I realize that equality was possible.

I did become Byoir's youngest vice president at age twenty-seven. But Gerry Swinehart said to me at the time, "We love you, Muriel, but you've gone as far as you can go. CEOs would never relate to a woman in senior management."

I'd reached what we used to call the "women's plateau." Our abilities and hard work brought us all the way to the middle. (The term *glass ceiling* had not been invented.) We quoted a comment made by Charlotte Whitton, mayor of Ottawa: "Whatever women do, they must do twice as well as men to appear half as good. Luckily, this is not difficult."

Said another maxim of the times: "Women in mid-level jobs are treated like mushrooms. They're kept in the dark and fed on manure. When they grow older, they're canned."

Despite our agency's collegial atmosphere, I had one adversary. Since he made no secret of his animosity, I'll mention his name. John Budd was a brilliant account executive who wrote a book on public relations and rose to be our agency's senior vice president, later executive vice president. John and I never had a disagreement, and I don't know why he disliked me. But he bad-mouthed me frequently. The problems began after John stole away my favorite staffer, Jim Gaylord, who was also my personal friend.

With his lucrative accounts, John used his clout and salary offers to lure away Jim and then my capable secretary, Cathy Morrissey. I learned one day that John had not been following agency practice in approving my expense accounts for meals with media contacts. Account executives were expected to initial our invoices and relay them to Accounting for payment. Instead, John threw my bills into a drawer. When John's misbehavior became known, he wasn't punished. Management simply told him to approve my expenses from then on. This episode, instead of reflecting on John, made *me* feel humiliated.

In the early 1960s, Byoir president George Hammond lectured the entire staff about the then raging protests against racism across the country. George said we must teach clients to behave in more enlightened ways. At one point he warned, "If our clients don't address racism intelligently, we can expect more protests in this country." Then, with a chuckle, he added, "Who knows, if this discontent catches on, workers might also complain about *sex* discrimination." The captive audience smiled at his humor.

When we discuss sex discrimination, we should remember the terrible way secretaries used to be treated. Today very few women hold that job. Thanks to computers, most executives do their own typing and filing these days; only top executives have an "administrative assistant," as they're called. But in the old days, practically every executive had at least one secretary. Bosses often referred to them as "my girl."

At the Byoir agency, prefeminism, a secretary had no chance of being promoted to a staffer's job. If she was ambitious, she'd eventually move to a smaller agency. One of my secretaries, Saralie Slonsky, did that and ultimately became executive vice president of the Burson-Marsteller agency. She thanks me for her early mentoring. I taught her how to write segments of our weekly radio show and gave her helpful corrections. But she held no chance of promotion at Byoir. Another secretary, Elsa Raven, became my close friend and was maid of honor at my wedding. Elsa left Byoir to pursue an acting career, taking character parts in Hollywood. I confess with shame that once, when I was asked, "How many men are in your department?" I replied, "Three men and two secretaries." (I counted myself among the men. At least I didn't say "two girls.")

The popular *Mad Men* TV series may have exaggerated sexual exploitation in the communications world, but not by much. Bosses did make advances toward their "girls," and their cavalier behavior was not challenged.

In my professional life, three executives tried to kiss me, and I brushed them off with a smile. My secure position and self-confident demeanor may have protected me from other encounters. Or maybe I was just lucky that it didn't happen more often. Too many women, especially secretaries and clerks, were victims of sexual harassment—feminists invented that term. It oppressed all women in jobs subservient to more powerful men. I had the advantage of being a white, educated, professional, native-born citizen. Millions of women lack that protection.

On October 21, 1966, at a Minneapolis conference of American Women in Radio and Television, the featured speaker was Leo Kramer, a management consultant. While outlining America's changing demographics, he remarked that it had been "a grave mistake" to add women to Title VII of the Civil Rights Act. I immediately raised my hand, stood up, and declared in a trembling voice, "Next week we're holding a conference in Washington that will fight to end that attitude. We're forming a new organization. It's called the National Organization for Women."

LOVE AND MARRIAGE

I had lots of dates, and several long relationships. I clung to the belief that "nice" girls didn't have sex before marriage. Psychoanalysis finally cured me. At the age of twenty-four, I made a deliberate decision to abandon virginity. I flew to Boston for a weekend with a charming journalist who had visited me several times in New York. The experience was pleasant but not earth-shattering. After that weekend, I never dated him again.

I almost became engaged to Dr. Bernard Burgin, an extraverted Baltimore internist. Bernie was exceptionally kind and loving. But I decided he didn't stimulate me enough intellectually. Also, I loved New York City too much to consider a move to Baltimore.

When I told my father on the phone about my promotion to head the TV-Radio Department, I recall his response: "Oh! Now you'll never get a husband!" In those times, popular dramas promoted the theme that career success made women less desirable for marriage. I recall one date (only one!) with a former high school classmate, Dr. Norbert Freinkel. Norbie was already on his way to fame as an authority on diabetes. We compared our experiences with psychoanalysis. Norbie was seeing an orthodox Freudian. On hearing my view that men and women should be equal partners, he assaulted me with the Freudian terms *castration complex* and *penis envy*.

I recall my mother urging me on my twenty-third birthday, "Don't get panicky, but let this be the year." By my twenty-sixth birthday, I worried. Would I become an old maid? (Nowadays, many women wait till their thirties before they begin to think about marriage. Or they decide not to marry at all. Times have changed.)

One day in the fall of 1954, I suggested lunch to my good friend Judy Krantz. (THE Judith Krantz who later wrote *Scruples, Princess Daisy,* and other best-selling novels.) Sophisticated, sociable Judy seemed to me the most likely friend who would know the right man for a blind date. Over lunch in Reuben's Restaurant, I proclaimed the following: "Judy, I'm tired of men in advertising and PR. They drink too much, and they can be insincere. They cheat on their wives. I've decided I'd like to marry a doctor. Specifically, an internist. An internist takes care of people, so he'll be kindly. Also, he could help look after my family. Of course, he'd have to be exceptionally intelligent." (This statement was rehearsed, but I swear that Judy is the only person to whom I ever delivered it.)

Judy's response: "Oh, you must meet my doctor. He's handsome and interesting, and he's been divorced for three years." Judy and her husband, Steve, arranged a double date with Dr. Shepard Gerard Aronson. We met on November 1, 1954, got engaged on April 1, and were married on July 1, 1955. It was a thrill for me to mail my engagement announcement to *The Miami News,* where I'd been bridal editor.

Our marriage lasted forty-eight blissful years, till Shep's death at the age of ninety. He was fifteen years older than I. Our tastes and values were compatible; and (I swear again) we did not have one fight in all those years. We'd both benefited from successful psychotherapy. Like me, Shep had been raised by an angry mother who felt trapped in an unhappy marriage. We knew we didn't want the squabbling marriage of our parents. When we disagreed about something, we talked it out

Muriel Fox and Dr. Shepard Aronson, a forty-eight-year marriage
Photography courtesy of Muriel Fox

sensibly. No need for an unpleasant battle. We relied on rational minds instead of prickly emotions.

It didn't go easily at first. Shep had been painfully damaged by his mother, who was even more hostile than mine. His first wife, New York City Opera prima donna Dorothy Sarnoff, divorced him because of sexual incompatibility. Shep and I were both undergoing productive psychotherapy when we met. My analyst, Dr. Ervin Maurer, talked to me about enjoying cuddly, erotic lovemaking with or without intercourse. Shep moved into my apartment in April. We began to experience successful, pleasurable sex every time. Thank you, Dr. Maurer! And thanks to Shep's psychoanalyst, Dr. Annemarie Weil.

Shep was an innate feminist. He took pride in my achievements, and he enjoyed smart women. A 1974 article about us in *Money* magazine highlighted our equal partnership in finances, with all money going into joint accounts. It pointed to a 1973 NOW resolution: "Each spouse shall share equally in the economic resources of the marriage." In those days, many wives secretly squirreled away money for a rainy day. (My mother certainly did.) If substantial wealth was involved, the man usually controlled accounts in his own name. Infinite jokes described the wife spending too much of her husband's money on nonessentials. If her husband died, many a widow felt unable to cope with the finances. I was the one who managed the finances in our marriage. Shep's eyes glazed over when money was mentioned.

My family did benefit, in important ways, from my marrying a doctor. There was a time when my mother suddenly showed a recurrence of pathological jealousy toward her new husband. (An article in *Psychology Today* called it "Othello syndrome," saying it was due to an overabundance of dopamine.) Shep persuaded my mother to take Stelazine, supposedly for her high blood pressure, and cured her, seemingly overnight. Years later, my brother, Jerry, suffered from serious mental problems. I asked Shep if Jerry could be "manic-depressive." (Now it's called "bipolar disorder.") Shep prescribed lithium for Jerry, and again my loved one was cured virtually overnight.

In October 1966, our son and daughter, ages six and five, flew with us to the founding conference of NOW. Shep escorted the children around Washington, with a visit to the Wax Museum. He did attend part of the conference, with the kids in tow. Months later, when someone at a cocktail party asked, "Shep, what's a doctor like you doing in the women's movement?" he replied, "I want my wife to make more money."

In 1967, when NOW launched its New York chapter, Shep was elected chairman of the board. It wasn't my idea—the members liked Shep and chose a male doctor to project a dignified image. After ferocious battles in our chapter's board meetings, Shep called that time "the worst year of my life."

In 1972, David Susskind interviewed Shep on his nationwide TV show. He talked with three husbands of feminists. In addition to Shep, they were Tim Cooney, husband of *Sesame Street* creator Joan Ganz Cooney, and Jerry Gardner, husband of NOW's Pittsburgh leader JoAnn Gardner. Susskind felt he was striking a blow against feminism when he asked Shep, "How would you feel if your wife made more money than you do?" Shep responded, "Relaxed." When Susskind declared, "My wife is my dearest treasure," Shep countered, "My wife isn't my treasure. She's my partner." On that same show, Tim Cooney remarked, "I am the wife who does volunteer work." (They later divorced. Joan complained about Tim's failure to seek a paying job. After the divorce, she insisted on paying him alimony.) JoAnn and Jerry remained active members of NOW. JoAnn adopted the last name Evansgardner.

LIFE IN FEMINISM

In 1963, soon after publication of *The Feminine Mystique,* I'd invited Betty Friedan to speak to American Women in Radio and Television. She agreed, on condition that we'd hire a stenographer to type up her speech for future use. Chatting before her speech, I mentioned growing talk about the need for an organization to combat sex discrimination. Said Betty, "You mean an NAACP for women?" Yes!

Her speech on "Television and the Feminine Mystique" on November 14, 1963, was electrifying. Half the women in the audience shared my enthusiasm for Betty's pronouncements. But the other half, women satisfied with the status quo of their middle-level jobs, found her comments unsettling. Several complained to me later about Betty's frequent use of the word *orgasm*.

I have a carbon copy of the thank-you letter I sent to Betty afterward. It referred to "the great need for a militant, intelligent organization devoted to women's rights."

In August 1966, as someone whose name was on Betty's huge Rolodex, I received from her the invitation to join NOW that's reproduced in chapter 2. I asked for two hundred applications to share with friends in AWRT. Betty invited me to her apartment in the Dakota. Waiting for me, in Betty's Victorian living room with its red flocked wallpaper, were Marlene Sanders of ABC and Betty Furness of NBC. (Marlene later moved to CBS.) Betty asked me to be publicity director of NOW. I agreed, with the understanding that I already had a more than full-time job with Byoir, plus a family with two young children.

In a speech about NOW's origins that Betty delivered in 1993, she cited me as an example of NOW's founders. "She had never even run a mimeo machine. But she ran one for NOW's first press release. We all jumped in to do whatever was needed."

After the founding conference of NOW, I arranged for Isot Weisberg, wife of a physician friend of Shep's, to work out of my office at Carl Byoir as Betty Friedan's secretary. I set up a chair, typewriter, and small table for Isot near my own desk. Byoir permitted this for over a month before the executive VP finally said, "Get the secretary out of your office." Isot had just resigned, complaining that "Betty was driving me insane." I hired another friend, who worked out of her own apartment.

MEDIA REACTION

I've previously described the enthusiastic media reaction to my press release on the October 29–30 NOW founding conference. Most, though not all, media agreed that we were making history. In the following few years, our releases, press conferences, interviews, demonstrations, marches, and other events enjoyed a welcome response from newspapers, magazines, and broadcasters. We owe much to the media for our early success.

A few journalists ridiculed us, or attacked what we were trying to accomplish. The night of our huge march on August 26, 1970, Bill Beutel remarked on ABC-TV News, "Now let's move on to other trivia." Megastar Andy Rooney of CBS-TV replied dismissively to my letter about NOW, saying, "We have a great bulk of film on women talking about themselves. I don't have the little relationships between men and women in an office. I don't have men doing small polite things they still do and are expected to do—opening doors, helping coats, etc." Rooney's widely hyped TV documentary about women, ignoring the material I'd sent him, proclaimed that a woman with a stroller is far more attractive than a woman with a picket sign.

Nearly all the women's magazines carried stories about our new movement, but their coverage was tempered by dependence on advertisers who paid them to exploit woman's role as consumer of household merchandise and beauty products. The message of fashion magazines continued to be "Girls, why settle for job equality when it's more fun to dream about finding a rich husband to support you?" In the late 1970s, *Vogue* editor Grace Mirabella broadened the magazine's coverage to include women's role in world events. We gave Grace an award for Leadership in Communications for a Just Society. (NOW LDEF had named that award after me and nicknamed it "The Foxy.") Other magazines eventually followed Grace Mirabella's lead.

Nearly all general-interest magazines ran stories about our movement. One of the first, *This Week,* presented a three-page picture story, "Sex and Civil Rights," to its 26 million readers.

OUR FIRST CHAPTER

When Betty Friedan realized in early 1967 that we were becoming a mass movement instead of the "elite cadre" she'd originally envisioned, she said to me, "NOW needs local chapters. Start one in New York." I phoned Shep's patient and friend Elizabeth Manning, who owned a public relations agency and an elegant town house on East Seventy-fifth Street in Manhattan. She lent us her town house for the founding meeting of New York NOW on February 6. I mailed postcards, over the signature of Betty Friedan, to local members of national NOW. My postcard ended: "And we'll begin to form local task forces to act on NOW's goals toward equal employment opportunity, a new image for woman, social innovations, etc. See you soon!"

Despite a snowstorm, seventy-five people showed up. I chaired the meeting until Betty arrived. I still have the sign-up sheet, on yellow lined paper, with many names that later became famous. Since we began as a chapter for the entire New York region, the sign-ups included Ithaca assemblywoman Constance Cook, as well as Shirley Chisholm, who would be elected the following year as congresswoman from Brooklyn. The handful of men at our meeting included James Beatty, legislative consultant to New York City councilman (later mayor) Edward Koch. Koch was a NOW supporter from the beginning. When he learned about our new organization, he phoned and asked, "How can I help?" (He told us later that the NOW member who answered the phone brushed him off because she wasn't interested in recruiting men.) (Fox 1991). At our Susan B. Anthony Birthday Party four years later, Koch was quoted as saying, "This is the most exciting night for me since I boycotted grapes with Gloria Steinem at Gristede's."

You'll learn later about our New York chapter's internal battles. But we did get a lot accomplished. More than two hundred feminists attended most of our meetings, and we had a roster of over three hundred members. As pioneers in America's media capital, we fought hard against discriminatory employment in the media, and against their stereotyped image of women. Lucy Komisar created small labels saying, "This ad insults women." We pasted them on stereotyped ads in subways and buses.

I organized a chapter press conference on October 4, 1967, supporting a forty-year-old steamship stewardess Pauline Dziob, who aspired to be a yeoman. A yeoman was a clerk-typist, but Moore-McCormack Lines designated it a "man's job." It paid well. Pauline had held the position temporarily, but Moore-McCormack demoted her back to stewardess because of her gender. She was replaced by an eighteen-year-old boy without experience, who quit two years later to return to school. Pauline sued the steamship line and also her union, the National

Maritime Union, which had declared that "women can only work as waitresses, stewardesses and child attendants but not yeomen; that is a male position." (In those days, alas, we fought numerous unions over sex discrimination.) *The New York Times* ran a story. With our help, Pauline won her lawsuit. In December 1967, the New York State Commission for Human Rights commanded the steamship line and the union to let Pauline keep the yeoman's job.

Jean Faust, president of our New York chapter, hailed this decision: "It makes the perfect illustration of why NOW was needed."

Another chapter project was support of Shirley Long, who'd been rejected for a job in the Parks Department because she was a woman. Fourteen feminists picketed the Department of the Interior building with signs saying, among other things, YOU DON'T NEED A PENIS TO PATROL PARKS.

Our chapter protested to Barnard College for threatening to expel sophomore Linda LeClair for living with her boyfriend off campus. Ultimately, Linda dropped out and moved to Vermont.

In 1971, the chapter prepared a marriage manual and a marriage test "like those for the driver's license." I no longer have copies of these. In 1979, our chapter sued the New York City Waterfront Commission and won work permits for more than one hundred women to become dockworkers.

In 1969, Betty Friedan decided that NOW needed a nontaxable, nonprofit affiliate to handle lawsuits and education activities, to be called the NOW Legal Defense and Education Fund, patterned after the NAACP LDEF.

The successful attorney in Pauline Dziob's lawsuit was a portly, gray-haired lawyer named Grace Cox. Betty and I were so favorably impressed by Grace's work for Pauline Dziob that we asked her to be NOW LDEF's legal director and to incorporate us as a nonprofit 501(c) (3). Grace agreed enthusiastically to do this, pro bono. But months passed without results. I grew so frustrated that I finally asked Grace, "Are you deliberately trying to sabotage us?" Grace replied, "Oh, I will. I've been busy." She never followed through. We learned that she was a good friend of Cardinal Terence Cooke of the Roman Catholic

Archdiocese of New York. Perhaps he had dampened her enthusiasm because of NOW's stand on abortion. I don't know whether the motivation for Grace's foot dragging was a procrastination problem or intentional sabotage. Finally, Marguerite Rawalt and Mary Eastwood picked up the assignment and incorporated NOW LDEF in D.C., rather than in New York as we'd originally planned.

POLITICS SLOWS US DOWN

The year 1968 brought sad news in the political arena. We suffered from the assassinations of Martin Luther King, Jr. and Robert Kennedy, then the election of Richard Nixon as president.

That summer, I volunteered for the presidential election campaign of Hubert Humphrey, whom I'd always admired as a champion of civil rights. At the Democratic National Convention in Chicago, I ran the Humphrey pressroom for New York State. Betty Friedan, who was working for Eugene McCarthy's campaign at the convention, threw me a really dirty look when she saw my Humphrey badge. I was heartbroken by scenes of police beating up young people in the park, and the stench of stink bombs in our hotel lobby.

We lost out in the November election. Nixon's administration appointed antifeminists to relevant government agencies, though he never tried to slow down our momentum with the EEOC. We especially lamented his veto of the Child Care Act we'd lobbied through Congress in 1971.

WILL THEY LET ME BE A REVOLUTIONARY?

John Budd, my only adversary at the Byoir agency, declared at an Executive Committee meeting in 1980 (after I'd been promoted to a place on the committee) that I should refrain from referring to the feminist movement as a "revolution" because the wording would alarm clients. He was wrong. By that time, my colleagues at the agency were untroubled by my association with feminist activism. The business world had learned how to coexist with our movement, and companies were beginning to boast about their gender "diversity." Byoir's presentations to prospective clients bragged about my outreach and expertise.

In the earliest days of NOW, I did have to be cautious. When I first requested permission to join the board of a new feminist organization in October 1966, I promised Byoir officers that I'd never embarrass our clients. In public pronouncements, I used Betty Friedan's name rather than my own. I recused myself from all discussions if NOW was weighing an action against a Byoir client. A decade after the birth of our movement, it had become respectable for a woman to be identified as a feminist leader. Ultimately, it became a badge of "influence."

In 1983, Byoir's internal newsletter ran a photo featuring twelve women who held executive or staffer positions. That was seventeen years after the founding of NOW, and thirty-three years after Al McMillan had told me "We don't hire women."

In the early years, I refrained from marching in public demonstrations. The only exception was a protest against Colgate-Palmolive in Louisville in 1968, outside a local supermarket. We were so far from New York that our clients wouldn't notice. In later years, I marched visibly and proudly as part of a mainstream revolution. In 1978, for our D.C. march to win extension of the ERA deadline, we were instructed to wear suffragist white. I looked so impressive in my daughter Lisa's white graduation dress, a Mexican wedding gown, that NOW officers asked me to head the march. My photo, with me holding the hand of seven-year-old Brooke Schafran while waving a NOW banner in my other hand, was reproduced in a NOW silver medallion that sold in NOW's offerings for years. On the opposite side of the medallion was Susan B Anthony's slogan, "A passion for the possible."

I wore the same white gown to lead NOW's ERA parade in Chicago on Mother's Day, 1980. My photograph, plus the dress itself, has been featured in several exhibits of the New-York Historical Society.

THE CONFLICT WITH *SESAME STREET*

Enough time has passed for me to reveal my role in a conflict between NOW and one Byoir client, Children's Television Workshop, producer of the trailblazing *Sesame Street* television show for children. I'd been a friend of CTW chair Joan Ganz Cooney ever since the 1960s, when I wrote a letter to Channel 13 chief Richard Heffner that helped Joan land a job with Public Television. Later, I wrote the original proposal that persuaded Children's Television Workshop to hire Byoir for the show's public debut. (I confess to saying *Sesame Street* was a terrible name when Joan first proposed it.)

One day I received an internal NOW memo proposing a nationwide boycott of *Sesame Street,* to protest the fact that none of the show's leading characters projected a positive image for girls. (I knew that one of Joan Cooney's major missions was to improve the self-image of Black *men* as authority figures in the home.) None of *Sesame Street*'s main puppets were female. The show's cohost, Susan, wore an apron and baked cookies.

I carried the NOW memo to our *Sesame Street* account executive at Byoir. He authorized me to arrange a meeting between NOW leaders and the *Sesame Street* producers. The meeting was amicable. The producers were sympathetic to complaints expressed by NOW president Wilma Heide, and agreed to revise future programs to feature more women in assertive roles. The two sides agreed to exchange letters on decisions reached at the meeting. Wilma Heide asked me to compose a letter to *Sesame Street* that she would sign, summarizing NOW's position. In the meantime, *Sesame Street* asked me to compose a letter to NOW on their behalf, summarizing the new understanding. I did both.

It may have been unethical for me not to tell the two sides that I was composing both letters. However, the result did benefit everyone. We succeeded in improving the portrayal of females on *Sesame Street.* And, we prevented a nationwide NOW boycott.

I thought of my connection with *Sesame Street* when I saw how the program illuminated the lives of my children, grandchildren, and great-grandchildren. A favorite doll of all three generations is Elmo.

NOW LEGAL DEFENSE AND EDUCATION FUND

Once we finally got NOW LDEF incorporated, it produced all-important victories for women and girls. These will be covered in later chapters on education, violence, the media, culture wars, and our relationship to business leaders.

I digress to pay special tribute to Mary Jean Crenshaw Tully, who brought it all together as president of NOW LDEF from 1971 to 1977. I met Mary Jean when I needed someone to replace me as editor of NOW's first national newsletter, *Do It Now*. She agreed to take over. Mary Jean later passed along that chore to another friend, so she could concentrate on her innovative work as president of NOW LDEF.

Mary Jean's husband, Bob Tully, was chief financial officer of Celanese Corporation. She used their social contacts to help NOW LDEF attract financial support from major companies. Corporate leaders and their wives felt comfortable with Mary Jean. One wife commented with white, wealthy hauteur, "She looks and sounds like us." Mary Jean invited Shep and me to her home several times for gourmet dinners with business executives who shortly became contributors.

You'll read later about NOW LDEF's "Hire him. He's got great legs" media ads. Mary Jean deserves credit for initiating that campaign, among others.

When I succeeded Mary Jean as president of NOW LDEF, I enlisted her business contacts to raise funds for corporate dinners and groundbreaking events. She introduced me to Coy Eklund, CEO of the Equitable Life Assurance Society. Coy was the first corporate CEO to go out on a limb as a champion of equal opportunity for women. He encouraged female employees to form a Women's Group at Equitable, one of the first in this country.

Coy gave us financial support for NOW LDEF's National Assembly on the Future of the Family, which he agreed to cochair with me. This full-day event on November 20, 1979, presented ten expert panels addressing the problems of evolving families. More than two thousand leaders participated from the worlds of community service, business, labor, academe, and government. *The New York Times* assigned a reporter to each of the ten panels. Its incomparable Enid Nemy wrote a summary that appeared in full-page coverage in the *Times*. In the women's section.

The Washington Post opened its story with the following: "The traditional American family with its breadwinner husband, homemaker wife and 2.5 children is rapidly becoming extinct, according to feminist Betty Friedan and futurists Isaac Asimov and Alvin Toffler. Families of the future will commonly come in multiple forms, including single-parent families, two-paycheck couples, and intergenerational communes, they told a sometimes-cheering audience of 2,000 Monday at a National Assembly on the Future of the Family in New York."

The following year, I organized another all-day event, our Convocation on New Leadership in the Public Interest. The program was attended by hundreds of prestigious leaders. The 422 participating organizations included universities, corporations, labor unions, government bodies, and civic groups, ranging from AFL-CIO to Xerox and the YWCA.

However, a gunshot wiped out our press coverage. That morning, on March 30, 1981, John Hinckley Jr. shot President Reagan.

For NOW LDEF, I chaired its Equal Opportunity Awards Dinner for twenty-two successive years. We raised twelve million dollars from corporations and guests. Equally important was that through this dinner we encouraged the business world to hire and promote capable women. We honored CEOs who announced at the dinner that equal opportunity for women is "good for the bottom line." The honorees, and my dinner cochairs, included top executives from major companies that were doing the right thing for diversity.

I'm proud of NOW LDEF's success in promoting women for nontraditional jobs. When our strenuous campaign led New York City to hire more women as firefighters and police officers, this inspired progress in cities across the country. We helped persuade builders and unions to admit more women into the building trades. I still wear a T-shirt we distributed after September 11, 2001. The front features a yellow hard hat with the slogan WOMEN REBUILD NEW YORK, NOW LEGAL DEFENSE AND EDUCATION FUND. The back says WOMEN REBUILD AMERICA.

NOW LDEF also helped persuade Congress to pass the FACE (Freedom of Access to Clinic Entrances) Act, making it a crime for antiabortion forces to blockade a reproductive-health clinic.

After my presidency of NOW LDEF, I served more than a dozen years as chair. The organization, with a loud but futile dissent from me, decided later to sever its official ties to NOW and change its name. Officers complained that media kept confusing the two organizations. With the advice of a focus group, the new name became "Legal Momentum, the Women's Legal Defense and Education Fund."

Legal Momentum still does important work. As chair of their National Advisory Committee, I often attend board meetings without a vote. Their Gender Equality Helpline is a free resource for people seeking information about rights or legal representation related to sex and gender discrimination, violence, and harassment. It's well staffed these days, with a grant from the Sy Syms Foundation.

When I sought support from a business executive (almost always *men* in the old days), I tried to find out if he had a daughter. I made a point of asking him about his daughter's education and career. It's no secret that men are more inclined toward feminism if they have a daughter. A study by the University of Rochester verified this tendency among judges. In a study of 2,500 votes by 224 federal appeals court judges, it concluded: "Having at least one daughter corresponds to a 7 percent increase in the proportion of cases in which a judge will vote in a feminist direction."

VETERAN FEMINISTS OF AMERICA

In 1993, I was asked by NOW pioneer Jacqui Ceballos to join a new organization called Veterans of Feminist Wars. I declined, because the title reminded people of all the wars we'd fought within the feminist movement. Soon after, Jacqui told me their name had been changed to Veteran Feminists of America (Veterans of Foreign Wars had nixed the VFW title); she asked me to serve as chair of the board. I agreed immediately. We're the foremost resource for information about the modern feminist movement. We offer these stories as inspiration to others for the work that still remains.

VFA's first event was a dinner honoring Catherine East. Other reunions followed, honoring Gloria Steinem, Kate Millett, midwestern feminists, radical feminists, labor union feminists, and others. At the dinner for Kate Millett, Betty Friedan apologized for her past homophobic behavior. Our Salute to Feminist Lawyers included Ruth Bader Ginsburg and Sarah Weddington, the attorney who won *Roe v. Wade*. You can access videos of these historic occasions on the website veteranfeministsofamerica.org.

I was the organizer of VFA's Salute to Feminist Authors and its Salute to Feminist in the Arts. At the art event I purchased June Blum's touching portrait of Betty Friedan. I remember the morning that June and I completed the sale, because that evening my husband, Shep, passed away.

In October 2014, the VFA produced a fund-raiser honoring me at the Harvard Club in New York City. With donations from friends from various phases of my life, the event was a financial success. Its highlight was a panel discussion that included Gloria Steinem, Rosie O'Donnell, Eve Ensler, Marlo Thomas, and Carol Jenkins.

To celebrate Betty Friedan's one-hundredth birthday on February 4, 2021, I produced a lively VFA webinar. You can access it free on YouTube. The webinar includes anecdotes from Betty's children, in addition to videos by Senators Chuck Schumer and Elizabeth Warren, columnist Gail Collins, Black Lives Matter cofounder Alicia Garza, and other leaders. It's an instructive introduction to the birth of our movement.

In a later chapter, I'll tell about the important book Barbara Love edited with help from VFA volunteers. *Feminists Who Changed America 1963–1975*, published by the University of Illinois Press, presents biographies of 2,200 women and men who were leaders in feminist history. Each made a difference. VFA now produces and disseminates oral histories of feminist leaders, with videos and transcripts. More than six hundred are available on its website. Apart from my files and my personal memories, these interviews provided the main resource for this book.

JUGGLING IT ALL

I'm often asked how we career women managed to juggle our lives with jobs and families. Although our careers in those days suffered from more egregious discrimination than the careers of today's young women, we did have one advantage: We could find (and afford to pay) women willing to clean our house, cook our meals, and help care for our children. They were mainly women of color from Latin America or the American South. Fortunately for minority women, most of them today can choose from a wide variety of jobs, of which housekeeping is just one option. (Critics of *The Feminine Mystique* rightly complained when Betty referred, perhaps insensitively, to "servant problems.") Our daughters don't have that assistance in the home today. When my children were little, I could afford to hire a housekeeper-cook and also a nanny. Today my granddaughter makes a high salary, but she struggled to find neighborhood child care. She and her husband manage housework together. Fortunately, he received generous parental leave when their two children were born.

I confess that I absorbed my mother's hostility to housework. When Shep proposed to me, I remember asking him, as I sat on his lap, "Can I have a maid?" I felt especially insecure about cooking. Although I did some cooking for the family on weekends, I felt fearful when following recipes.

Sure, I was privileged to have had help with the housework. But I felt perpetually stressed by all the other demands of balancing family, career, and feminist activism. The clock was my taskmaster. I didn't get enough sleep. And I never enjoyed moments of optional leisure. I never had time to ask myself, "What would I like to do today?" Fortunately, I loved my family and my job and the women's movement, so life was rewarding, if exhausting. Because I went home each night to a loving and supportive husband, I felt basically comfortable with life. Setbacks in the job did not overwhelm me.

I'm well organized and a fast writer, so I managed my days and nights efficiently. But the biggest regret of my life is that I didn't somehow find more time to spend with our children. I did attend every school play and parents' meeting (fathers didn't attend then), but I wish I'd found more time for just having fun with the kids. Fortunately, Shep hung out with them more than most fathers in those years.

In those busy, busy times I did not have a girlfriend. There were good friends who happened to be associated with my work. I had only one best friend: Shep.

I've thought about working mothers who struggle today without the help and luxuries that I enjoyed. When I compare my life to the lives of most single mothers, I shouldn't feel sorry for myself.

Like all children, mine guilt-tripped me often. They complained when I went out of town on a business trip or a NOW assignment. But today Eric and Lisa reassure me that they didn't feel especially deprived by having a working mother. In August 1972, *Good Housekeeping* ran an article headlined "What Does Mommy Do?" It included interviews of a dozen children of prominent women. My ten-year-old Lisa ended her interview by saying, "I like her working. I don't get bored of her and she doesn't get bored of me."

I did believe there was a stigma attached to children whose mothers worked outside the home. This belief is reinforced in a book I recently read about Sylvia Plath. Heather Clark writes about Plath's mother, Aurelia: "Aurelia's experience assured Plath that it was possible to join a profession and raise a family, yet the stigma of a working mother was very real in white, middle-class, mid-century America." (Clark 2020, p. 125)

While we're discussing family pride and prejudice, permit me to brag about my family's feminist genes, in addition to Shep's and mine. My brother, Jerry Fox, an alumnus of *The Yale Law Journal*, was vice president of NOW's New York chapter. He represented NOW in negotiations with *The New York Times* to desexigrate the "Help Wanted" ads. My first cousin, Marcia Federbush, wrote the country's first study of sex discrimination in a public school system, entitled "Let Them Aspire! A Plea and Proposal for Equality of Opportunity for Males and Females in the Ann Arbor Public Schools" (1971). My second cousin Marjorie Rosen wrote the best-selling *Popcorn Venus*, the first book about sex discrimination in the movie industry. My daughter, Lisa Aronson Fontes, Ph.D., has published four books about the abuse of women and children. Lisa's *Invisible Chains* is the first popular treatise on coercive control, a form of violence against women that is now receiving increased attention. My son, Eric Aronson, Psy.D., is a clinical psychologist much appreciated for his feminist insights. Eric served as an escort for abortion clinics and is active in feminist causes. My granddaughter Marlena Fontes is national organizing director for the Climate Organizing Hub. In her previous labor union job she led a widely publicized strike that won better staffing conditions for nurses. My granddaughter Analua Fontes is a speech therapist who's been teaching trans people how to speak in their new gender identity. My grandson Gabriel Fontes is a schoolteacher who's been deeply involved in gender studies, as well as African American studies.

TIME TO RETIRE

Life never stands still. I had serious disagreements with the decisions of new leadership at Carl Byoir, and decided to retire. The firm gave me a gala retirement party, which Betty Friedan and a number of well-known friends attended.

I began working around the clock on a semi-autographical novel. It was a roman à clef about the women's movement, with thinly disguised portraits of leading characters. Alas, when I completed the book, publishing experts told me it did not work as fiction. The plot wasn't "grabbing" enough. Now, years later, I've returned to telling the story through nonfiction.

SENIOR LIVING

Shep retired from his medical practice around the time I retired from Byoir. He embarked on a new career as an impartial expert witness in lawsuits involving medical malpractice. He died in 2003, at the age of ninety. During these semiretired years, we traveled widely. Shep once perused a United Nations list and said we'd visited eighty-seven countries together. I've visited another two dozen countries since Shep's death.

One highlight was a trip to Saudi Arabia. In their drab capital city, Riyadh, I did not see a single woman walking outdoors. Nor did I see any with a shopping cart or baby carriage, let alone a briefcase.

Since 2010, I've lived in the lifetime care community of Kendal on Hudson, located in Westchester County, New York. Every day, facing west on my balcony, I'm delighted by ever-changing views of the Hudson

River. I've been busy with activities such as the Residents Council, *Kendal View* magazine, the Opera Committee, the Ping Pong Committee (which I founded after a bad knee ended my tennis days), and the Dining Advisory Committee. When I arrived at Kendal, I learned they didn't have a New Year's Eve show. I now produce that celebration every year, along with an annual Fourth of July celebration.

I believe our community is living proof of Betty Friedan's insistence that people can lead happy, active lives at an advanced age. I have dozens of really good friends. Two are 104 years old. Two others are a married gay couple.

Now for a revisionist view on another subject: sex. Since Shep's death, I've enjoyed three rewarding romances. All three men eventually died; most men live shorter lives than women. I hereby testify that women can enjoy screaming multiple orgasms in their nineties. There are numerous cuddly, thrilling ways to enjoy sex in our later years. One of our Kendal residents, sex psychologist Marian Dunn, confirmed this in a recent lecture. Marian offered to escort residents to a local sex shop and advise them on purchases.

The feminist movement has continued to campaign for greater respect and rewards for older women. Gail Collins, the much-enjoyed *New York Times* columnist, celebrates our possibilities in her best-selling book *No Stopping Us Now: The Adventures of Older Women in American History.* Gail says I inspired her to write the book when I told her about my love affairs. She recently wrote a column with the headline "Is 90 the New 60?" I'd given her that quotation.

As an activist statement, I reprint here a sonnet I composed for a recent significant other in response to a poem he'd written to me.

Sonnet to a Late Love

I never hummed so merrily before
Or caught my breath when Someone rang the bell.
I do know how to kiss and ask for more—
Full seven decades taught me very well.
The world is wrong. They see a pair near death,

Our walk unsteady, our necks bent to the right.
They can't conceive your sweet and loving breath
Upon my cheekbone, gleaming through the night.
Tonight I'm violin to lover's bow.
You say my crinkled upper arm is soft.
I trace your many wrinkles, placed just so.
Miraculous! We're children borne aloft.
That time of year thou mayst in me behold
When burning whispers shield me from the cold.

HOW DO I LOOK?

I've always been concerned with my appearance. This may seem super-ficial or reactionary to some feminists. I suffer from memories of a dirty, disorderly childhood, in which I was dressed in torn, ill-fitting clothes, and was always scratching my itchy scalp. Never again.

The only childhood toys I remember were my treasured paper dolls, which I adorned in paper dresses. In high school and college, I admired girls who were well dressed and well put together. They seemed to be in control of life because they looked neat and pretty, and this became one of my goals.

I wanted to look like the popular, privileged women I envied. I underwent plastic surgery to have my too-long nose shortened. I still watch my weight and still wear makeup—lipstick and eyeliner every day. I had a face-lift at age seventy-five. I will never stop dying my hair because I think of myself as dark-haired rather than gray-haired.

I paid a voice coach in 1956 to help me overcome my unpleasant northern New Jersey accent. I spent weeks practicing correct vowel into-nation in words like *now* and *can't*. This helps me feel more acceptable.

Superficial or not, I believe those "improvements" helped me advance in the professional world. (Experts have written about the "Pretty Privi-lege" that gives attractive people more advantages.) Other feminists make other choices. Our movement is about choices. It's regrettable that men in power may pay closer attention to young, attractive, white women. As more women of all shapes and sizes improve the world through their brains and talent, I hope their example will lead to a fairer environment, where employers judge people by what they can contribute rather than by appearance, skin color, or ethnic background.

FINALLY . . .

What else have I left unsaid about myself? I'm fortunate to enjoy loving relationships with my two children, three grandchildren, and two great-grandchildren.

Also, a word about my lifetime profession of communications. I'm grateful for the skills that enabled me to spread the word about our feminist revolution. But on the other hand, I'm saddened by the destructive role our profession is playing in the moral disruptions of the world. In my opinion, self-seeking capitalist patriarchal interests wield too much power to underwrite sophisticated campaigns that disinform the public. It's a special evil in social media. Now there's a new threat involving the falsehoods spread with artificial intelligence. I hope that humanity-loving activists—those who share our feminist values—will find ways once again to reestablish truth and kindness.

9

WE WIN BIG IN EDUCATION

PASSING TITLE IX

Our movement's greatest successes have been in education. Women now head major universities and large school systems. They've achieved equality as school principals. But, even though women outnumber men as elementary and secondary school teachers, they still have far to go when it comes to the faculty of universities.

Equality in education has always been a major focus of our movement. Seven university professors and administrators served on our founding board of NOW. One of these, Professor Carl Degler of Vassar, told me he'd joined us because he was saddened by seeing some of his brightest women students lose their ambition and end up frustrated in a secretarial pool. Carl declared in one speech, "We have to broaden the expectations of young women. . . . As a society we have to act as if we believe that women are entitled to careers as well as to babies and husbands. . . . And even for those young women who do elect not to take a job or pursue a career when they marry, they should know that . . . raising a family is, in fact, not a lifetime job." (Degler 1966)

Earlier in this book there appears an image of a NOW LDEF poster topped by the photo of an elegant diploma: "Congratulations. You've just spent twelve thousand dollars so she could join the typing pool. WOMANPOWER. It's much too good to waste!"

Our struggle was not easy. Even the enlightened Adlai Stevenson believed the mission of education for women was to produce intelligent wives and mothers. His infamous 1955 speech to the Smith College graduating class, titled "A Purpose for Modern Woman," advised women graduates to welcome "the humble role of housewife, which, statistically, is what most of you are going to be whether you like the idea or not just now—and you'll like it!" (Clark 2020, p. xvi) Infuriating!

Title IX of the 1972 Education Amendments created a huge turnaround in education. After watching televised events showing young women's victories in athletics, some people mistakenly believe that Title IX covers only sports. But it also created new opportunities in school admissions, scholarships, and every phase of employment in all education systems. In November 1983, when I presented an award to astronaut Sally Ride for NOW LDEF, Sally told me publicly, "I owe my success to Title IX." In turn, all of us owe the existence of Title IX to Edith Green.

EDITH GREEN: IT'S COMPLICATED

Edith Green served ten terms as a Democratic U.S. congresswoman from Oregon, from 1955 to 1974. In her first year in Congress, she introduced the Equal Pay Act, the very first act that specifically outlawed sex discrimination. It prohibited "discrimination on the basis of sex in wages for equal work on jobs requiring equal skill, effort and responsibility." Green's bill was passed in May 1963, over fierce opposition from the Chamber of Commerce. Business executives testified against it.

Edith Green played a complex role in feminist history. On the negative side, she was the only congresswoman who voted against adding sex to prohibited discriminations in Title VII of the Civil Rights Act of 1964. Why? She explained: "At the risk of being called an Aunt Jane, if not an Uncle Tom, let us not add any amendment that would get in the way of our primary objective.... For every discrimination that has

Edith Green
Photograph by Harris & Ewing, courtesy of the
Library of Congress

been made against a woman in this country there has been ten times as much discrimination against the Negro." (Davis 1991, pp. 31, 141) Green believed the addition of sex would hinder passage of the bill. As she predicted, every southern congressman voted against the Civil Rights Act, but President Johnson muscled it through to passage.

Feminists can forgive Green's vote in Title VII because we owe her everlasting thanks for introducing and passing Title IX.

Edith Green was the daughter of two schoolteachers, but she became a teacher herself only after advisers warned her not to pursue her preference of electrical engineering, a field unfriendly to women. After her election to the House of Representatives, as chair of the Subcommittee on Education, she became known as "Mrs. Education" for her sponsorship of important bills.

In 1972, she quietly introduced thirty-seven momentous words into the annual congressional budget bill on education: "No person in the United States shall, on the basis of sex, be excluded from participation in, be denied the benefits of, or be subjected to discrimination under any education program or activity receiving Federal financial assistance." Green advised feminists against publicly lobbying for Title IX. She didn't want to call attention to her words. The bill passed without controversy on June 8, 1972, and was signed by President Nixon on June 23. As for getting Title IX *enforced,* that proved more difficult.

Edith Green's contradictory stands through the years also involved the Equal Rights Amendment. In 1962, when she chaired the Committee on Civil and Political Rights of the Commission on the Status of Women, Green shared Pauli Murray's contention that women should fight discrimination not through the ERA but through the Fourteenth Amendment to the Constitution. Both Pauli Murray and Edith Green later changed their minds and fully supported the ERA.

Certain historians say that Green joined forces with longtime ERA opponent Emanuel Celler because, as a supporter of protective labor laws, she found the ERA threatening. However, her views did evolve. In 1972, she was an invaluable ally in helping feminists move the ERA to passage in Congress. When Celler worked to get the bill recommitted to his Judiciary Committee for certain death, Green told Congress it was incredible that they were still debating "whether or not the majority of the American people have equal rights under the Constitution . . . it is time for profound social change."

Edith Green also forced the Job Corps to include more women. Corps director Sargent Shriver replied to her sharp questions by admitting that yes, the program was ignoring women, in violation of Title VII. He agreed to give more training slots to women.

It should be mentioned that Green was one of only seven House members to vote against President Johnson's 1965 escalation of military involvement in Vietnam. She was known as a maverick and an original thinker. Her chief of staff once bragged, "I was always very proud of the fact that the assembly hushed when she got up to speak."

GETTING TITLE IX ENFORCED

After Edith Green won passage of Title IX, government officials failed to take it seriously. The Department of Health, Education and Welfare (HEW) refrained from issuing any regulations at all for Title IX until June 1974; then they failed to enforce their own regulations. The National Women's Law Center filed a lawsuit in 1974, but the lawsuit dragged on for years. It took Bernice Sandler and Holly Knox and millions (yes, millions) of activists, educators, and students to light a fire under HEW. Their success should inspire future generations of feminists who fight for social justice. It can be done!

Our feminist campaign had two parts. Bernice Sandler and the Women's Equity Action League (WEAL) headed our fight in higher education. Holly Knox and the Project on Equal Education Rights (PEER) of NOW LDEF led the way in elementary and secondary schools. Both groups mobilized school boards, educators, parents, and hundreds of influential organizations to force HEW to do its job.

Dr. Bernice "Bunny" Sandler embarked on her inspiring career as "the Godmother of Title IX" in reaction to being rejected for promotion in the University of Maryland's education department. Her rejection was explained thus: "You come on too strong for a woman." Thanks to Bunny, that stereotyped sex discrimination is now illegal under Title IX.

In 1970, after Bunny had fully informed Congresswoman Edith Green about sex discrimination in education, Green hired her to organize seven days of congressional hearings. Women's groups embarked on a two-year campaign of agitation.

In 1970, through WEAL, Bunny launched a class-action complaint with the Department of Labor against all colleges and universities in the country, attacking their industry-wide pattern of sex discrimination in hiring, promotions, and salaries. Her complaint was documented with eighty pages of shocking examples. She pointed out that numerous university departments observed quotas for women, or hired no women at all. For instance, Harvard did not have a single tenured

Dr. Bernice Sandler
Photographer Jo Freeman, courtesy of the photographer

woman professor. Often, women students were denied scholarships, with the excuse that they were married.

Within the next two years, WEAL filed complaints against 250 institutions. NOW chapters filed complaints against one hundred others. Bunny urged that the federal government must withhold financial support from schools that violated President Johnson's Executive Order 11375, mandating affirmative action for women.

Bunny Sandler made close to three thousand presentations on college campuses to improve education methods. In addition to her portfolio with WEAL, she was a leader in the Project on the Status and Education of Women, the Women's Institute for Freedom of the Press, the Center for Women Policy Studies, and the Women's Research and Education Institute.

Bunny Sandler pinpointed another problem that still needs remedy today: She labeled it the "Chilly Classroom Climate." Female students are still called upon less often by teachers; they get less eye contact and less encouragement. Boys receive more classroom computer time than girls. (Sandler, Silverberg, and Hall 1982)

These days, experts frequently comment on the relatively poor showing of boys in our schools. But it's not because boys lack attention from teachers. The problem is that schools need to develop *different kinds* of education for boys, and different forms of motivation. Boys' brains may be wired differently. Educators may need to devise different books and methods to keep their attention. However, there's another aspect to this discrepancy: The 2022 book *The Crisis of Men and Boys* says an extensive survey found that "Women are just more motivated, work harder, plan ahead better." (Brooks 2022)

Holly Knox
Photograph courtesy of Holly Knox

Holly Knox deserves the most credit for government enforcement of Title IX in elementary and secondary schools.

In the summer of 1974, Holly left her job with HEW because the agency was dragging its heels with regard to enforcement of Title IX. Mary Jean Tully, innovative president of NOW LDEF (now known as Legal Momentum), hired Holly to create and head its Project on Equal Education Rights. I'm proud of my work with Holly and Mary Jean in the multiyear campaign to enforce Title IX.

After Title IX had been passed by Congress in 1972, *all* HEW secretaries failed to take it seriously. That includes secretaries under Richard Nixon, Gerald Ford, and Jimmy Carter. In 1976, we learned that the Office for Civil Rights had a backlog of more than three thousand unattended Title IX cases.

Carter's Democrat appointee, Joseph Califano, proved no more helpful than his Republican predecessors. He was aware of strong opposition from the National Collegiate Athletic Association, bankrolled by colleges with big-budget men's sports teams. NCAA kept fighting to get Title IX eviscerated or repealed. Fortunately, we had strong (and smart) activists fighting on our side.

PEER was financed primarily by the Ford Foundation in a program led by Terry Saario. Mary Jean Tully, who had recruited Holly and then Terry for our cause, once said to me, "Joe Califano is a lousy excuse for a Democrat. We're gonna make that bastard do his job."

PEER, working with WEAL and other organizations, established the National Coalition for Women and Girls in Education (NCWGE). It's still a powerful lobbying organization in D.C. It mobilized and trained parents and educators to force their local school boards to demand enforcement of Title IX. Holly Knox explained to us, "Local school boards are the key to putting pressure on the government."

Hundreds of NOW chapters gave all-out support to our campaign. During the summer of 1974, they engineered ten thousand comments to Congress—a powerful instance of NOW chapters and NOW LDEF working together.

Government officials had written their (unenforced) regulations for implementing Title IX in complex legalese. To overcome this problem,

PEER translated the regulations side by side in plain English and distributed the publication through NOW chapters. PEER held schools and school boards to account for obeying these simplified orders.

PEER's newsletter was mailed to local school boards and distributed to parents by NOW chapters. PEER also published a report called "Stalled at the Start," which revealed the shocking fact that HEW— whatever else it might be doing—was neglecting gender problems. HEW was reviewing an average of three-tenths of one sex discrimination complaint per investigator per year. *The Washington Post* and other newspapers published PEER's revelation on their front pages. Joe Califano was finally pressured to "do your job."

At a press conference in 1979, PEER announced its Silver Snail Awards to states that lagged behind in education equality. Among other criteria, it listed the percentage of women hired as school principals, the percentage of girls in vocational education classes, and the percentage of girls in high school sports programs. The state receiving the first Silver Snail Award for terrible performance was Alabama.

In 1974, feminists successfully pressured Congress to pass another important bill: The Women's Educational Equity Act, known as WEEA, mandated HEW to develop nondiscriminatory curricula, career counseling, and sports programs and "other programs designed to achieve equity for all students regardless of sex." The act funded projects to eliminate sexism in textbooks, and it funded women's studies programs in colleges. WEEA was absorbed quietly into the annual education bill. Thus, like Title IX, it eluded debate in Congress.

Big colleges with revenue-producing men's sports programs lobbied intensively (and expensively) to scale back the regulations for Title IX and defeat WEEA. But women's organizations fought back hard and won. Holly tells me that she and Pat Reuss, who will be discussed in chapter 10, lobbied the wives of Republican congressmen and found them helpful in lobbying their husbands. All wanted to support the education of their daughters.

Men's sports coaches at all levels of education opposed us strenuously. They attacked Title IX with comments such as "If they go too far with the competitive stuff, girls lose their femininity," or "If a boy loses to a girl, think what that could to a young boy's self-image." Those were actual comments, and not infrequent.

Holly shared an opinion with me about one public error: Although Congresswoman Patsy Mink of Hawaii was the hero who introduced WEEA, Holly says Mink had not contributed much to the passage of Title IX. Because of active campaigning by Mink's admirers, more and more people came to believe that she was the coauthor of Title IX. On June 20, 2007, the U.S. Congress officially proclaimed that the fateful thirty-seven words will now be known as the Patsy Takemoto Mink Equal Opportunity in Education Act. Holly and I believe that Title IX should have been named after its true author, Edith Green, rather than Patsy Mink.

With funds supplied by the Ford Foundation, Holly established a pilot project called Michigan PEER in 1979. In addition to activating local school boards, Michigan PEER helped to defeat Congressman Jim O'Hara in a Democratic primary. O'Hara had lined up with the NCAA in an attempt to weaken Title IX. Our Michigan success inspired feminist groups in other states to campaign locally against sex discrimination.

10

VIOLENCE AND HARASSMENT

GETTING TO THE VIOLENCE AGAINST WOMEN ACT (VAWA)

We still have far to go to protect women from violence. Homicide rates of men murdering women are as high as ever. (In contrast, fewer women kill men than in the past. Instead of killing their abusers, women now flee to shelters, which didn't exist before.)

According to the National Council Against Domestic Violence, one out of five American women have been subjected to attempted or completed rape in their lifetime. One out of thirty-three men have had that experience.

Although rape by strangers has decreased, rape by intimate or casual acquaintances is more common than ever. Psychologists point out that when a woman faces acquaintance rape, shock and fear at the moment of rape may disarm her more than a weapon. Ten million people in the United States are abused every year by an intimate partner, according to the National Council Against Domestic Violence.

Among other contributing causes, there's a growing problem with "roofies" and other drugs surreptitiously slipped into women's drinks. All too often an unknowing victim complains, "I only had two drinks. I don't know why I passed out."

Acquaintance rape is a major concern of our movement, especially in colleges and high schools. I once wrote a song, "No Means No," highlighting our feminist slogan, but I didn't succeed in signing up a music publisher.

Nearly all colleges have issued directives on refraining from sex without specific permission of both parties. California was the first state to proclaim "Yes Means Yes." Without specific assent to go ahead, it's considered acquaintance rape, and is subject to consequences.

Many colleges prohibit drinking in fraternities and dormitories on campus. They also issue directives to discourage drinking in fraternities off campus. Unfortunately, it's still an uphill battle. According to the National Institute on Alcohol Abuse and Alcoholism, more than 97,000 college students a year become victims of sexual assault related to alcohol.

Some fraternities and sororities have taken action to reduce or abolish consumption of alcohol. In 2019, the two fraternities of Swarthmore College in Pennsylvania voluntarily disbanded altogether because of sexual assaults related to binge drinking in their houses.

Feminists have made progress against another menace, marital rape. They've succeeded in pushing nearly all states to criminalize marital rape. That took years of public pressure. In political campaigns we've defeated unyielding officials like the California state senator who complained, "If you can't rape your wife, who can you rape?"

Feminists also achieved passage of rape shield laws. Defendants' attorneys are no longer permitted to ask a victim in court about her previous sexual history. In the early days of our movement, ACLU opposed rape shield laws because they eroded a court weapon of defendants. But today the ACLU supports us, with some exceptions that are still controversial.

Fortunately, I've never been a victim of rape. But two members of my family were raped by acquaintances. Both were scarred by the violation. In the case of my cousin, the trauma may have been a cause of her descent into schizophrenia.

In 1951, I had a distressing experience. A male coworker phoned me late at night. "I missed the last train to Greenwich. Could I sleep on a sofa in your apartment?" Foolishly, I agreed. When he arrived, I laid out linens and blankets on the sofa and went back to sleep in my bedroom. In the middle of the night, he suddenly jumped on top of me. I pushed him off and shouted, "I'm a virgin!" (True at that time.) If I hadn't said that, would he have persisted? He backed away. Neither of us ever referred to the incident.

DO THEY BELIEVE WOMEN?

It's true that women sometimes commit violent acts against men, but not frequently. Far too often today, violent attacks are not penalized. Most police departments follow a policy of mandatory arrest if there are signs of injury. But this policy can work against a woman if her injuries are invisible.

In the old days, violence in the home was ignored as "just a family matter," not to be interfered with. Finally, we've forced local governments and police departments to treat domestic violence as a crime. But the crime is still all too common—especially for women with children, who don't have the means to escape from a threatening relationship.

When a victim of violence testifies against her assailant in court, she may suffer from not being "the perfect victim." Perhaps she doesn't cry enough, or she cries too much and seems hysterical. Perhaps she seems too angry and confrontational. Perhaps her clothes give a bad impression. As for the perpetrator, law enforcers admit, "Minorities are immediately put away. But if they're clean-cut . . . We look the other way. We don't want to ruin their lives." (Sanday 1993) Speaking of ruined lives . . . A study of women who'd been raped found that more than 30 percent of them suffered from post-traumatic stress disorder throughout their lives. (U.S. Department of Veterans Affairs)

Sexual assaults by domestic partners still oppress countless women and children. Lynn Schafran of Legal Momentum pointed out to me that, for some reason I cannot understand, judges often award custody to the husband if the wife accuses him of sexually abusing their child. How can this be? Perhaps the accusation is so unbelievably terrible that judges somehow think the complaining wife is making it up. Tragically, fear of this bias leads women to avoid making the accusation, on the advice of a lawyer. Abused children are then subjected to unsupervised visits with abusers.

PAT REUSS, JOE BIDEN, AND THE VAWA

Through heavy pressure on law enforcement agencies and expanded education of the public, our movement has made tremendous gains against violence. Our greatest weapon is the Violence Against Women Act, first passed in 1994 and then reauthorized in 2000, 2005, 2013, and 2022. In the old days, congressional votes for VAWA were overwhelmingly bipartisan. Not today. (Feminists affectionately pronounce the act "VAH'-wah" without a "the" in front of its name.)

We might never have passed VAWA without Pat Reuss and then Senator Joe Biden. Pat affirms that Biden's campaign literature is telling the truth when it credits him with declaring, one day in 1990, "Let's pass a bill that deals with domestic violence, especially marital rape, and has a civil cause of action."

Biden first introduced VAWA in Congress on June 20, 1990. His staff conferred with NOW LDEF, which helped him improve the bill. We were aided by the visionary feminist academic Professor Catherine McKinnon. In 1991, Helen Neuborne, executive director of NOW LDEF, hired Pat Reuss, then working for NWPC, to help us move VAWA through Congress.

Pat Reuss, a feminist whom history should not forget, had been our WEAL ally years earlier in the fight to get Title IX enforced. Pat brought together a wide range of experts and organizations in a coalition to improve VAWA and get it enacted. This large, diverse National Task Force to End Sexual and Domestic Violence is still a powerhouse. It works effectively with Congress on VAWA bills and related legislation. Early meetings of this task force were held in NOW's D.C. headquarters, or in the United Methodist Building across from the U.S. Supreme Court.

Our lobbying campaign to pass the first VAWA faced fierce opposition. But after four years we succeeded by folding it into the Violent Crime Control and Law Enforcement Act of 1994. The bill was controversial for various reasons. We knew we were making a difficult compromise by

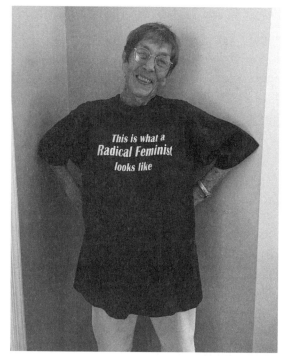

Pat Reuss
Photograph courtesy of Pat Reuss

supporting the entire crime bill. Several of the bill's provisions proved harmful to communities of color and families on welfare. Pat led our lobbying efforts to soften the bill's harmful effects.

VAWA changed how our entire criminal justice system treated violence against women. It provided billions of dollars for protection and aid. For the first time, police were trained—in fact, *required*—to treat domestic violence as a crime, instead of looking the other way. It doubled the penalties for repeat sex offenders. It criminalized stalking. It helped launch a large network of family shelters that has continued to expand through the years. These shelters make it possible for battered women to flee, with their children, from dangerous situations. Battered women often face the question "Why can't she leave him?" VAWA provides a hopeful answer.

This protection is nationwide. VAWA requires every state "to afford full faith and credit to orders of protection issued anywhere in the

United States." Since the passage of VAWA, domestic violence in the nation has decreased by more than 50 percent. That's encouraging, though not good enough.

We tried but failed to pass a provision stating "No state can receive VAWA money if it does not have a law criminalizing marital rape." Neither Biden's state of Delaware nor Hatch's state of Utah had a marital rape law. Therefore, our two champions did not pursue this requirement.

Pat Reuss worked closely with Republicans as well as Democrats to get VAWA passed and then reauthorized. I admired her success with very conservative Republican senator Orrin Hatch of Utah. Hatch's valued staff woman, Sharon Prost, was a former battered spouse. Hatch proclaimed his support for VAWA as a matter of morality, "to protect our daughters." Today the political situation has changed. Most Republicans now vote against VAWA out of party loyalty. In 2022, the only Senate Republicans who voted for VAWA reauthorization were two women, Lisa Murkowski of Alaska and Joni Ernst of Iowa.

I recall a NOW LDEF luncheon organized by Pat Reuss to thank Senator Joe Biden for his vision and persistence in establishing VAWA. Biden grinned proudly as we expressed our appreciation. He'd worked with us every step of the way to win VAWA's passage in 1994, and he continued helping us in subsequent years to win reauthorizations.

The reauthorization of VAWA in later years has added billions more dollars and more support for victim services. It improves protection for immigrants, communities of color, Indigenous peoples, and other underserved populations. It educates judges, prosecutors, probation officers, health-care professionals, ministers, and survivors themselves. It forbids authorities to charge rape survivors for sexual assault examinations and rape kits. Yes, many states used to charge the victims. Even more egregiously, many thousands of rape kits are still gathering dust, unprocessed, on the shelves of law-enforcement offices.

Pat Reuss served feminism in numerous ways, apart from her landmark work in education and violence. She lobbied for passage of the Consolidated Omnibus Budget Reconciliation Act (COBRA) of 1985. Years of feminist pressure preceded final passage of COBRA. The law gives workers who lose or leave their jobs the right to continue benefits provided by their group health plan for a limited period of time. Pat Reuss also headed our lobbying work to win pension reforms for women.

As I write this book, Pat is still operating telephone banks to contact voters for feminist political campaigns.

Authorities have begun to recognize a pervasive form of domestic violence that was not addressed in the past, although it always persisted. It's known as coercive control. Authorities and victims alike are beginning to realize that domestic abuse is broader than physical violence. Through coercive control, men (usually, but not always men) dominate their targets by isolating them from friends and family, regulating their everyday behavior, depriving them of their usual support systems, and/ or manipulating them sexually. Coercive control is treated as a crime in England today, and in several American states. My daughter, Dr. Lisa Aronson Fontes, wrote the first popular book on the subject. She and other experts are frequently asked to testify in lawsuits where women have been victimized by this pervasive oppression.

HARASSMENT IN THE WORKPLACE

Nobody knew about the term *sexual harassment* until our feminist movement publicized the concept. According to the EEOC, sexual harassment consists of "unwelcome sexual advances, requests for sexual favors, and other verbal or physical harassment of a sexual nature in the workplace or learning environment." The EEOC says one in four women have faced harassment at work.

Legal Momentum and other groups have published guidelines for companies to help them prevent and respond to this crime. Finally, most states do consider it a crime.

Legal Momentum won an important lawsuit, *Robinson v. Jacksonville Shipyards*, establishing that it's sexual harassment to post pictures of nude women in the workplace. Federal courts agreed that this once common practice is illegally intimidating and humiliating for female workers. We all remember pretending not to notice the girlie calendars that were once common in offices and factories. If sexual materials create a hostile work environment, it's illegal sexual harassment.

The act of sexually "putting women in their place" involves power more than lust. Men in power use intimidation, and worse, against less powerful women to remind them of their vulnerability. Women at all levels endure it, for fear of being fired or demoted. It's still true that "imbalance of power leads to abuse of power." (Suk 2020, p. 109) People in power do cruel things because they *can*.

In the twenty-first century, feminists took a giant step forward against hostile workplaces with the #MeToo Movement. The name for this movement was originally coined in 2006 on MySpace by Tarana Burke, an activist survivor of sexual assault. The movement took off virally in 2017 when the extreme behavior of movie mogul Harvey Weinstein hit the headlines. Accelerated by heavy publicity, #MeToo has caused the downfall of innumerable people in power, including some instances of man-on-man harassment. It's been especially visible in the entertainment and music industries, but #MeToo also brought down figures in government and other fields. Without a doubt, it's making people in power think twice before they harass an employee.

The fallout from #MeToo is 99 percent a positive gain for humanity. But we should avoid the 1 percent side effect that could thwart the ambitions of mid or upper-level women in the business world. We should not let fear of criticism hamper healthy camaraderie between the sexes. The word *camaraderie* partly explains why male bosses usually promote other men—they feel more comfortable with people like them. This problem has contributed to the glass ceiling that keeps women down.

I hope fear of criticism won't prevent a boss from mentoring a female employee. Or inviting her to lunch. Or asking her to accompany him, legitimately, on a business trip that could help her career. Some of my friends, successful female executives, say they've wondered about this too. It's mostly conjecture on our part, since my friends and I are retired.

Although I did not feel oppressed if a boss complimented me on a new outfit I was wearing, or if he patted my shoulder in a friendly way, it's definitely sexual harassment if a boss compliments a woman's appearance too frequently or touches her inappropriately.

Eventually, people will feel more comfortable when assessing what is and is not acceptable in work situations. Meanwhile, feminists must continue to fight against sexual harassment in all circumstances. This pertains to behavior between teacher and student, pastor and parishioner, doctor and patient, and all relationships of unequal power.

11

EQUAL OR DIFFERENT?

TWO KINDS OF FEMINISTS

The battle over protective labor laws caused a lot of grief in the early years of our movement. Supporters of protective laws were known as "difference feminists." They focused on women's physical differences from men and special laws to keep us safe. On the other hand, equality feminists fought against laws that barred us from better jobs and equal justice.

Beginning in the nineteenth century, labor unions struggled hard to pass laws that protected women, with their "softer bodies made for child-bearing," from working long hours, working at night, carrying heavy weights, or otherwise burdening their constitutions. On February 24, 1908, crusaders finally achieved their goal with the Supreme Court decision in *Muller v. Oregon*. This decision upheld an Oregon law barring women from working more than ten hours a day in factories or laundries. The Court reasoned that "the child-bearing nature and social role of women provided a strong state interest in reducing their working hours."

The decision covered single women as well as married ones, on the grounds that long hours might endanger their ability to bear children in the future. (Davis 1991, p. 31) The Court declared that women's physical well-being "becomes an object of public interest in order to preserve the strength and vigor of the race." In the early years of EEOC, the agency upheld this viewpoint, declaring that state protective laws could not be overruled by the federal government's civil rights laws.

Not all protective laws made sense. Nine states barred women from working behind a bar. The state of Ohio forbade women to read gas meters, work as bellhops, work in shoeshine parlors or poolrooms, or set pins in bowling alleys. (Carabillo, Meuli, and Csida 1993, p. 53) Utah banned women from jobs where they'd lift more than a mere fifteen pounds.

During congressional hearings on the Civil Rights Act of 1964, powerful labor unions testified against including sex in Title VII because it would "inhumanely" threaten the protective laws.

After women had won the vote in 1920, a schism arose between difference and equality feminists. The National Woman's Party, led by Alice Paul, fought on the side of equality. The NWP proposed an Equal Rights Amendment (ERA) with twenty-four powerful words: "Equality of rights under the law shall not be denied or abridged by the United States or by any State on account of sex."

Equality feminists insisted that protective laws banning truly harmful conditions should be changed to protect *men* as well as women. I remember arguing in early 1967 with Catherine Conroy: "Don't men get hernias if they carry something heavy? And don't they deserve decent hours, so they can spend time with their family?"

Equality feminists held the upper hand in NOW. Our Legal Committee labored to overturn practices that treated women workers differently from men. Our early cases supported women who were barred from lucrative jobs that would require them to work nights as supervisors, or carry a heavy burden.

Evidence indicates that Eleanor Roosevelt did not endorse the ERA because she supported the protective labor laws. Protectionists had a strong champion in Deputy Secretary of Labor Esther Peterson, the highest-ranking woman in our federal government during the 1960s. Peterson was seconded by Mary Keyserling, head of her department's Women's Bureau.

On the equality side, a vociferous champion was Congresswoman Martha Griffiths, who insisted, "The main function of protective labor laws for women is to protect men's rights to the best paying jobs."

THE BATTLE OF JUNE 30, 1966

When agitation for the ERA began to stir up both political parties, Esther Peterson proposed to President Kennedy a device to appease the agitators. At Peterson's suggestion, JFK created the Presidential Commission on the Status of Women on December 14, 1961, to advise the president on women's issues. Headed by Eleanor Roosevelt, the PCSW was heavily stacked with anti-ERA protectionists. The PCSW proposed various improvements, such as fair hiring practices, paid maternity leave, and affordable child care.

An offshoot of the national PCSW, similar commissions were created in each state to address women's issues. Most members of state commissions favored protection rather than equality.

Betty Friedan's paranoid streak led her to accuse Kay Clarenbach of being "Mary Keyserling's pawn" and "the darling of the Women's Bureau." Once Betty used the word *agent*. There was also friction between NOW's midwesterners and easterners. Betty told me the midwesterners considered her a "wild New York radical."

For the legendary meeting in Betty's hotel room at the SCSW conference on the night of June 29, 1966, Betty objected at first when Catherine East included Kay in the invitation list. Kay originally believed the gathering was "just a social meeting to have a drink," and she invited her Wisconsin friend Nancy Knaak to join them. Dorothy Haener later criticized Nancy to historians, saying Nancy had insisted, "Do you really think we need another women's organization?"

Some writers accuse Nancy of vigorously opposing Betty's call for an "NAACP for women." In later years, Nancy refuted this impression. She said she just wanted the group to examine all alternatives before creating a new organization. She knew all along that a new organization was inevitable. She was one of those who signed up for

NOW membership the next day. Nancy has insisted, "I cared a whole lot." (Carabillo, Meuli, and Csida 1993, p. 23)

In a later conversation with me, Mary Eastwood recalled, "After Nancy Knaak suggested delay, Betty opened the door to her room and screamed at Nancy: "Get out! . . . This is my room and my liquor!" Nancy remained seated on the floor. "I will not. I'm having too good a time." At that, Betty rushed into her bathroom and locked the door, not to emerge for fifteen minutes.

As a compromise, Kay Clarenbach suggested, "Let me talk to Esther Peterson and Mary Keyserling. I can persuade them to allow a vote on our proposals." She didn't succeed. The following morning, Esther Peterson rejected Kay's request. That triggered the lunchtime birth of NOW.

The difference group's leader within NOW was Catherine Conroy of Milwaukee. Catherine, active in the Communications Workers of America, supported protectionism and opposed the ERA. At the SCSW final luncheon on June 30, instead of sitting at the union table, Catherine joined the main feminist table. For the new organization about to emerge, Catherine was already prepared with a list of a proposed steering committee. Her list omitted the name of Betty Friedan. She announced, without asking for a vote, that the temporary chair of the committee should be Kay Clarenbach. She also declared that the group's headquarters would be in the Midwest, where protectionist union leaders held control.

I have a copy of NOW's first "Invitation to Join." It was signed by a steering committee headed by Kay Clarenbach. The name of Betty Friedan was not listed among the signers.

As reported previously, Catherine's ploy failed. Within the next few weeks, Mary Eastwood and Betty Friedan maneuvered a place for Betty on the steering committee—as NOW's president. And they persuaded the committee to establish headquarters on the East Coast "because that's where the media are located."

I was not involved in NOW at the time. Mary Eastwood has told me that Catherine Conroy also brought to the table an outline for a "Statement of Purpose" espousing protection rather than equality. Betty ignored their suggestions and spent the summer writing NOW's beautiful, historic "Statement of Purpose." It promotes equality rather than protection. Despite our differences, Catherine Conroy remained one of NOW's most active supporters. She enlisted hundreds of loyal members.

The ERA controversy came to a head the following year, in November 1967. At NOW's national conference in D.C., the United Auto Workers contingent resigned in protest when we passed a resolution supporting the Equal Rights Amendment. UAW executive Dorothy Haener, our devoted workhorse as NOW's de facto secretary-treasurer, had begged us to "wait another year" to help her wean the UAW from its protective position. But ERA activists refused to wait, and overnight we lost valued colleagues in the labor movement.

Dorothy Haener deserves a special tribute. Dorothy mobilized the Women's Department of the United Auto Workers to manage all of NOW's clerical work in our first year. Under Dorothy's supervision, that department handled our finances, memberships, mailings, and all our printing. I wonder if we could have grown so quickly without that help. (Dorothy's boss in the UAW, Caroline Davis, was officially our secretary-treasurer. But Caroline was ill, and Dorothy did all the work. Caroline never came to a NOW event.) We were sad when Dorothy ended the UAW operation after NOW voted to support the ERA. Dorothy continued her personal membership in NOW but could no longer remain active.

Dorothy kept lobbying the UAW to change their position on the ERA, and finally succeeded in 1970. Soon after, she joined the board of NOW LDEF. Dorothy was also active in WEAL, the Older Women's League, the NWPC, and the Michigan Task Force on Sexual Harassment in the Workplace.

As a delegate to the 1976 Democratic National Convention, Dorothy worked hard for a provision in the party platform protecting a woman's right to choose her own reproductive life. (Love 2006, p. 195)

Although Catherine Conroy and her Communications Workers were opposed to the ERA, Catherine's union allowed her to remain active in NOW despite the conference vote. Later she created NOW's innovative delegate voting system.

Dorothy Haener
Photographer Jo Freeman, courtesy of the photographer

EQUALITY LAWSUITS

Ultimately, equality feminists consolidated their victory. Several of NOW's trailblazing lawsuits established forever that sex discrimination for "protection" was illegal under Title VII of the Civil Rights Act of 1964.

Equality feminism led us to four all-important lawsuits, which I've described previously. *Mengelkoch v. Industrial Welfare Commission* argued against policies that barred women from promotion to jobs involving night work. *Weeks v. Southern Bell* and *Bowe v. Colgate-Palmolive Company* involved policies that barred women from lifting over a certain weight. In the *Colgate* case, we fought additionally against separate seniority lists for male and female workers.

Feminists found the *Phillips v. Martin Marietta Corp.* especially infuriating. Martin Marietta had refused to accept job applications from women with very young children. With our victory in the Supreme Court in that case, feminists advanced the concurring opinion of Justice Thurgood Marshall that hiring practices "must not justify stereotypical characterization of traditional gender roles."

Bear in mind that protections against nighttime work or heavy lifting had never applied to cleaning women, domestic workers, or thousands of other women in the lowest-paying jobs.

YES, THERE'S A DIFFERENCE

We did recognize one area where women are different and deserve assistance: Feminists persuaded the EEOC in 1972 to issue new guidelines treating pregnancy the same as other temporary disabilities. The Pregnancy Discrimination Act, passed in 1978, prohibits discrimination on the basis of pregnancy, childbirth, or related medical conditions.

Later, in the 1980s, the issue was refined further. In the case of *California Federal Savings & Loan Association v. Guerra*, the Supreme Court ruled that companies should treat pregnancy like other medical conditions and should not terminate a woman's job if she took time off to have a baby. NOW LDEF argued that *all* employees should be granted a leave for medical reasons if necessary. We declared that parental leave should be available to fathers as well as mothers.

Another battleground for difference feminists was identified by Harvard psychologist Carol Gilligan. She attributed our societal gender gap to the fact that girls are born different from boys, and raised differently. Females are taught to value "helping others," while boys are raised on issues of abstract morality, justice, and human rights. Men work in hierarchies; women work in supportive networks. Carol's 1982 book, *In A Different Voice,* insists that the different values maintained by women and girls should be celebrated, rather than punished.

Carol brought us to another epiphany. A research study she led from 1982 to 1985, covering thousands of girls from various backgrounds, found that many girls begin to lose confidence in their capabilities after the age of eleven. By the age of fifteen or sixteen, girls have become more hesitant and less assertive. Recently, thanks to feminist campaigns and educational reforms, we're taking steps to overcome this confidence gap.

Today experts say boys, too, need special attention and supportive education, in light of genetic differences in learning abilities. A 2022 book by Richard V. Reeves, *Of Boys and Men,* suggested that boys should start school a year after girls because the cerebellum and pre-frontal cortex, which govern self-regulation, develop later in boys than in girls. (Brooks 2022) However, this might present other problems, since boys in a classroom would be older and bigger than the girls.

ALICE PAUL, FIRST WAVE AND SECOND WAVE

Alice Paul was our great equality feminist. She will be remembered by history as a leader of three feminist campaigns: (1) She led the final suffragist push for passage of the Nineteenth Amendment to the Constitution, giving women the vote at long last; (2) she lobbied to include women in Title VII of the Civil Rights Law of 1964; (3) she was *the* person who introduced the Equal Rights Amendment in 1923. Alice was our hero in both the first wave and second wave.

Women nicknamed Alice "the Lenin of Suffragism" because of her success in pressuring President Woodrow Wilson to keep his World War I promise to pass the proposed Nineteenth Amendment through Congress at long last.

In 1916 Alice had declared that the National American Woman Suffrage Association (NAWSA) was not militant enough, so she founded the National Woman's Party (NWP). She and her followers endured prison, hunger strikes, forced feeding, sanity examinations, and chaining themselves to White House fences. Most leaders who had demanded

Alice Paul
Photograph by Underwood and Underwood,
courtesy of the Smithsonian Institution Archives

women's suffrage at the Seneca Falls Convention of 1848 did not live long enough to see their final victory.

In 1923, at another historic Seneca Falls Convention, Alice Paul introduced the Equal Rights Amendment, which she coauthored with attorney Crystal Eastman. Alice promptly delivered the resolution to Congress that same year. She originally called it the "Lucretia Mott Amendment," named after the famous suffragist. But in 1943, activists correctly renamed it the "Alice Paul Amendment."

Even though the ERA was finally passed by Congress in 1972, and its expiration date was extended in 1978, it has still failed to become law, as I write in 2023. If a Democratic, pro-feminist Congress is elected in the near future, this could change. Our lawmakers might agree to recognize the ratification votes we've already secured in the necessary thirty-eight states. An alternative would be to pass the ERA through Congress once again, and once again ratify it in thirty-eight state legislatures.

In working for the ERA, Alice Paul was aware that southern states lagged behind other states. Not until the period between 1969 and 1971 was the Nineteenth Amendment ratified by the southern states of Florida, Georgia, Louisiana, North Carolina, and South Carolina. Mississippi didn't ratify votes for women until 1984! (Women in those states did enjoy the *nationally* enforced right to vote, even if their states delayed official ratification.)

Alice was a close friend of southern congressman Howard W. Smith. For twenty successive years, Smith sponsored the ERA in Congress. This complicates the mystery of Howard Smith's motives. Did he propose the inclusion of sex in Title VII in order to scuttle passage of the entire civil rights bill? Or did he really believe in women's rights? Probably both.

Though we all revered Alice Paul, she's been accused of racism and insensitivity to the needs of Black women. Also, NOW leaders were distressed by her role in the defection of Mary Eastwood's group in late 1968. Perhaps Mary's group might not have fled from NOW, taking with them our key lawsuits, if Alice had not written a check for them.

After a lifetime of activism, Alice suffered a stroke in 1974. Her nephew placed her in a nursing home and criminally depleted her estate. After Alice's penniless condition became known, a fund for indigent Quakers supported her.

KAY CLARENBACH

Kathryn Clarenbach is another leader who should be remembered by history as an influential organizer of our movement. Kay never expressed strong feelings about the issue of protective labor laws—or other controversies, for that matter. But in the beginning, she sided with her midwestern sisters, favoring protectionism.

Because of Kay's intelligence, kindness, and ability to befriend activists of all persuasions, she was elected to chair several major feminist conferences. Everyone liked and respected her. A distinguished-looking

gray-haired educator, Kay smiled a lot. She almost always had a ciga-
rette in her hand and smoked so heavily that she ultimately died of
emphysema.

After Betty Friedan sidestepped Catherine Conroy's early efforts to
install Kay as president of NOW, we elected Kay our first national chair.
She recruited many members from the Midwest.

Mary Eastwood once said to me, "I became very fond of Kay after I
got to know her. . . . She always said she was a little naïve, and I think
that accounted for her going along with the Women's Bureau initially."
Betty Friedan gradually transitioned from her original attacks against
Kay. In the August 1979 issue of *Cosmopolitan* magazine, she referred to
Kay as a "peer mentor," saying "she was a good countervail to me." (In
that same article, Betty said I was her other peer mentor. "To this day,

Kay Clarenbach
Photographer Diana Mara Henry, copyright © Diana Mara Henry

when I have a tricky decision to make involving the women's movement, I check with Muriel.") (*Cosmopolitan* 1979, p. 206)

Kay pioneered continuing education programs for women that were adopted throughout the country. Her numerous chairmanships included the National Women's Political Caucus. Getting along with both Betty Friedan and Bella Abzug was no easy feat. In 1977, Kay was chosen as coordinator of the historic National Women's Conference in Houston, celebrating International Women's Year. She also served as president of NOW LDEF in 1981. NOW LDEF was suffering from serious personnel problems at the time, and I argued with Kay about her reluctance to address the conflicts decisively.

Kay's passivity in challenging a status quo included her early opposition to NOW support for lesbianism as a feminist issue. She declared it would be a "disastrous blunder" to involve NOW in that cause. (Self 2012, p. 178)

RUTH BADER GINSBURG MERGES EQUALITY AND DIFFERENCE

Ruth Bader Ginsburg, an equality feminist, scored important victories for women by proving that *men* suffer, too, when the two genders are treated differently. She directed the Women's Rights Project of the American Civil Liberties Union, a major force in feminist progress. Ruth won five trailblazing cases before the Supreme Court:

In *Frontiero v. Richardson in* 1973, she established that husbands of servicewomen must receive the same rights as service wives when the government allocates military housing allowances, medical care, and other benefits.

In *Weinberger v. Weisenfeld* in 1975 and *Califano v. Goldfarb* in 1977, she won equal Social Security child-care benefits for husbands as well as wives, and for widowers as well as widows.

In *Duren v. Missouri* in 1979, she struck down a state law that made jury duty optional for women but compulsory for men.

In *Reed v. Reed* in 1971, she used the Fourteenth Amendment to overturn preference for men in selecting administrators of estates.

Ruth Bader Ginsburg
Photographer R. Michael Jenkins
Photograph courtesy of the Library of Congress

(Until the Equal Rights Amendment finally becomes part of the Constitution, the Fourteenth Amendment and Title VII are our main weapons for gender equality.)

Ruth joined the board of NOW LDEF in 1972, while I was chair. NOW LDEF and the ACLU often worked together to support feminist goals.

Ruth was living proof of the benefit to society when women are finally admitted into men-only professions. When she graduated first in her class at Columbia Law School, she didn't receive a single job offer from a law firm. Perhaps employers realized their mistake later when they saw Ruth shine as a professor, a feminist lawyer, and then the second woman to serve as a Supreme Court justice.

Ruth's many contributions as a justice included her oft-quoted majority opinion in *United States v. Virginia* in 1996. In overturning Virginia Military Institute's refusal to accept female students, she wrote that while Virginia "serves the state's sons, it makes no provision whatever for her daughters. That is not equal protection." (Love 2006, p. 174)

Like Gloria Steinem, Betty Friedan, and me, Ruth publicly lamented the frustrated life her mother had endured. She once declared, "I pray that I may be all that she would have been had she lived in an age when women could aspire and achieve, and daughters are cherished as much as sons. (Love 2006, p. 175)

My husband, Shep, was family doctor for Ruth and her lawyer husband, Martin Ginsburg, when they lived in New York City. Once, after Shep learned that we'd all be vacationing at the same time in the south of France, the four of us arranged to lunch together at a three-star restaurant. I recall that Marty did most of the talking and Ruth hardly said a word. She did remark, "In our house, the first person who gets home at night does the cooking." In their later years in D.C., Marty cooked all the meals.

Ruth was a big believer in a mother and father sharing child-care duties equally. For this purpose, she offered the same flexible work schedules to her male and female court clerks.

I cherish the handwritten note Ruth sent me, signed "Ruth & Marty," after Shep's death. Among other consolations, she wrote, "The life partnership you had with Shep was something to celebrate."

I remember sitting next to Ruth at lunch during a VFA event honoring feminist lawyers. She seemed fragile at the time. I urged her, "Please take good care of yourself, Ruth. The world needs you." Ruth replied, "I do my best. I've had a trainer for years, and I drop everything for my workouts." She knew that Republican senators would insist on replacing her with a more conservative justice. Alas, she died during Donald Trump's presidency and was replaced by conservative Amy Coney Barrett.

NINE WOMEN

When Ruth Bader Ginsburg was asked what would be the right number of women justices for the Supreme Court, she replied, "Nine women." This reminded me of NOW's earlier demonstration on February 16, 1973. Nine of us, dressed in justices' robes, appeared together for a photograph on the steps of the Supreme Court. The caption in the NOW newsletter declared, "The demonstration served notice, not only that NOW's national Conference was in town, but that we were still waiting for women to take their rightful places on the bench of the high court." Seven years later, in 1980, when Ronald Reagan was running for president and the press asked him about the ERA, he promised to appoint the first woman to the Supreme Court. We've indeed made some progress.

12

NOT JUST A HOUSEWIFE

IN THE EARLY DAYS OF OUR MOVEMENT, we concentrated on women in the paid workforce. We fought to make employers treat them fairly in hiring, salaries, promotions, and benefits. But how about the homemaker? After a short time (not short enough, perhaps) feminists began to insist that the homemaker, too, is a workingwoman. We lobbied to win her greater financial security, recognition, and fair compensation for her labors in the home.

In our fight for the ERA, our opponents told married women that "gender neutral" laws might deprive them of alimony and other special protections. Feminists tried to prove this was inaccurate. We kept reminding the public that feminists were fighting to help homemakers by winning them the compensation they deserved in Social Security, pensions, and other benefits. We were fighting to protect wives justly in case of divorce or the death of a spouse.

Betty's *Feminine Mystique* focused on educated women who felt unfulfilled because their lives were limited to housework. Every time I appeared in a public place with Betty, women rushed up to her with the same words: "You changed my life!" These women, inspired by Betty's book, had decided to launch a career, or enter law school, or embark on other pursuits in the outside world. Betty's book was less popular with women who remained in the home. Many reacted furiously, feeling disrespected. After Betty's book appeared, she was ostracized by neighbors in Rockland County. Women complained, "She makes me feel patronized. To her I'm just a housewife."

In the early days, feminists did undervalue the contribution of homemakers. At our first press conference, our usually gracious Kay Clarenbach remarked, "There's no value in being a housewife. It's boring." As NOW's vice president for public relations, I immediately changed the subject. I later advised our members to keep stressing that "housework is real work and should be rewarded with respect and financial security." We should refer to women with a paid job as "women who work outside the home" rather than "women who work."

I instructed colleagues to use the word *homemaker* instead of *housewife* and to point out that NOW favors *choices* for women. We kept repeating the slogan "Every mother is a working mother."

In later years, dozens of newspaper columns pounced on stories about successful professional women who chose to drop out of their career to stay home and raise children. That's an option, too—though most of those professional dropouts cited by the newspapers happened to have husbands earning huge salaries. Again, we emphasize the all-important need for *options* and for treating women fairly wherever they work, whether in the home or in the paid workforce.

Sociologists everywhere did find that women who brought home a paycheck received more respect from their husbands and children. A feminist in Afghanistan was quoted recently as saying, "As soon as women bring money into their household, their voices begin to be heard." (Shahalimi 2022)

The feminist struggle for equality becomes complicated when we discuss marriage, divorce, and the family. Most regulations are decided by the states, rather than by the federal government.

In some states, NOW chapters fought vigorously against no-fault divorce and other laws that make divorce easy to obtain, because easy divorce deprives a wife of her bargaining power. (NOW lost those battles. Since 2010, most states have adopted no-fault divorce.)

Child custody is another complex problem. Men's groups complain that judges give unfair preference to mothers. Men press for joint custody, which sounds like a noble idea. But many NOW chapters fight against it. That's because some divorcing husbands use joint custody as a cudgel to extract a better financial settlement from their wives. Also, presumption of shared custody can be dangerous for parents who share a child with a violent partner. We're still working through these issues, and it isn't simple. Legal Momentum has published helpful brochures advising women on their legal rights state by state.

In some cases, a mother with a full-time job loses custody rights if a judge thinks the children would be better off with the husband's stay-at-home mother or his new stay-at-home wife. Statistics show that husbands after divorce are usually more prosperous than wives who have divorced. They can afford more comfortable homes. Most important—divorcing husbands can afford the best lawyers.

In 1989, a new issue arose for mothers whose jobs involve long working hours. The *Harvard Business Review* published a controversial article by Felice Schwartz, founder of Catalyst, an admirable organization that serves women executives. Felice's article proposed that law firms should create an optional career track for women attorneys with children. Mothers should be permitted to work fewer hours, so they could attend to their families. In exchange for this privilege, they would forfeit their chance of ever becoming a partner in the firm. Feminists pounced on this suggestion immediately. Although Felice had not used this phrase, the new term *mommy track* enraged us. We pointed out that law firms demand too many work-hours from *all* employees, and mothers should not be singled out for career limitation. Felice was a friend of mine, and I was one of many feminists who tried to make her back off from her suggestion. But she stuck to her guns.

Our early efforts for homemakers did not take into account the problems of lesbian homemakers, disabled homemakers, and trans homemakers. Most especially, single mothers who depend on welfare payments have special needs that require special attention.

13

WOMEN'S HEALTH, WOMEN'S SEX

THROUGHOUT HISTORY, many women had no time for world affairs because they were perpetually pregnant, perpetually involved in raising children, and maintaining a home for the family. Today, because women in most societies have control over their pregnancies, we can be more active in the world outside our homes.

Attempts at birth control go way back. The first condoms, made of animal and fish bladders, were introduced as long ago as 3000 B.C. The first family-planning clinic in the United States, established by Margaret Sanger, appeared in 1916. She was arrested for distributing illegal information. Sanger told the world, "Enforced motherhood is the most complete denial of a woman's right to life and liberty." Our liberation finally became a possibility in 1960, when the Food and Drug Administration approved the first birth-control pill. However . . .

BARBARA SEAMAN AND WOMEN'S HEALTH

The Pill caused serious health problems for many women. No experts objected to its side effects until Barbara Seaman published *The Doctors' Case Against the Pill* in 1969. Barbara deserves an honored place in feminist history. As an active feminist, she was grateful for the Pill's

Barbara Seaman
Photography courtesy of the National Women's Health Network

protections from pregnancy. But she insisted that its high-estrogen dosage had to be changed because it was endangering women's lives.

In response to Barbara's accusations, the U.S. Senate launched the Nelson Pill Hearings. Unbelievably, these hearings did not include any women as witnesses. Feminist activists kept interrupting and protesting. We called those protests "the Boston Tea Party of the women's health movement." Widespread publicity led to the first informational insert ever placed inside a drug package. Pharmaceutical companies did further research, not revealed to the public. Finally, they bowed to feminist pressure and revised the Pill to just a fraction of its original estrogen dosage. High-dose pills were banned in Europe in the late 1970s, but not in the United States until 1988. Shameful!

My husband, Shep, reacted defensively at first, in loyalty to his physician brothers. He questioned Barbara's right to challenge medical experts. But her statistics finally persuaded him. Then Shep pressured his colleagues in the New York County Medical Society to recognize the indisputable facts in Barbara's book. Doctors everywhere began to respond to those facts. Pharmaceutical companies never forgave

Barbara for her attacks. Women's magazines refused to run ads for any of her books.

The National Women's Health Network (NWHN), cofounded in 1975 by Barbara Seaman, Alice Wolfson, Belita Cowan, Mary Howell, and Phyllis Chesler, became a trailblazing "watchdog for women's health." According to author Barbara Ehrenreich: "Barbara Seaman proved that women can talk back to doctors—calmly, rationally, and scientifically. For many of us, women's liberation began at that moment."

NWHN soon turned its attention to another abuse, the dangers of estrogen replacement therapy (ERT). At first, experts claimed that estrogen doses after menopause would prevent heart disease, in addition to keeping women young-looking longer. Barbara Seaman was convinced that ERT had contributed to the death of her beloved aunt. She publicized scientific observations that ERT might increase breast cancer, heart attacks, strokes, and blood clots. ERT treatments screeched to a halt.

Today, five decades after Barbara's NWHN crusade, we learn that the ERT story is more complicated than once realized. Studies by the North American Menopause Society have found that side effects from ERT can be mitigated by prescribing smaller doses of estrogen, combined with progestin. Also, treatment is more helpful and less harmful if it's started early, when a woman is under the age of sixty. (Dominus 2023, pp. 22–44) If Barbara had lived long enough, she surely would have acknowledged these complexities.

The NWHN also promoted natural childbirth. It insisted that the United States had a higher rate of infant mortality than other developed nations because our obstetricians interfered too much with medications to hasten the birth process instead of patiently allowing birth to take its course. Today, natural childbirth is more popular in the United States than ever before.

PAY ATTENTION TO NURSES AND WOMEN PATIENTS!

In response to Barbara's accusation that doctors don't listen attentively to women patients, Shep organized a special meeting with women's groups for fellow board members of the New York County Medical Society. Copies of his report on the meeting were distributed to doctors nationwide. *The New York Times* carried a long story.

Energized by that meeting, Shep created a special Medical Society committee to address condescending, dismissive behavior toward nurses by many doctors. His committee established a precedent by including an equal number of doctors and nurses.

Since those days, doctors' attitudes toward women patients have greatly improved, but not completely. Studies in 2022 showed that doctors and emergency room staff still pay less attention to women's pain complaints than to men's and that women receive fewer painkillers.

Black patients fare especially poorly. Innumerable studies show that they receive less attention, fewer painkillers, and fewer health safety measures than white patients. In one study, half of medical school students revealed they believed the following: "Black people's nerve endings are less sensitive than white people's." "Black people's skin is thicker than white people's." "Black people's blood coagulates more quickly than white people's." (Sabin 2020)

Black women suffer especially from maltreatment, including abusive hysterectomies and sterilizations and inadequate medical attention. Infant mortality is several times higher among Black families. Even the wealthiest Black women die in childbirth more often than the poorest white women. (Hill 2022)

The National Council of Negro Women (NCNW), a valued ally of NOW, has emphasized women's medical issues since 1935. In 1941, NCNW was the first national women's organization to endorse birth control.

In Barbara Seaman's widely read book *Free and Female,* she pointed out that women have certain sexual advantages over men, especially a capacity for multiple orgasms. But *society* gives more advantages to men than to women. A double standard penalizes women more than men for adultery or prostitution.

Barbara stayed in close contact with Betty Friedan. In April 2002, she drove Betty from the airport to our Veteran Feminists of America Salute to Feminist Authors. Betty was living in an assisted living facility in D.C. at the time, and struggling from memory deficit. Barbara whispered to me before Betty's speech, "You shouldn't put her on the program. She's in bad shape." Nevertheless, Betty gave a brilliant talk at our conference, with no perceivable problems.

OUR BODIES, OURSELVES

Feminists point out that many women are seriously uninformed about their bodies and sexual functions. This problem was brilliantly addressed in 1970 when the Boston Women's Health Book Collective published *Women and Their Bodies*. They priced this revolutionary 136 page booklet at thirty-five cents. In 1971, the title was changed to *Our Bodies, Ourselves*. In its various editions, the book has sold over four million copies in thirty-three languages.

Later editions cover subjects such as women's sexual health, lesbianism and bisexuality, birth control, abortion, pregnancy, childbirth, violence, abuse, menopause and—in recent years—transgenderism. The collective always emphasizes the need for reproductive justice.

When I presented the collective with a VFA award and thanked Judy Norsigian for giving women previously taboo information, she replied, "It isn't just about information. We want women to exult in their bodies. And enjoy their sexuality."

TABOO SUBJECTS

Feminists began to pursue sexuality further by *demonstrating* what it's all about. Carol Downer and Lorraine Rothman traveled to twenty-three cities across the United States, introducing thousands of women to self-examination and seeing their cervixes for the first time. Hundreds of local clinics and self-help groups sprang up across the country. At the 1971 NOW national conference, where I was elected chairwoman, Carol and Lorraine rented a booth. Would we permit them to conduct clinics there? Of course!

Even more controversially than self-examination, these clinics promoted the practice of menstrual extraction, using an inexpensive

187

Del-Em suction device that Lorraine had invented. It can be used for abortion. Today, nonphysicians employ medical extraction in performing over a million abortions in countries such as Cuba, Bangladesh, Korea, Singapore, Hong Kong, Thailand, and Vietnam. (Mosher 2001)

Feminists advanced from self-examination to self-pleasuring. Betty Dodson traveled widely with sex lectures and an array of sex products. Dell Williams, an active member of NOW's New York chapter, built a successful business called Eve's Garden. She offered a wide variety of vibrators, plus recordings to keep women aroused as they self-pleasured. Before she died, Dell sold Eve's Garden to an online marketing company, and it's still thriving. Dell was an energetic campaigner for "sexual self-care and wellness." She once informed us that May is International Masturbation Month and that International Masturbation Day was first declared on May 7, 1995. As might be expected, the initiator was a company that sold vibrators.

Women's sexuality was also advanced by the popularity of Eve Ensler's play *The Vagina Monologues*, which has informed and entertained audiences throughout the world since its debut off-off-Broadway in 1996. It's still a favorite production on college campuses everywhere.

SHERE HITE GETS IT RIGHT

Women's sexuality received meaningful support from the works of Shere Hite. History must remember Shere. I remember the evening when Shere first introduced her proposed survey to a meeting of NOW's New York chapter. Her questionnaire did not receive the enthusiastic response it deserved. We failed to realize the important knowledge Shere's study would contribute to world understanding of women's sexual needs.

I called the survey "self-selecting." I objected to Shere's opening one question with "*When* you masturbate" instead of "*If* you masturbate."

Shere mimeographed and distributed the survey herself. She spent five years compiling the information. Fortunately, when her survey was completed, it reached the attention of Regina Ryan, an astute editor at Macmillan publishers. Regina titled the book *The Hite Report* and arranged massive publicity. It was favorably reviewed in *The New York*

Shere Hite
Photographer Bernard Gotfryd
Photography courtesy of the Library of Congress

Times Book Review by Erica Jong, author of the sex-absorbed *Fear of Flying*. Erica's funny, exciting bestseller had introduced the term *zipless fuck* to American literature. Shere's book, published in 1976, was an instant bestseller. Sales have exceeded 48 million copies worldwide. It became the thirtieth-best-selling book of all time. I happened to be supervisor of the Macmillan account at my PR agency; I confessed to Regina how wrong I'd been when Shere first introduced her survey.

More than 70 percent of the survey's three thousand respondents reported that women need clitoral stimulation to reach orgasm, rather than vaginal intercourse with a penis. Shere insisted that the reports of Alfred Kinsey and Masters and Johnson had been incorrect in placing too much emphasis on male thrusting. Shere said it's men, rather than women, who require stimulation from the entire vagina.

This same conclusion had been reached in Anne Koedt's 1970 article, "The Myth of the Vaginal Orgasm." Anne and Shere both berated Sigmund Freud's contention that women are emotionally immature if they seek clitoral rather than vaginal orgasm.

The Hite Report provoked a furor in the male establishment. *Playboy* magazine dubbed it "The Hate Report," and Shere received death threats. Gloria Steinem decried those male attacks as "against the rights of women everywhere."

Later books by Shere Hite produced further revelations. She highlighted women's "increasing emotional frustration" in their relations with men. Her subsequent survey of men reported that more than 70 percent of married men have affairs outside marriage. The media attacked Shere's methodology and called her "unprofessional." They inevitably mentioned that she'd once posed nude for *Playboy* while studying for her Ph.D. at Columbia. She received so many death threats that in 1995 that she surrendered her American passport and moved to Europe.

I had lunch with Shere during one of her visits to this country. She expressed uncomprehending frustration with the American press. Her first marriage, to a German concert pianist nineteen years younger, ended in divorce. Her second marriage, to an Englishman, lasted until her death.

Books by Australian Germaine Greer also became bestsellers, beginning with *The Female Eunuch* in 1970. Germaine's shocking statements include "Women who fancy that they can manipulate the world by pussy power . . . are fools." (Cohen 1988, p. 257) Her attacks on outmoded ideas of "womanhood" and "femininity" charged that women are too submissive in agreeing to serve as "fulfillment for men's sexual fantasies." She supported the women's liberation wing of feminism, insisting that women must combat the patriarchy by deciding their own values and fate. She belittled NOW's struggle for legal equality, which she dubbed "assimilation."

Germaine agreed to fly to America for NOW's April 30, 1971, debate at New York City's Town Hall, moderated by macho novelist Norman Mailer. Other speakers were our chapter president Jacqui Ceballos, literary critic Diana Trilling, and *Lesbian Nation* author Jill Johnston. The encounter is immortalized in a documentary film titled *Town Bloody Hall.*

In my opinion, the six-foot-tall Germaine far outshone Norman Mailer with her insistence that discrimination damages men as well as women. Diana Trilling said we're all victims of "a culture that makes people believe there's no such thing as a female orgasm." Jill Johnston's segment was the most remarkable. Jill declared, "All women must accept themselves as lesbians, loving themselves in order to be equal to men." At that moment, two lesbians jumped onstage and began kissing and rolling on the floor. Norman Mailer shouted, "Come on, Jill. Be a lady." The documentary is still available online.

THE CRIME OF FEMALE GENITAL MUTILATION

We cannot overlook the worldwide crime of female genital mutilation (FGM), a painful procedure designed to prevent females from enjoying their sexuality. Ritual FGM involves cutting out all or part of a young girl's clitoris. Some societies also remove all or part of her external genitalia. According to UNICEF, more than 200 million women and girls alive today bear the scars of FGM.

Through the ages, the practice was mislabeled as "female circumcision." Activists got this terminology changed half a century ago to stress that it's cruel mutilation. There's no way to compare it to male circumcision. I've wondered how an inhumane practice like FGM ever came into existence in the first place. It's an extreme but too common instance of the patriarchy's subjugation of women.

The United Nations condemned FGM, and most countries have declared it illegal, but it's still practiced in thirty nations in Africa, Asia, and the Middle East. Feminists and other humanitarians fight desperately to persuade societies to abolish this inhuman ritual.

14

NOW AND BLACK FEMINISM

IN THE WORDS of Black lesbian feminist Audre Lorde, "I am not free while any woman is unfree, even when her shackles are very different from my own." What did NOW do for Black women? Not enough, but more than some people realize. I do believe that Black women today enjoy more security, opportunity, and self-esteem than they did before 1966, and the feminist movement helped bring this about.

How did feminism change the lives of Black women? NOW ended blatant discrimination against *all* women in education, "Help Wanted" ads, factory promotions, union seniority lists, credit cards and mortgages, health care, the justice system, places of public accommodation. NOW opened up affirmative action for millions of workingwomen.

The link between sexism and racism was highlighted by Pauli Murray, who added to NOW's "Statement of Purpose" the declaration that "human rights for all are indivisible." Pauli's influential paper with Mary Eastwood, "Jane Crow and the Law," equated women's problems with racial problems. With Pauli's encouragement, most of our early lawsuits concerned low-paying jobs that especially impacted Black women.

Black women understood NOW's antidiscrimination goals even sooner than white women did. A 1972 poll found that 67 percent of Black women approved of our movement at a time when only 35 percent of white women approved. (Smeal and Steinem, 2020) The "Combahee River Collective Statement" points out this commitment: "Black, other Third World, and working women have been involved in the feminist movement from its start . . ." (Combahee River Collective 1977)

But where has NOW failed the needs of Black women? I wish NOW could have succeeded in fighting for universal child care, and pressing for child-care workers to be paid well and offered good benefits. If our child-care campaigns had prevailed, more Black mothers could have participated in the movement.

If NOW had promoted more Black women to its leadership from the very beginning, we might have worked harder and sooner to overcome racism, infant and maternal mortality, sterilization abuse, ghettoized housing, culturally biased school tests, inadequate health services, unemployment, illiteracy, lack of interpreters for service-seeking women who don't speak English, etc. As for Black *men*, we could have done more to combat their oppression by white institutions. Also, we might have paid more attention to Black men's treatment of Black women, which is a complicated subject.

In promoting feminist studies in schools, NOW was late to promote the study of African American foremothers such as Frances Ellen Watkins Harper, Josephine St. Pierre Ruffin, and Maria W. Stewart. Our feminist educators should have directed readers to *A Voice from the South: By a Black Woman of the South,* written in 1892 by Anna Julia Cooper, and to inspiring revelations about Black women by W. E. B. Du Bois in his *Darkwater: Voices from Within the Veil.* (Guy-Sheftall 2023)

I recall writing letters to officers of the Leadership Conference on Civil Rights, urging them to include us in their actions. The conference soon admitted us as a member in the spring of 1967.

NOW chapters frequently took independent local actions that aided women of color. A NOW chapter in California sponsored a welfare rights conference in 1971 in collaboration with the United Farm Workers. And dozens of chapters acted in support of the 1975 acquittal of Joan Little, an imprisoned Black woman who killed a prison guard when he tried to rape her. As part of this action, NOW sponsored a press conference in Washington, D.C., with Congresswomen Shirley Chisholm and

Yvonne Burke, demanding a federal study of the conditions of women in prison. (Turk 2023, pp. 119–120)

Betty Friedan once remarked to me, "When lesbians felt that NOW didn't address their needs, they responded by transforming NOW. There were times when they almost seemed to be taking us over. But when Black women became unhappy with NOW, they just left flat out. They moved to Black feminist organizations." Why the difference? The truth is, I don't know. But I do know that NOW lost some members because of one woman's decisions. That woman was Aileen Hernandez, whom we elected the second president of NOW, after Betty Friedan's term had ended.

AILEEN HERNANDEZ: GREAT LEADER, HARSH CRITIC

During her eighteen-month term as NOW president, from March 1970 to September 1971, Aileen Hernandez led us brilliantly and effectively. She captained our successful August 26 March. She advanced actions that sparked new laws in Congress. She activated new chapters across the country. She established NOW's National Task Force on Minority Women. She inspired us to work harder for racial justice. History should not forget her.

When Aileen's term as NOW president ended, she declined to run for a second term, explaining to colleagues that her professional life was "fully overcommitted." Those were her words. She wanted to devote more time to lucrative consulting work. And she couldn't afford the thousands of dollars she was spending on NOW travel and expenses. (We were not compensated for expenses in those days.) Some historians claim mistakenly that Aileen resigned from NOW's presidency abruptly, out of frustration with our "racial inequities." (Aileen's Wikipedia biography says she resigned from NOW's presidency.) But this is not accurate. There was no resignation and no condemnation. While declining to run again for the presidency, Aileen agreed immediately to chair NOW's National Advisory Committee. The post was mainly ceremonial but gave her a seat at board meetings. She encouraged NOW to

Aileen Hernandez
Photographer Jo Freeman, courtesy of the photographer

elect Wilma Heide as president, and me as chair of the board. All very friendly.

I have a copy of the inspiring speech Aileen delivered at our 1971 conference as our outgoing president. There were no accusations. Aileen approved our conference press release, which stated that NOW recognized the "double oppression of minority women by both racism and sexism." The press release declared, "We abhor all efforts to divide us as disadvantaged groups."

I remember having lunch with Aileen in earlier days, during a board meeting in 1969. I asked her, "How can we do better to have more Black women in our membership? She replied, "It won't be easy. Needless to say, very few have servants to help with the children." (A later study by NOW found that mothers who lacked child care found it almost impossible to serve actively in the organization.)

In her early days with NOW, and especially during her presidency, Aileen said frequently that NOW must keep Black women's special needs in mind. But she admitted that there were obstacles. Aileen organized a NOW survey that found only 10 percent of our members were women of color.

I have pleasant memories of Aileen's days in NOW in the early 1970s, after her presidency had ended. I recall no animosity, despite what some historians claim. I remember Aileen leading us as we joined hands and danced around the room singing Helen Reddy's "I Am Woman." I recall her initiating a round of applause for me in 1973 after I'd led the national board through a contentious weekend meeting. Her attitude seemed to change in 1974.

I don't know if her feelings were influenced by the contract that Sears, Roebuck signed with Aileen C. Hernandez Associates in 1974. By the year 1977, this contract earned her firm $46,000 yearly ($205,000 in today's money). (Turk 2023, p. 180). Our February 1974 national conference in Houston focused on NOW's major lawsuit against Sears, which involved more than one hundred chapters. Mary Jean Collins, who led the Sears campaign with Ann Ladky, told me that Aileen was observed during the conference talking into the ear of Ray Graham, Sears's director of equal employment opportunity, who attended the conference along with thirty-five Sears employees. At this conference, Mary Jean was running for the national presidency of NOW, in addition to chairing a workshop on the Sears action.

One historian states that Sears's original plans for their contract "had Hernandez helping Sears beat NOW," but Aileen then broadened the contract's wording to include dialogue with "minority and women's groups and organizations." (Turk 2023, p. 177)

At our board meeting held early in 1974 in San Francisco, and again at the Houston conference later that year, Aileen condemned NOW LDEF's widely heralded ad campaign, themed "WOMANPOWER. It's much too good to waste." She introduced a resolution, which was defeated, stipulating that every ad showing a white person must also include a Black person. In some ads—as I look back now—the inclusion of a Black person might have made good sense. But in other ads, doing so would have diluted our message on sex discrimination. One ad, featuring a baby, proclaimed "This normal healthy baby has a handicap. She was born female." Although race discrimination is abhorrent, addition of a Black baby would have complicated our ad campaign against sex discrimination

From 1974 to 1979, Aileen played an active role in the Majority Caucus faction within NOW, led by Eleanor Smeal. But their collaboration ended abruptly at NOW's national conference in Los Angeles in October 1979. President Smeal supported a slate of five officer candidates that failed to include a woman of color. Aileen, furious, resigned from NOW with a harsh statement. She soon persuaded the women's caucus of the Black American Political Association of California to pass a resolution urging Black members of NOW to send back their membership cards "and not to rejoin until NOW takes meaningful action to eliminate racism."

Aileen's outspoken criticism of NOW continued from then on, even when NOW adopted a sweeping affirmative action plan to guarantee board seats for women of color. Article VII, Section 3 of the NOW bylaws says that "any electoral district with a delegation that includes a person of color may have an additional member elected to the National Board from any state in the district." As a result of these bylaws, eight out of fifteen NOW board members in 2023 were women of color. Aileen never applauded this affirmative action plan, which was a rare move in nonprofit organizations at that time. In a 1996 interview about various topics, Aileen dismissed the NOW plan: "It's not very much better." In my opinion, that judgment was unfair.

On August 25, 1979, NOW held a Minority Women's Leadership Conference in D.C. The theme was "Racism and Sexism—A Shared Struggle for Equal Rights." Unfortunately, our October national conference, two months later, blighted this effort with that all-white slate for the executive committee. At the October conference, I recall that Patsy Fulcher, our western regional director, called NOW "a racist organization." She resigned soon after. Incidentally, Patsy had joined Aileen W. Hernandez Associates as a senior officer in 1977.

I mention in passing that Aileen was an out lesbian. I never heard her mention this, and never heard her speak out on NOW's lesbian issues.

NOW AND BLACK FEMINISM

From the beginning, Betty Friedan pointed out that Black women suffered from sexism as much as white women, though they also suffered from racism. NOW has accomplished "a lot, but not enough" to help Black feminists. NOW strongly supported Black women who ran for office, beginning in 1972 with Betty Friedan's endorsement of Shirley Chisholm for president. Betty and other members of NOW quoted widely this advice from Shirley: "If they don't give you a seat at the table, bring a folding chair." (Suk 2020, p. 113) Carol Moseley Braun of Illinois, the first Black woman elected to the Senate, thanked NOW effusively for its all-out, door-to-door work, which helped her win her election.

NOW has worked collaboratively with the National Welfare Rights Organization (NWRO), the National Domestic Workers Alliance, and other organizations that promote laws helping low-income women, predominantly women of color. NOW made low-income women a focus of its Mother's Day actions in 1973. It designated that entire year as NOW's "action year against poverty." It attacked Richard Nixon's administration for "not being in the interest of minorities." It demanded a higher minimum wage, public financing for day-care centers, and "a national welfare program under which no woman with pre-school or school-age children will be forced to work." (Shanahan 1973)

I recall NOW's sixth annual conference, held in Washington, D.C., in February 1973, when we declared the action year against poverty. Wilma Heide was reelected president. I concluded my term as national chair, moving into a less time-consuming position as chair of the National Advisory Committee. Judy Lightfoot succeeded me as chair. NOW entered a year of bitter internal battles. These hampered NOW's antipoverty work, even though the national conference had directed all of the organization's four hundred chapters to establish committees on poverty.

NOW didn't always agree completely with the National Welfare Rights Organization. In 1970, the NWRO executive director met with the NOW board and revealed that the organization's main goal was to "put men back at the head of the Black family." He said the NWRO was not concerned with economic advancement for Black women. NOW objected. But on occasions when its goals coincided with those of NWRO, NOW's Task Force on Women in Poverty supported them.

Early in 1972, NOW's Task Force on Women in Poverty joined with the NWRO in protesting that poor women were being exploited in federal manpower (*sic*) programs. NOW's press release said women were "being used as cheap labor in federal agencies and are receiving little or no real training."

In 2020, charismatic Black feminist Christian Nunes was elected NOW's president after president Toni Van Pelt was ousted, having been accused of "racial insensitivity." (Toni resigned before her term ended, blaming illness.) Christian has led NOW effectively, with a strong focus on "intersectionality," which addresses the relationship between all forms of discrimination, including gender, race, age, class, socioeconomic status, physical or mental ability, sexual identity, religion, or ethnicity. Christian won reelection easily in 2021.

NOW has often worked closely with Dorothy Height, who served as president of the National Council of Negro Women for forty years. We also collaborated with the National Black Feminist Organization (NBFO), which was founded in 1973 by four hundred women led by Michele Wallace, Faith Ringgold, Doris Wright, Flo Kennedy, and Margaret Sloan-Hunter. When they were getting started, they worked out of the office of NOW's New York City chapter. Many women were members of both NBFO and NOW. I followed the pronouncements of NBFO eagerly.

Like many organizations of the time, NBFO suffered from internal disagreements. Their Boston chapter broke away in 1974 to form the Combahee River Collective, whose widely circulated Statement in 1977 identified its members as Black lesbian socialists. The rebels cited "serious disagreements with NBFO's bourgeois-feminist stance and their lack of a clear political focus." (Combahee River Collective 1977)

NOW proclaimed allegiance to NBFO's call for reproductive justice, moving beyond reproductive rights. In addition to insisting that
women must be able to choose whether or not to have children, and to
raise children in a healthy and safe community, NBFO says women of
color must also have access to family planning, sex education, and
assisted reproductive technologies (ART), which are too often
denied because of poverty or class oppression. (Morgan 2022) Did
NOW work hard enough to help Black feminists meet those objec-
tives? Probably not.

Today we're looking at a new statistic: More than one-third of U.S.
Black families now live in suburbs. Activists realize that the interests of
many Black women now include middle-class issues, such as better
schools, more housing, less crime.

15

LESBIANS AND NOW'S EVOLUTION

WHEN OUR MOVEMENT WAS BORN, most founders (including me) believed that lesbianism was a separate issue from feminism. Although we opposed discrimination against gay people, we didn't want the issue of homosexuality to distract from our mission of combatting sex discrimination. Even Pauli Murray, a closeted lesbian and perhaps a suppressed transsexual, held this view.

The word *evolved* would correctly describe how our perceptions— and then our behaviors—turned around within five years after NOW was born. At our national conference in September 1971, the same conference that elected Wilma Heide president and me national chair, our members voted almost unanimously that lesbianism is indeed a feminist issue. We understood at last that lesbian issues are intermingled with a woman's role in the world. Besides, our opponents call us lesbians anyway.

Despite the progress we made in later years, some feminists still refer to NOW as "anti-lesbian." Much of that misapprehension can be blamed on the misplaced language of our first president, Betty Friedan. The memory of Betty's early vitriol still lingers in the unforgiving air of many gender studies courses and writings.

Betty first referred to "the lavender menace" at a 1970 NOW board meeting in New Orleans. I was there. Betty claimed that lesbian issues would detract from our campaigns in employment, education, and other feminist priorities. And she warned that the visibility of lesbian activists would discourage housewives from joining. Also, she believed that some lesbians were actively "recruiting" other members—a euphemism for seduction—by saying, "You can't be a feminist if you love men." This issue swirled through our early meetings as we debated whether lesbianism should be part of our feminist agenda. Rita Mae Brown, editor of the New York chapter newsletter and later famous for writing the lesbian-oriented novel *Rubyfruit Jungle,* aggravated these rumors by joking that her friends had assigned lesbians to seduce Betty and me and other leaders. Just a joke.

In January 1970, Rita Mae published her own five-page addition to the chapter newsletter. She resigned from NOW with an attack on our "racist and sexist" leadership. Two other women signed the document. Rita Mae charged that the slightest mention of lesbianism gave our leaders "a heart attack." She deplored other behaviors, including that "the nat'l President is not the only NOW woman who employs a black maid and sends her children to expensive private schools." Rita Mae joined Redstockings but resigned soon after. She accused them, too, of antilesbianism.

In February 1970, as I reported previously, Betty Friedan persuaded our national executive committee to dismiss executive director Dolores Alexander. Betty called Dolores "disobedient and disrespectful." To force our unwilling acquiescence, Betty blackmailed us by threatening to call a press conference about "the lavender menace" if we didn't fire Dolores. Apart from that threat, Betty's phone call to the executive committee never mentioned lesbian issues. Her only complaint was Dolores's insubordination. Betty did not say that Dolores herself was a lesbian (she was not at that time).

I've often spoken out against the widespread interpretation by respected historian Flora Davis, inaccurately linking together Rita Mae's resignation and Dolores's firing as NOW's "first lesbian purge." (Davis 1991, pp. 263–264) Wrong. There never were *any* lesbian purges in NOW. Most lesbians remained as members, earnestly debating policy with other members. Throughout 1970 and 1971, NOW chapters held heated arguments on whether or not lesbianism was a feminist issue. Public relations executive Toni Carabillo of our Los Angeles chapter sent out intelligent, well-reasoned position papers. These gradually helped to persuade us.

In January 1971, lesbianism was the subtext of our New York chapter's annual election. Should we reelect our popular president, Ivy Bottini, who was urging NOW to support lesbian issues? Ivy was one of numerous feminist mothers who had divorced their husbands and come out as lesbians after joining NOW. Mary Jean Collins recalls Ivy first appearing "in a little dress, with a pompadour hairdo." Early in the 1970s, Ivy transformed herself with butch clothing and a mannish haircut. Undoubtedly, supporters of both candidates were making a statement with their January vote. We loved Ivy. But because of the lesbian subtext to that 1971 election, a majority of chapter members voted for Jacqui Ceballos to replace Ivy as president. Flora Davis referred to this election as NOW's "second lesbian purge." Wrong again. Nobody, not even Ivy, felt pressured to resign from NOW. Ivy and others remained in NOW to continue arguing their cause.

On May 1, 1970, Rita Mae Brown organized a widely publicized stunt during the second Congress to Unite Women in New York City, an event convened by NOW with other feminist organizations. The lights suddenly went out. When light reappeared, it shone on a chorus of women wearing LAVENDER MENACE T-shirts. They recited in unison, "We are your worst nightmare, your best fantasy." We all laughed— some of us uncomfortably.

Marlene Sanders, a CBS-TV journalist and a NOW member, told me later that someone stole the film reel for her planned telecast about the Congress, which would have covered feminism favorably. Rita Mae bragged later of stealing Marlene's reel and dumping it into the Hudson River.

At our 1971 national conference the following year, there was only one dissent against hundreds of "yes" votes when NOW resolved that lesbianism is a feminist issue and NOW must fight actively for lesbian rights. This vote was historic. Mary Jean Collins, a prominent lesbian activist, says our decision was "earlier than any other organization I'm aware of." (Mary Jean had originally opposed NOW's taking a stand on lesbianism, but she later changed her mind.)

Our lengthy resolution acknowledged that "lesbians were never excluded from NOW, but we have been evasive or apologetic about their presence." It resolved "that a woman's right to her own person includes the right to define and express her own sexuality and to choose her own lifestyle" and further resolved "that NOW acknowledge the oppression of lesbians as a legitimate concern of feminism."

During the next few years following this vote, lesbian women flooded into NOW. Some had a proudly butch appearance. Many were elected to boards and committees. Our national conferences added a dance on Saturday night. Since there were hardly any men among the women, planners intended the Saturday dance "to make a statement." Was our recruitment of housewives impeded by a roomful of women closely embraced in dance? I believe it was. But on the other hand, NOW did benefit from the influx of new lesbian members, who worked tirelessly for *all* feminist causes, including abortion rights. Straight members greatly appreciate their involvement.

Eventually, housewives became members again. As America's largest feminist organization, NOW enjoyed its greatest influx of both straight and lesbian women during the presidency of Eleanor Smeal, who in 1977 became our first homemaker president.

KATE MILLETT ATTACKS SEXUAL POLITICS

Kate Millett was a leading force in educating the world on woman's sexual oppression. She enlivened NOW campaigns from 1966 on. During NOW's Park Avenue demonstration against Colgate-Palmolive, Kate provided the toilet (originally displayed as a sculpture) into which protesters threw the company's products. In Kate's later years, she also joined New York Radical Women, Radical Lesbians, and Downtown Radical Women while maintaining her links to NOW.

I recall vividly the 1968 New York NOW chapter meeting when Kate delivered her survey, *Token Learning: A Study of Women's Higher Education in America*. With acid sarcasm, Kate recited sexist excerpts from brochures of the country's foremost women's colleges. She charged that the woman's college "has violated its public trust. . . . It now spends

206

Kate Millett picketing for abortion rights, February 1968
Photograph courtesy of Muriel Fox

its time, its money and its academic energies in preparing women for marriage and homemaking, marginal or menial employment, merely token representation in the professions, and only occasional academic education. If not in the home, nowadays a woman must be very near it: nursing the sick, dispensing charity, caring for children or performing a wifely obedience function in the tedious and unrewarding labor of a secretary." (Millett 1968, p. 3)

The front cover of Kate's report featured a half-eaten apple. She described it as "the apple of knowledge which Eve tasted of and thereby freed herself from the dubious 'paradise' of being Adam's Rib: for it was Eve who nibbled first at knowledge." (Millett 1968, p. 57)

NOW members were thrilled when Kate's book *Sexual Politics,* derived from her doctoral thesis, became an overnight bestseller. Her book blamed the patriarchy for spreading a false belief in men's superiority to women. She called for a sex-role revolution, with a radical revision of the traditional family. Kate enjoyed instant fame in the media. *Time* magazine featured Kate on its cover for August 31, 1970.

Then it suddenly fell apart. That same *Time* magazine, on December 8 of the same year, attacked Kate for being bisexual. It was brutal. *Time* said Kate's bisexuality disqualified her as a feminist spokesperson. Two days later, thirty feminist leaders, led by Ivy Bottini and Barbara Love, staged a press conference, announcing "solidarity with the struggle of homosexuals to attain their liberation in a sexist society." Gloria Steinem and Bella Abzug issued statements in support of Kate. So did Aileen Hernandez, then our national president, and Wilma Heide, national chair. Betty Friedan declined to do so. (Two decades later, at our Veteran Feminists of America dinner honoring Kate, Betty extended a public apology to Kate for her behavior.)

Kate later wrote several other books about feminism, and about her years of struggle with mental illness and confinements in mental hospitals. In 2005, she spoke out at the United Nations against the use of psychiatric torture, during compilation of the UN's *Convention on the Rights of Persons with Disabilities.*

Kate married Japanese sculptor Fumio Yoshimura to help him obtain an American green card. She said she and her husband were "friends and lovers." He accepted her relationships with women. After twenty years, they divorced. Kate later married photographer Sophie Keir, who remained her devoted partner for thirty-nine years.

BARBARA LOVE FIGHTS FOR FEMINISM

Barbara Love played two valuable roles in the advancement of feminism—as a powerful champion for lesbian rights and as the producer of trailblazing events and publications. I first encountered Barbara as a fashionably dressed executive of the CBS network. I agreed to serve on the board of a new directory she was publishing, titled *Foremost Women in Communications*. In 1970, after the book's debut, Barbara phoned me about "something important": She said she was a founding member of Daughters of Bilitis, the pioneering organization of American lesbians. I advised Barbara not to make public statements on the subject. In those early days, it could hamper her career. Barbara disregarded my advice, left CBS, and began to speak widely on lesbian issues.

With her then partner Sydney Abbott, Barbara published *Sappho Was a Right-On Woman: A Liberated View of Lesbianism*. In welcoming this book, the *Los Angeles Times* pointed out that lesbian women were "shadowed by the constant fear of being fired from jobs, spurned by parents, doomed to a life of almost total isolation." (Green 2022)

Barbara and Sydney said their ambition was to avoid discrimination and just be "ordinary." On the other hand, their book claimed that lesbians were *extraordinary* in pursuing a promiscuous sexual lifestyle, in contrast to the less interesting lifestyle of heterosexuals.

Barbara crusaded for lesbian causes through NOW, Daughters of Bilitis, and Parents and Friends of Lesbians and Gays (PFLAG). She cofounded Identity House, a walk-in counseling center for gay people. She joined Rita Mae Brown and others in launching the first lesbian consciousness-raising group.

In the early 1980s, Barbara told us about her plan to create a book with biographies of active feminists. I'd nurtured a similar idea, a directory to be titled *What I Did in the Revolution*. Barbara committed her personal funds and years of hard work to make her project come true.

Barbara Love
Photograph courtesy of Eleanor Pam

It could make a major contribution! Several times Barbara wanted to quit; the endeavor was overwhelming. In the book that finally emerged, she gives me credit for nagging her to continue plowing ahead. We succeeded in recruiting members of Veteran Feminists of America to help round up stories of feminists from all sectors of the movement. I proofread all final submissions.

Barbara was conscientious about checking back with all biographees for their fact-checking approval. It was a monumental ten-year achievement. She contracted with the University of Illinois Press to publish *Feminists Who Changed America 1963–1975* in 2006. The book lists the feats of 2,200 women and men. Each was a leader who made a difference in the feminist revolution. I enlisted the distinguished historian Nancy F. Cott to write a foreword. Nancy proclaimed, "The biographies herein provide a precious resource for the future. Read them for a hedge against forgetting, a vital collective portrait, and a deep well of inspiration." (Love 2006, p. ix)

Barbara's "FWCA," as we refer to it, is accessible on Kindle and through VFA's website. It was my primary source of information for this book. (My second resource was VFA's trove of oral histories in its Pioneer Histories Project.)

In October 2014, at a time when VFA was struggling financially, Barbara put us back on our feet by organizing a well-attended fundraising luncheon at the Harvard Club in New York City. I was the honoree, and friends in the business and professional world made generous contributions. Barbara produced a lively panel of feminists, including Gloria Steinem, Rosie O'Donnell, Eve Ensler, Marlo Thomas, and Carol Jenkins.

Barbara and Sydney Abbott broke up as a couple. Barbara later married educator Donna Smith. Numerous lesbian couples have activated our movement: Toni Carabillo and Judith Meuli were especially influential, as were Del Martin and Phyllis Lyon. In 1968, NOW accepted the ten-dollar "Husband and Wife" combined membership application of Del and Phyllis. (Individual memberships cost $7.50.) Responding to feminist opposition against special benefits for marriage, we omitted the "Husband and Wife" category after the first year.

A LESBIAN CHAPTER?

In December 1972, in my capacity as chair of NOW and supervisor of new chapters, I faced an unexpected question: A group in New Jersey wished to form a chapter with only lesbian women. I told the organizers that this would be discriminatory, and they must include members of all sexual preferences. They agreed to comply.

THE OTHER INITIALS IN LGBTQ

Today some feminists call NOW's hard-fought 1971 stance on lesbianism "old-fashioned." Civilization has progressed to further stages, building on questions raised by feminists about what it means to be female or male. Some emphasize the letter *B* in the LGBTQ spectrum. They circulated a humorous saying, "Homosexuals are people who don't have the courage to face their bisexuality." Other feminists embrace the transgender movement. Others have moved along the gender spectrum to non-binary identity, with continuous fluidity between male and female. They refuse to identify with one sex or the other. Instead of referring to women, they refer to "people with a uterus." More and more progressives choose to use the pronoun *they* instead of masculine or feminine pronouns.

Some observers are asking whether Joan of Arc, Pauli Murray, and Louisa May Alcott were trans men. Author Katha Pollitt refutes the question: "Longing for masculine freedoms and advantages does not constitute Male Identity Envy." On the other side of the question, were certain nonconforming men throughout history basically trans women? Discussions will continue, as well as arguments.

Today some prominent feminists battle bitterly with trans leaders over regulations in women's sports and women's colleges. The acronym for their group is TERFs, transgender-exclusionary radical feminists. Tennis icon Martina Navratilova, a longtime lesbian activist, attacks the participation of trans women in women's sports. She complains about their birth-given "testosterone advantage." It's complicated.

Some radical feminists have warred against trans women since as far back as 1973. When prominent activist Robin Morgan spoke at the West Coast Lesbian Conference, she attacked the conference's organizer, Beth Elliott, a transgender woman. She insisted on referring to Beth not as a woman but as a "transsexual male," using male pronouns to describe her. She called for a vote on whether to eject Beth from the meeting. Two-thirds of the audience voted for Beth to remain. The conflict continues.

I conclude this chapter with comments made by Betty Friedan in November 1975 at the Houston conference, when she apologized for her "lavender menace" remarks: "I am considered to be violently opposed to the lesbian movement and in fact I have been. This issue has been used to divide us and disrupt us and has been seized on by our enemies to try and turn back the whole women's movement. . . . We've all made mistakes in our view of the issue, but we all have learned. . . . It's the duty of the women's movement to help [lesbians] win their civil rights." (Shteir 2023, pp. 209–210)

16

WOMEN, BUSINESS, AND POWER

WE PROVED THAT FEMINIST PROTESTS can make a difference. Our early attacks on EEOC decisions finally forced the agency to pay attention to sex discrimination. The EEOC became an active supporter of women's rights. Once activated, they put heavy pressure on businesses to set goals and timetables for hiring and promoting higher percentages of women. And the government penalized companies that exhibited "patterns and practices" of sex discrimination. One by one, nearly all large American companies introduced affirmative action programs for women. NOW focused its pressure on especially backward corporations. In 1973, NOW chapters coordinated in sending "bills" totaling four billion dollars to AT&T for back pay owed.

A TALE OF TWO COMPANIES, AT&T AND SEARS, ROEBUCK

The turnaround of AT&T set an example. Other large companies watched closely, and followed suit. Under heavy pressure from the EEOC, AT&T settled two NOW lawsuits with huge consent decrees of $30 million in 1973 and $45 million in 1974, covering back pay and future wage adjustments for women employees. AT&T agreed to overhaul its entire system of hiring, salaries, and promotions. They even promised to hire more *men* as telephone operators and clerks in order to reduce age-old sex stereotyping. The business world's response to this settlement "revolutionized corporate affirmative action." (Love 2006, p. 211)

As president of NOW LDEF, I set out to befriend AT&T executives. Through mutual acquaintances I met with William Sharwell, their fair-minded executive vice president, and invited him to join our board of directors. Bill served us as a committed feminist board member for nearly two decades.

In 1979, Bill escorted me to the AT&T executive dining room for lunch with senior officers. I made a special effort to create a rapport, and brazenly asked CEO Charlie Brown if he'd had the dining room painted blue to match his blue eyes. Brown agreed to accept an award for AT&T at NOW LDEF's first annual Equal Opportunity Awards Dinner in November 1979. In his acceptance speech, Brown told the world that our NOW consent decree had been "the best thing that ever happened to us" because it spurred the company to make fuller use of talents and energies of women employees.

Since that time, AT&T has maintained a mostly friendly collaboration with the feminist movement. Today, despite the government's 1984 breakup of the Bell System and other problems, AT&T is the world's largest telecommunications company, with more than $170 billion in annual sales. Let's compare them to Sears, Roebuck.

In contrast, Sears responded to a NOW lawsuit with a strenuous counterattack. Eventually, Sears won their legal battle. The government never required Sears to change its ways. In 2018, Sears, once the world's largest retailer, filed for Chapter 11 bankruptcy. Financial analysts blamed "changing consumer behavior." Would Sears have benefited from AT&T-type concessions, leading to greater input from innovative women?

In our Sears lawsuit, NOW charts proved widespread discrimination. Entire job categories, those offering the highest salaries, had no women employees at all. High-commission products, such as appliances and auto equipment, were sold only by men. Women sold lower-price products, such as socks and toys. Sears hired male college graduates as assistant buyers; female graduates became "buyers' assistants."

The EEOC issued a report fully supporting our lawsuit, charging Sears with extensive sex discrimination. However, Sears ultimately succeeded in forcing the agency to table its report. Sears's main weapon was accusing the EEOC of collusion with NOW. They linked their complaint to the fact that EEOC officer David Copus was living with NOW leader Whitney Adams.

Brilliantly, Sears hired attorney Charles Morgan of Birmingham, Alabama, to captain its response to our lawsuit. Morgan had built a reputation as a champion of Black civil rights. He retained Barnard College professor Rosalind Rosenberg as an expert witness. (She wrote the book about Pauli Murray that I mentioned previously.) In her testimony, Dr. Rosenberg claimed that women actually preferred the lower-paying jobs, for family reasons. Columbia professor Alice Kessler-Harris testified with an opposing opinion, agreeing with NOW that women were flagrantly victimized by Sears' discrimination.

Sears also launched a longtime "urban affairs consultancy" with Aileen C. Hernandez Associates. Aileen had been the second president of NOW and was admired in the civil rights world.

Mary Jean Collins, who cochaired NOW's Sears campaign, was a feminist hero whom history should not forget. In 1970, she was elected president of our Chicago chapter. That same year, she also became NOW's Midwest regional director. She led our 1970 Women's Strike for Equality in the area, and helped recruit fifteen thousand marchers to downtown Chicago. She directed our ERA campaign in Illinois and led our actions against discrimination in higher education. Mary Jean also led a national action and boycott against General Mills.

In 1982, NOW elected Mary Jean our national action vice president. In 1985, she left NOW to fight for abortion rights as deputy director of Catholics for a Free Choice. She still serves our movement as historian of Veteran Feminists of America. She cochairs VFA's Pioneer Histories Project, which provides valuable information about second-wave feminism.

With Ann Ladky, Mary Jean led our all-out nationwide action against Sears, Roebuck, using data supplied to NOW chapters by local

Mary Jean Collins
Photograph courtesy of the National
Organization for Women

Sears employees. They mobilized one hundred NOW chapters to picket and leaflet Sears stores.

From 1970 to 1974, Mary Jean's husband, Jim, operated NOW's national office in Chicago. Jim received a modest salary to handle our printing, finances, and membership services, and Mary Jean worked in the office without pay. She earned our gratitude with tireless, unsalaried labors day and night. In those days, as I recall, she looked red-eyed and exhausted. Jim's contract in 1973 paid him $50,500. They mailed out 55,000 documents and printed over a million impressions. (Turk 2023, p. 188)

Jim and Mary Jean used the last name Collins-Robson after their marriage in 1968. Hyphenated names were a new idea at the time. But in 1975, when they divorced, they reverted to Jim Robson and Mary Jean Collins. That year, she came out as a lesbian.

At NOW's February 1974 national conference in Houston, the opposing candidates to succeed Wilma Heide as president were Mary Jean Collins and Karen DeCrow. We expected Mary Jean to win easily, thanks to her high-profile leadership of the Sears action.

In her campaign for NOW presidency, Mary Jean focused on Sears. Her campaign's T-shirts, referring to Sears owing women $100 million in back pay for sex discrimination, carried the slogan SEARS, $100 MILLION AND NOTHING LESS.

I was told that Sears sent thirty-four women employees to sign up for NOW membership at our Houston conference. These women kept disrupting our Sears Workshop at the conference, conducted by Mary Jean and Ann Ladky. Our new members from Sears also voted in the presidential election—against Mary Jean, I presume.

That 1974 election introduced sophisticated political maneuvers we'd never seen in NOW before. In addition to Karen and Mary Jean, two other candidates were recruited into the race at the last minute. This deprived Mary Jean of her anticipated majority, and revotes became necessary. For the first time in a NOW election, Karen attacked the character of her opponent. She claimed that Mary Jean and Jim were profiteering unscrupulously from their NOW contract. Mary Jean says members asked her, "Is it true that you made a million dollars out of NOW last year?" (Turk 2023, p. 198)

On Candidates Night, Karen DeCrow declared, "I'm fed up with all this corruption." This shocked all of us on the national board. It implicated not only Mary Jean but also outgoing president Wilma Heide. Wilma remained silent in the contest to choose her successor.

Aileen Hernandez was chosen to chair Candidates Night. All candidates attacked Mary Jean and "the Chicago Machine." After a night of revotes in four ballots, with "lots of marijuana in the air," Karen DeCrow won the presidency by forty votes.

The next NOW presidential election, held in Philadelphia in 1975, again pitted Mary Jean against Karen. Sears was again an issue. Once more, Karen defeated Mary Jean. The newly elected NOW board voted, by a narrow margin, to discontinue the Sears fight. Members of a new NOW faction, the Majority Caucus, called Mary Jean and Ann Ladky "socialists" for pursuing the action. That ended NOW's last nationwide employment campaign.

A WIN IN THE COURTS

In the years before AT&T's consent decree of 1973, we sued one of its affiliated Bell System companies for using state protective laws to bar women from promotion to good-paying jobs. Our victory in this important lawsuit, *Weeks v. Southern Bell,* told companies they could no longer say "It's a man's job." NOW participation began with Marguerite Rawalt, who read in a newspaper that a Georgia woman named Lorena Bell had lost a lawsuit against Southern Bell Telephone Company. Lorena had sued for the right to be promoted to a switchman's job. She was rejected because a Georgia state law "protected" women from lifting more than thirty pounds. (How many women carry babies weighing more than that?) Marguerite referred this lawsuit to feminist attorney Sylvia Roberts of Baton Rouge, Louisiana.

Sylvia won Lorena's case for us on appeal. Sylvia was five feet tall and weighed only one hundred pounds. Her long dark hair fell in curls. During her final speech to the jury, Sylvia walked back and forth, carrying the heavy equipment used by switchmen. Her victory on March 4, 1969, won Lorena $31,000 in back pay and the right to be a switchman. For women everywhere, Sylvia's victory established that employers cannot bar a woman from a position "unless all or substantially all women could be proved to be unable to do the job."

Southern Bell dragged their heels in enforcing the lawsuit verdict. To force compliance, NOW chapters across the country demonstrated against the company. Lorena finally received her award and her job.

Sylvia Roberts is another feminist hero whom history should not forget. We elected her general counsel of NOW, and later president of NOW LDEF. Another lawsuit headed by Sylvia represented Dr. Sharon Johnson, who'd applied for tenure at the University of Pittsburgh. I remember Sylvia in tears, telling us we'd lost Sharon's lawsuit and she was denied tenure. But Sylvia did establish an important precedent: She obtained an injunction stating that a woman could not be fired if

Sylvia Roberts (left) at NOW LDEF with Mary Jean
Tully (third from left) and others not identified.
Photo Credit: Sylvia Roberts papers (NA-282),
Newcomb Archives and Nadine Robert Vorhoff
Collection, Newcomb Institute of Tulane University

she failed to obtain tenure for reasons not related to her qualifications.
That was a time when very few women received tenure, just because
they were women.

Sylvia then represented a woman named Selina Martin in challenging a Louisiana law that referred to husbands as (are you ready for this?)
"head and master." Head and master laws in several states gave the husband power to make all decisions about property shared with his wife,
no matter whose name was on the deed. In 1980, Louisiana became the
final state to repeal its head and master law.

In later years, Sylvia turned her attention to cases involving domestic violence. She campaigned to prevent teen dating violence. And she
assisted people who'd been wrongly committed to mental hospitals.

In 1980, Sylvia Roberts launched NOW LDEF's National Judicial Education Program to Promote Equality for Women and Men in the Courts. She worked with our legal director, Phyllis Segal, and advisor Marilyn Hall Patel, who later pursued a long, distinguished career as a United States district judge. They enlisted the newly formed National Association of Women Judges as our cosponsor in forming NJEP.

We'd envisioned this program as early as 1970, but it took ten years to make NJEP a reality. At the beginning, experts said we could never persuade judges to self-scrutinize their own gender biases. But NJEP eventually won broad acceptance because its programs were scrupulously designed and fair-minded.

The project presented its first course for judges in 1981. In 1986, NJEP and the National Association of Women Judges published a how-to manual detailing how to create state supreme court task forces on gender bias in the courts. In 1998, it developed a model judicial education curriculum titled "When Bias Compounds: Insuring Equal Justice for Women of Color in the Courts." In 2005, it produced a one-thousand-page resource manual for the U.S. Air Force to help them prevent and treat sexual assault. Lynn Schafran has led NJEP brilliantly since 1981. It's been supported financially by the administrations of all Democratic and Republican presidents, including Donald Trump.

THE OLD GIRL NETWORK ARRIVES

Through the centuries, professional women had to compete with the old boy network. Men helped one another by sharing information, ideas, and—best of all—personal contacts. A feminist activist, Elinor Guggenheimer, finally created that same reality for women by founding a trailblazing organization she named the Women's Forum. It converted the noun *network* into a verb.

Elly was a wealthy New York philanthropist with visionary ideas. Among her creations were the Child Care Action Campaign (I helped Elly launch CCAC and served on its first board), the Council for Senior Centers and Services, and the New York Women's Agenda. It was in Elly's

Park Avenue apartment that Betty Friedan convened the predecessor to the National Women's Political Caucus.

In the spring of 1974, Elly invited two other friends and me to lunch. The Women's Forum later honored us as the "2 Elinors and 2 Muriels" who cofounded the organization. The two other founders were Muriel "Mickie" Siebert, the first woman to gain a seat on the New York Stock Exchange, and Eleanor Holmes Norton, then chair of New York's Human Rights Commission.

Elly told us of attending a NOW chapter meeting where feminists interviewed candidates for New York City mayor. The interviewers were unfamiliar with city government, and focused their questions on lesbian issues rather than civic policies. She asked us to help organize an "admittedly elitist" network of professional women that would be more influential. Until that time, she lamented, "there was no way for powerful and accomplished women to speak out as a group or to communicate with each other." (Women's Forum 2009, p. 10) The four of us assembled a list of New York women preeminent in business, government, education, and the arts.

The Women's Forum held its first luncheon meeting at the until recently male-only Harvard Club. Each member stood up and introduced herself. *Sesame Street* creator Joan Ganz Cooney established a key mission for our new organization. Joan declared, "It's a shame that Mayor Beame hasn't reappointed Eleanor Holmes Norton yet to continue heading the Human Rights Commission. Let's all go back and write him a letter about this on our professional letterheads." Again and again in subsequent years, Women's Forum members would utilize their prestige to advance other women.

I used to keep the Women's Forum membership directory in my desk drawer. Nearly every day, I referred to the list for help when I needed information or contacts. An article about the Women's Forum in *The New York Times* quoted me: "Because there are so few of us at a certain level, we really help each other—it's like a sisterhood."

Ms. magazine publisher Betty Harris became the first president of the Women's Forum, and I was elected the second. To mold us into a supportive "sisterhood" rather than a hive of self-serving "queen bees," I organized a series of rap sessions in members' apartments. For the first session, we sat on the floor of my living room and talked about our mothers. Bess Myerson confided that her mother "never thought I was good enough" and Betty Cott's mother had called her unattractive.

A later session on our daughters was tearful. With one exception, every woman in the room said she did not get along with her daughter. One member, a judge, sighed and said, "I'm close to my son, but my daughter hates me." Mary Nichols, a city official several years older than the rest of us, offered consolation: "Don't worry. They'll be friendlier when they get older. Especially when they have daughters of their own." When I told my daughter, Lisa, about that session, she offered this explanation: "You're competitive women. You raised your daughters to compete with you." At that time, Lisa and I struggled through an up-and-down relationship, but today we're close buddies. Mary Nichols was right.

A rap session I'd planned about men surprised me. I didn't want Women's Forum members to feel left out if they had no man in their life, so I announced the program title as "Men and Power." It turned out that nobody was interested in talking about men. They preferred to discuss their feelings about power. A week before this meeting, I'd shared a taxi with Joan Ganz Cooney. Joan confided, "I admit that I love power. Women shouldn't be ashamed of this." Joan's confession was a revelation to me at the time. In the subsequent Women's Forum rap session, other women experienced a hunger for power that had previously been identified with men and testosterone.

Many Women's Forum members became my personal friends. Donna Shalala, who served as President Clinton's secretary of Health and Human Services, told us a joke. She was told she'd changed the old game of little girls playing doctor with little boys. Instead of always playing the nurse, girls now could say, "You be the doctor, and I'll be the secretary of Health and Human Services."

Elinor Guggenheimer engineered the creation of allied Women's Forum groups throughout the United States. In 1982, she founded the International Women's Forum, with headquarters in D.C. We've since held meetings across the globe for chapters with 3,000 influential members in twenty-four countries on five continents.

A favorite memory for many of us was our first national Women's Forum meeting, held in Phoenix. The New York Women's Forum performed a humorous musical written by Elly. Our high-kick dancing was hilariously out of step. In one skit, actress Polly Bergen, our only professional performer, sang to the tune of "Alice Blue Gown" a lyric that ended thus:

> I can steadily rake in the loot
> For I never, no never, look cute.
> In my little bow ties I'm just one of the guys,
> In my very appropriate suit.

Alas, our brainy Elly ended her days suffering from Alzheimer's disease. She died at the age of ninety-six.

Some of us were disappointed when the Women's Forum declined to take a stand on political issues. Mary Jean Tully and several others circulated open letters of resignation, blaming the Women's Forum for not getting involved with problems of women at lower rungs of the ladder. Mary Jean circulated the following statement, attributed to the New York State Commissioner of Education: "Equality is not when a female Einstein gets promoted to professor; equality is when a female schlemiel moves ahead as fast as a male schlemiel."

ARE WOMEN BOSSES DIFFERENT?

Today we see a variety of management styles among women; female bosses are becoming numerous and varied. But it's still a new phenomenon. Betty Friedan used to quip, "Young women say, 'I'm not a feminist, but I want to become CEO of IBM.'" That goal seemed unreachable when Betty joked about it. But today, IBM has had a woman CEO. So have General Motors, Xerox, Pepsi-Cola and other major corporations. In 2023, 15 percent of the CEOs in the Fortune 500 are women. (One day in the future, we'll look back on this percentage as outrageously unfair.) Our movement has brought women a long way since the time when the

Harvard Business Review canceled its study of women executives because "the barriers are so great that there is scarcely anything to study."

I recall a long-ago conversation with ABC News executive Nick Archer. Nick opined, "Women can't be bosses because they can't give orders." Capable women bosses have disproved Nick's statement. However, women may give orders in a different way. This was the contention of the Stanford Research Institute. The SRI presented a revealing research paper on female bosses at NOW LDEF's Convocation on New Leadership in the Public Interest, which I organized in 1981. The SRI maintained that women bosses are more collegial and encouraging than their male counterparts, and that we lead by eliciting cooperation, rather than submission. Successful female bosses have proved the truth of that thesis. The SRI referred to the collaborative technique of female-style bosses as "beta" leadership, and the previous style of bosses as "alpha"—as in alpha males who fight to lead packs of animals. Needless to say, there are exceptions. Some "Iron Lady" bosses have governed well through fear rather than collegiality.

NOW chapters protested frequently at annual meetings of corporations that promoted no women to their executive suites or boardrooms. Most companies have made progress in recent decades, but a glass ceiling mentality still dissuades many men at the top from choosing women for leadership positions. We don't look or speak or act like the male colleagues they're used to. Corporations may appoint one or two women to their board of directors, but seldom more.

When we're elected to corporate boards, are we mere tokens? I asked myself that question when I served on the boards of the Harleysville Mutual Insurance Company and the Rorer Group, the international pharmaceutical company. I influenced a few decisions, but not many. I did succeed in protecting the job of one female executive whom managers considered abrasive. But at Harleysville, I was unanimously outvoted when I suggested gender-neutral insurance rates.

Americans for Democratic Action gave me their Business Leader of the Year award in March 1979. In all honesty, they may have chosen me as a token. Perhaps they'd decided to recognize a woman executive that year.

MUST A FEMALE BE "FEMININE"?

We've succeeded in proving that women can be strong as well as smart. Definite progress from the days when the Merrill Lynch brokerage had a rule against allowing women customers to trade in commodities, saying that women are "too emotional." But now there's a reverse side to this bias. Not only must ambitious women prove they're sturdy enough to be bosses, but they also must conform to traditional concepts of feminine agreeableness. They're punished by "sex stereotyping."

In 1989, the U.S. Supreme Court quoted from an amicus brief of NOW LDEF in deciding the case of *Price Waterhouse v. Hopkins*. Ann Hopkins, who had outperformed many of her male coworkers in the financial firm, was twice denied promotion to a partnership because of stereotyping. Her boss said she needed to "walk more femininely, dress more femininely, wear makeup, have her hair styled and wear jewelry." The Supreme Court agreed with NOW that companies are violating Title VII of the Civil Rights Act if they base a female employee's career success on outmoded ideas of how a woman should look and behave.

This decision reinforced for us the value of filing amicus curiae (friend of the court) briefs in lawsuits. The Supreme Court used NOW LDEF language extensively in its decision.

The victory of Ann Hopkins has been especially helpful to LBTQ women, and to women in "appearance-conscious" jobs. Several women journalists on television have won discrimination rulings based on the Hopkins ruling. The unspoken, unfair requirement for women to be "courageous but charming, assertive but adorable" still exists, but employers can no longer use illegal stereotypes in personnel decisions.

The Hopkins case made me think twice about my own standards. I realized that I'd paid too much attention through the years to outmoded ideas about female appearance and personality.

In a landmark case in January 1981, Christine Craft sued KMBC-TV, Kansas City. They'd removed her as a news coanchor after a focus group opined that she was "too old, too unattractive and wouldn't defer to men." She was thirty-seven years old! A federal jury awarded her $500,000 in damages. (The Supreme Court ultimately overturned that verdict on a technicality. The single dissent came from the Court's only woman, Sandra Day O'Connor.)

MENTAL HEALTH? WRONG!

Betty Friedan led the way in a feminist attack against stereotyped teachings of psychotherapists. She zeroed in on Sigmund Freud's proclamation that women suffer from a "castration complex" if they seek equal partnership rather than subservience. In our lifetime, we've seen a 180-degree change in psychotherapy attitudes. Even Freudian analysts recognize today that women have a right to be forceful and ambitious. I'm sure that Dr. Freud, who once said "I am not a Freudian," would have revised his teachings if he'd lived long enough.

In the early days of NOW, we fought against the psychological tests that companies were using in hiring decisions. A 1970 study found that testers held a warped concept of the psychologically mature woman. They considered a woman to be well adjusted and fully mature if she was "more submissive, less independent, less adventurous, more easily influenced, less aggressive, less competitive." On the other hand, psychologists considered men *less* mature if they exhibited those same traits. (Dominus 2023, pp. 22–44) Some, but not all, of those psychological tests have been revised. More employers are hiring adventurous, risk-taking women and sensitive, considerate men. It's good business.

17

MINDS, WORDS, MEDIA

I'VE SOMETIMES BEEN INTRODUCED as "the Communicator of the Revolution." I'm grateful that widespread communications played a role in the rapid growth of our movement. But the media are fickle. Their enthusiasm waned after our first few years. Once we'd achieved societal change throughout the world, and millions of women had begun to realize a new self-image, the media considered us "yesterday's news." It became more difficult to attract media attention for important feminist issues, and for the work that still needs to be done. To arouse media interest, there had to be a fight between leaders. Or stunts by small groups such as Women's International Terrorist Conspiracy from Hell (WITCH). Or a "man bites dog" story about a woman somewhere who opposed the feminist movement. In the world of drama and fiction, plots continued to promote false stereotypes of "what is masculine or feminine."

We faced so much media criticism that feminism became the f-word. Even our supporters said publicly, "I'm not a feminist, but . . ." Betty Friedan complained. "The leaders of a number of major women's organizations told me that they could not . . . speak out against sex discrimination . . . for fear of being called 'feminist.'" (Friedan 1967)

Our opponents continued to claim that men find feminists unattractive. With varied success, we've counterattacked media celebrities who perpetuate the myth. We've boycotted adversaries like Rush

Limbaugh, who ridiculed us as "feminazis" and repeated such mantras as "Feminism was established so as to allow unattractive women access to the mainstream of society."

LADIES' HOME JOURNAL TURNS AROUND

Savvy women in the movement attacked our media problem head-on. First they targeted the women's magazines, which earned big profits from persuading women to buy lots and lots of household items and beauty products. Top editors of the magazines were all men. Feminists staged the famous *Ladies' Home Journal* sit-in on March 18, 1970. Over one hundred women took over the New York City office of the magazine's editor, John Mack Carter. Their ranks included New York Radical Feminists, Media Women, NOW, Redstockings, and a group of angry Barnard College students.

I did not participate. As a public relations executive, I'd be fired immediately if I assaulted the media. The magazine's senior editor, Lenore Hershey, was a friend of mine. I didn't forewarn her about the impending sit-in.

The protesters met at a nearby church and entered the building at 9:00 A.M., using a diagram drawn by a former employee. On the way to Carter's office, they talked to secretaries and clerks and explained their mission.

To everyone's amazement, Carter didn't leave the room during the entire eleven hours of the sit-in. He listened politely when protesters urged him to step down as editor in chief and hire an all-female editorial staff. They also insisted that the magazine should provide free on-site child care for employees, raise women's salaries to a minimum of $125 a week, hire nonwhites in proportion to the U.S. population, and stop running ads that degraded women.

Agitators came prepared with a twenty-page mock magazine titled *Women's Liberated Journal*. They flew a banner with that title from Carter's office window. The cover of their magazine featured a pregnant picketer with a sign saying UNPAID LABOR.

The women issued a press release accusing *Ladies' Home Journal* of presenting no alternatives to marriage, even though one out of three American women were single, divorced, or widowed.

Carter refused to resign. But he agreed to print more feminist columns every month, and to explore on-site child care for employees. He contracted with the protesters to produce an eight-page section titled "New Feminism" for the magazine's August issue. They were paid ten thousand dollars, which they donated to create the first women's center in New York City.

John Mack Carter became a good friend of our movement. When he later moved to *Good Housekeeping* magazine, he did as he had done at *Ladies' Home Journal,* assigning an increasing number of feminist articles.

Here's an interesting fact: Our two strongest supporters in the world of women's magazines were John Mack Carter and Sey Chassler, editor of *Redbook*. Both men were born twin brothers to twin sisters! John and Sey served diligently on committees for NOW LDEF's Equal Opportunity Dinners.

GLORIA, OUR CHIEF PHILOSOPHER AND PERSUADER

When people consider the feminist movement, the name that comes to mind most often is Gloria Steinem. That's a great advantage for us, because nearly everyone admires and trusts Gloria. She knows how to explain complex feminist issues, and she wins us millions of recruits with her wisdom and humor.

In quoting some of Gloria's persuasive aphorisms, where should we start? "A woman without a man is like a fish without a bicycle." "It took us forty years to prove that women can do what men do. Now we have to prove that men can do what women do." (That's my favorite.) When I moderated a Rollins College panel with Gloria and Congresswoman Pat Schroeder and asked them what was the most important achievement of our feminist movement, Gloria replied, "We proved to the world that we're not crazy."

Gloria Steinem and Muriel Fox, 2009
Photograph courtesy of Muriel Fox

Gloria had not yet crossed over to feminism when she covered NOW's Plaza demonstration on Lincoln's Birthday, 1969. Her "click" occurred soon after, while she was covering the Redstockings abortion action. Gloria had once had an abortion.

Gloria led the group of journalists who created *Ms.,* the first prominent magazine owned and controlled by feminists, in December 1971. She served as its editor for fifteen years. The articles in *Ms.* introduced consciousness-raising epiphanies, such as Jane O'Reilly's "click" in "The Housewife's Moment of Truth" and Judy Syfers's plea, "I Want a Wife." The many contributions of the Ms. Foundation included Take Our Daughters to Work Day.

I believe our movement is blessed with two especially good human beings. If I weren't antifundamentalism, I'd call them saints. Those two people are kind and considerate, always eager to help others, and primarily motivated by ideology rather than power. One is Heather Booth, whom you'll meet in the next chapter. The other is Gloria Steinem. Gloria gives readily of her time and devotion to hundreds of people and to many good causes. She once commented, "For sure, my funeral will be a fund-raiser." Gloria disagreed with me when I told *People* magazine, after Betty Friedan's death, "It takes hostile people to make revolutions." She insisted to me that benevolent, caring people can also make revolutions. Gloria proves that to be true.

Some people in our movement have portrayed Gloria as far from a saint. In May 1975, the New York radical feminist group Redstockings staged a press conference and issued a sixteen-page press release attacking Gloria as a CIA pawn. Gloria had worked briefly for the Independent Research Service, which sent liberal American college students to overseas youth festivals in 1959 and 1962. The CIA underwrote the program. Feminist historian Sheila Tobias has admitted, "We were a front for the CIA." (Cohen 1988, p. 110) Gloria says, in retrospect, that she made "a mistake" in being involved with the project, but that sending students to the Helsinki Youth Conference was "CIA's finest hour." (Cohen 1988, p. 371) Redstockings accused Gloria of providing the CIA with "political dossiers" on the conference organizers; but Gloria responded, in a six-page release, that the "dossiers" were biographies in an information pamphlet sent to libraries. After the Redstockings attack, prominent feminists rushed to Gloria's support. I'm confident that history will treat Gloria with reverence.

The attack on Gloria epitomized the destructive practice that tore our movement apart in the 1970s. We called it "trashing." Disparaging feminists waged public attacks against any sister who achieved too much prominence.

Also, radicals blamed reformers for not trying harder to overturn the entire patriarchal system. They called *Ms.* magazine "inauthentic." Ellen Willis accused *Ms.* of "promoting a mushy sisterhood that tells its readers to work within the system . . . rather than for economic radicalism and integration of feminism with the revolutionary left." (Franks 1975) Ellen joined Redstockings in charging that *Ms.* "takes upper-middle-class privileges and values for granted."

Ironically, while radicals were accusing Gloria of being a right-wing pawn, the FBI at the same time designated her a security risk. The Department of Justice had asked the FBI to run a security check on Gloria when it planned to hire her as a consultant on sex discrimination. J. Edgar Hoover's FBI replied that it would be inadvisable to hire Gloria because of her leftist associations. (Franks 1975) The DOJ never offered her a job.

As soon as Gloria proclaimed her feminism, the media embraced her overnight as our spokesperson. She was beautiful, witty, and gracious. Unlike Betty Friedan, she didn't hang up on reporters. Her smiling image appeared everywhere. Al Capp, on *The Dick Cavett Show,* called her "the Shirley Temple of the New Left."

Reporters didn't always get their stories right. For instance, after Gloria appeared by chance in the same photo as Henry Kissinger, columnists described her as "Kissinger's girlfriend." The two celebrities hardly knew each other.

I prefer feminist author Vivian Gornick's depiction of Gloria to Al Capp's: "She is to feminism what Yasir Arafat is to the Palestinians . . . the glamorous woman among us is the one who, more than any other, continues to hold the inner attention of depressed housewives, expectant schoolgirls, angry waitresses and restless academics." (Hole and Levine 1971, p. 273)

Deposed by Gloria's sudden fame, Betty responded angrily and destructively. As I reported earlier, *McCall's* magazine held a press conference to publicize Betty's article in their August 1972 issue, which called Gloria and Bella Abzug "female chauvinist boors." Gloria refrained from fighting back. However, her *followers* jumped at opportunities to support Gloria in opposition to Betty. *Ms.* magazine hardly ever carried a story about NOW in the 1970s. I have no doubt the reason was NOW's association with Betty. When I complained to Gloria about the inattention *Ms.* displayed concerning NOW, she rebutted by mentioning a couple of brief items in the magazine. But in truth, her followers refrained for over a decade from giving Betty's NOW the attention it deserved.

Even if *Ms.* did not extol NOW as an organization, it was an invaluable influence in awakening American women to our feminist ideals. And that's still true today!

Gloria and Betty did work together in feminist activities. I remember one march in Detroit. It was raining. I had no trouble persuading Gloria to share her umbrella with Betty, I don't recall if they talked to each other.

In 1981, Betty Friedan did apologize for her brutal attacks on Gloria, who had sent her a birthday card. She thanked Gloria for the card and wrote about "the transcending of previous hostilities, misunderstandings, or real differences between us. . . . I am grateful for your continued contribution and commitment to the women's movement." (Shteir 2023, p. 247) There is no record of a reply from Gloria. Unfortunately, Betty did continue to criticize Gloria in the media in years that followed. In February 2022, Gloria graciously sent us a video tribute for use in a webinar I produced for Veteran Feminists of America to salute Betty Friedan on her one-hundredth birthday.

Gloria was a rock-star celebrity. The media followed every aspect of her life. When she gave up her eyeglasses for contact lenses, the *Arizona Daily Star* ran a long article headlined "Steinem Changes Her Look But Not Her Convictions."

Gloria claimed that she was shy, and "conflict is very, very hard for me." But she crossed the country, giving innumerable speeches for feminism. She nearly always insisted on sharing the platform with a woman of color; her cospeakers included Margaret Sloan, Dorothy Pitman Hughes, and Flo Kennedy.

During the 1970s, her speakers' bureau, Harry Walker Associates, booked me for several engagements as a substitute when Gloria was too busy (or too expensive). I did not turn out to be a fascinating speaker at the time because I tried to make our movement sound respectable. Most of my speeches took place on college campuses, and the students would have preferred more inflammatory language.

NOW leaders were unhappy when Gloria founded the Women's Action Alliance, supporting feminist activities in local communities. I complained to Gloria that WAA was siphoning off donor money that NOW desperately needed. But she stressed the need to encourage small local groups, in addition to big national organizations. Funders flocked to Gloria's causes.

Despite several highly publicized romances, Gloria remained unmarried until the age of sixty-six. Then she married David Bale, a South African businessman, environmentalist, and animal rights activist. During our Rollins College conference, a student asked Gloria publicly why she'd decided to marry after all those years. She replied, "He needed a green card." (Kate Millett married a man for the same reason.)

Fate was unkind to the newlyweds. After one year of marital bliss, David was stricken with lymphoma, confusion, and paranoia. He died two years later. I recall a memorial for feminist hero Mary Jean Tully, where Gloria and I spoke. We'd both just lost our husbands. Gloria wept openly.

SUSAN AND ROBIN MAKE A DIFFERENCE

Fortunately for the movement, author-activists wrote excellent books about its achievements. Apart from accounts by Betty Friedan and Gloria Steinem, nearly all these books were written by the those in the radical feminist wing. Susan Brownmiller has been described as "a midwife of the second wave." Her crusades revised public opinion about two serious abuses of women: rape and pornography.

Susan was an active member of New York Radical Women and then New York Radical Feminists. With the former, she engaged in consciousness-raising sessions, reporting that she'd had three illegal abortions. With the latter, she led its *Ladies' Home Journal* sit-in and highlighted its 1971 speak-out on rape. She spent four years researching the history of rape. Her 1975 book, *Against Our Will: Men, Women and Rape*, was electrifying. Susan declared that rape is not a crime of passion, but an instrument of control. No animals commit rape in their natural habitat. But among humans, she claimed, rape is "a conscious process of intimidation by which all men keep all women in a state of fear." (Some feminists disagree with Susan's condemnation of "all men," and insist that women and men can work together to eliminate rape.) She became an advocate for supporting rape victims

Susan's stand on pornography was controversial. She cofounded Women Against Pornography in 1979. This organization helped change the climate of opinion about pornography, which until then had been viewed by the public as trendy chic. One of her later books, *In Our Time: Memoir of a Revolution*, published in 1999, won new converts to the feminist cause.

Also influential is Robin Morgan, compiler/editor of the classic anthologies *Sisterhood Is Powerful* (1970), *Sisterhood is Global* (1984), and *Sisterhood Is Forever* (2003). Robin was editor in chief of *Ms.* magazine during the crucial years 1989–1994. She typified the dynamic energy of radical feminists at the time: She cofounded New York Radical Women and WITCH and was active in the Feminist Women's Health Center, the Feminist Alliance Against Rape, National Battered Women's Refuge Network, Women Against Pornography, and the National Women's Political Caucus. She also gets credit as chief organizer of the 1968 protest against the Miss America Pageant. With Anita Rapone and Anne Koedt, she edited the influential "Notes from the Third Year."

As evidence of Robin's versatility, she is also listed as an American poet. She began her varied career as a child actor. At the age of four, she starred in the *Little Robin Morgan Show* on New York radio station WOR.

Robin fell victim to an outbreak of radical feminist trashing after she became a media celebrity. When she was working on the underground newspaper *Rat,* she and other feminists reacted against the sexism of the paper's male editors and staged a takeover of *Rat.* Robin attacked that sexist mentality in a classic article titled "Goodbye to All That."

In 2005, Robin Morgan, Jane Fonda, and Gloria Steinem founded the Women's Media Center, whose mission is "to make women powerful and visible in the media." The WMC produces programs and conducts valuable surveys on women's visibility (or lack of it) in the media.

MEDIA WOMEN SUE AND WIN

Just as today's young people find it hard to imagine that ads once said "Help Wanted Male" and "Help Wanted Female," they're also shocked to learn of the hiring practices women encountered at *Time* and *Newsweek*. Both influential news weeklies hired only men as reporters. Women, no matter their background or ability, could never be more than researchers. Osborn Elliott, editor in chief of *Newsweek* from 1961 to 1976, cited "a news magazine tradition going back almost 50 years."

Sixty women at *Newsweek* were the first feminists to sue major media for sex discrimination, in May 1970. Their lawyer was Eleanor Holmes Norton, future chair of the EEOC. The date of their landmark settlement with *Newsweek* happened to be August 26, celebrated for ratification of the Nineteenth Amendment. In addition to awarding a modest cash settlement for back pay, *Newsweek* promised to hire and promote women as reporters and editors. To prove their new commitment to equality, *Newsweek* agreed to recruit men as researchers.

The women at *Time*—147 of them—filed a class-action suit after hearing about their sisters at *Newsweek*. On February 5, 1971, *Time* settled for a similar agreement. Soon after, women at *The New York Times* sued and won. To illustrate the effectiveness of "suing the bastards," look at this contrast: Before the lawsuit, only 7 percent of new hires in reporting and editing at the *Times* were women. In 1973, one year after the suit had been settled, 47 percent of new hires were women. (Randolph 2015, p. 158)

Women then sued and won at other media outlets. NBC was the first network targeted by a women's lawsuit; it ended in a settlement. Then women's groups at ABC and CBS won employment agreements without having to go to court. The women at CBS, not satisfied with their agreement, later came back with a more demanding lawsuit. In October 2000, CBS settled for eight million dollars in compensation plus a four-year hiring program to be supervised by the EEOC. This settlement rewarded women technical workers and executives, in addition to writers and editors.

The famously conservative *Reader's Digest* responded to its women's lawsuit with a $1.5 million settlement. In addition to back pay and salary increases, the magazine agreed to hire and promote women for top editorial jobs.

WORDS, ADS, AND BACKLASH

We approached our battle for people's minds in micro and macro ways. I previously mentioned New York NOW's micro subway stickers saying "This ad insults women." For a macro approach, we attacked how women were treated by TV networks.

From the earliest days, we worked to change specific words that disempower women. Young girls through the centuries have been discouraged from realizing their dreams when a career is cited in words like *businessman, assemblyman, policeman, fireman, switchman,* or *congressman.* Feminists successfully promoted nonsexist descriptions, such as police officer, firefighter, business executive, or (somewhat less effectively) congressperson. Instead of *chairman,* the word *chairwoman* is a bit clumsy, but some people use it. More and more now, however, use the word *chair.*

Some efforts ended in failure. When I was elected as national chair of NOW, I was horrified to see myself listed officially as "chairone." Whose idea was that? Instead, I referred to myself as "chair." Today, in the 2020s, we see mixed reactions to the term *Latinx,* which is unpalatable to some Latino or Latina people. We had great success installing *Ms.* as the alternative to words indicating marital status, such as *Mrs.* or *Miss.*

We've added new words to popular vocabulary. These include *macho, machismo, chauvinist, sexism,* and *sexigrated.* The word *sexism,* first used by Pauline Leet in a 1965 speech, was a natural corollary to the specter of *racism.* Soon after, people began to think in terms of *ageism, weightism, ableism, sanism,* and *speciesism.* (The last, created by a philosopher in 1970, described a bias toward humans as opposed to other animals.)

One widely popular term in the late 1960s was *MCP.* A male chauvinist pig was guilty of extreme misbehaviors and misstatements. Although the term has disappeared from use today, MCP behavior has not disappeared.

I was especially delighted when the word *sexism* appeared on the scene. At that time, we were reeling from Betty Harragan's lost lawsuit against advertising agency giant J. Walter Thompson. Along with other unsuccessful female plaintiffs, Betty learned that a woman could be denied promotion if lawyers could prove in court that she was "abrasive." In 1971, to atone for JWT's unfair verdict against Betty Harragan, a group of women at JWT agency obtained permission to work pro bono for NOW LDEF in creating a new ad campaign on gender discrimination. I suggested the theme "Were you a sexist today?" But the JWT team came up with a better idea: "WOMANPOWER. It's much too good to waste."

Their ads were brilliant. TV stations and newspapers were happy to carry them without charge. CBS produced two thirty-second TV spots on the theme, for use across the country.

One poster, still sold on eBay, became a classic. It depicts a knobbly-kneed man with his trousers turned up. Below him, the line runs "Hire him. He's got great legs." The JWT team also produced a poster, reproduced in this book, that features a college diploma with the line "Congratulations. You just spent twelve thousand dollars so she could join the typing pool."

I previously mentioned the campaign's poster with a baby, captioned "This normal healthy baby has a handicap. She was born female." Another ad used my head superimposed on the body of a male business executive, in suit and tie, at a boardroom table. The caption read "How many of your key men are women?"

The chair of that ingenious JWT creative team was Anne Tolstoi Wallach, who later won fame as a novelist. I wrote the letter that persuaded the Advertising Council to endorse their eye-opening campaign.

In 1979 NOW LDEF ran another well-received public service campaign created by our board member Jane Trahey (whose "What becomes a legend most?" campaign had put Blackglama mink on the map). The caption on one of Jane's witty ads was "He calls it Fun, we call it Sexual Harassment." Another: "When I grow up I'm going to be a judge or a senator or maybe president. Oh no, you're not, little girl."

Our efforts to sway minds didn't always succeed. Despite my expertise in public relations, I never persuaded the media to retract a cover story that appeared in *Newsweek* in 1986. It quoted a Yale sociologist's claim that women college graduates over age thirty have only a 20 percent chance of getting married—and only a 5 percent chance at age thirty-five. The study was deeply flawed statistically.

Some of the media damage against us was skillfully engineered by right-wing opponents. Susan Faludi summed up their motives in her 1991 book, *Backlash: The Undeclared War Against American Women,* when she stated, "The antifeminist backlash has been set off not by women's achievement of full equality but by the increased possibility that they might win it. It is a preemptive strike that stops women long before they reach the finishing line."

One organization in the antifeminist backlash is still active today. The Independent Women's Forum was founded in 1992 by women who supported Clarence Thomas in his Supreme Court battle against Anita Hill. One of its founders, Lynne Cheney, was the wife of the then powerful secretary of defense, Dick Cheney. Their organization is often confused, very intentionally, with the influential International Women's Forum, which we launched in 1974 to promote networking among women.

WE DISAGREE ON PORNOGRAPHY

Feminists split nearly fifty-fifty on the media question of pornography. Susan Brownmiller, Robin Morgan, and other prominent feminists claimed there's a connection between pornography and assaults against women. Robin declared in 1974, "Pornography is the theory, and rape is the practice." They campaigned for a bill proposed by law professor Catherine MacKinnon and author Andrea Dworkin, seeking permission for women to sue the makers and distributors of pornography that had harmed them. Such a bill was enacted in Canada.

This created a firestorm of controversy. Feminists for Free Expression, whose ranks included Betty Friedan, Nora Ephron, Susan Jacoby, and Nadine Strossen, campaigned against the antipornography bill, under the banner of free speech. They insisted that women do not need "protection from explicit sexual materials." They added, "Women are as varied as any citizens of a democracy; there is no agreement or feminist code as to what images are distasteful or even sexist."

KATHY HITS TV STATIONS WHERE IT HURTS

Our youngest hero was Kathy Bonk. As an eighteen-year-old college student, Kathy was active in NOW's Pittsburgh chapter. In 1971, all of Pennsylvania's TV stations were coming up for license renewal. Station WLBT-TV in Jackson, Mississippi, had recently lost its license because of race discrimination. This led Kathy and other chapter members to challenge Pennsylvania stations on the new battleground of *sex* discrimination.

Station WTAE-TV of Pittsburgh became the first station in the country to sign an agreement with NOW. WTAE-TV committed to hiring and promoting more women. Other terms of the settlement sound modest today: They agreed to present a weekly five-minute show on women's issues, to produce a special about women's rights once a year, and to refrain from mother-in-law jokes.

Encouraged by Joanne Evansgardner and other NOW leaders, Kathy Bonk developed workshops to be used by all NOW chapters in challenging FCC license renewals of TV stations guilty of sex discrimination.

Kathy moved to D.C., where she helped NOW members pressure the Gridiron Club to admit women journalists. At that time, women reporters were still barred from important events at the National Press Club, or forced to sit in the balcony.

To celebrate August 26, Kathy and other feminists created a large poster that said FBI, FEMINISTS BUREAU OF INVESTIGATION, listing ten most wanted men for crimes against women. During the night, they distributed three thousand posters throughout the capital. Their actions put pressure on all D.C. media, including the NBC, CBS, ABC, and PBS networks.

Working for the government, Kathy Bonk wrote recommendations for an official document titled *To Form a More Perfect Union.* This offered guidelines for media on their coverage of women's issues, with directives for improving the image of women and girls.

In 1977, Kathy ran press operations at the National Women's Conference in Houston, servicing more than one thousand reporters from around the world. She was twenty-three at the time.

Kathy Bonk
Photograph courtesy of Kathy Bonk

I'm proud that Kathy refers to me as her mentor. She came to work at NOW LDEF as head of Media Relations. This involved far more than seeking publicity. Our main goal was to eliminate sex discrimination at TV stations.

Through the FCC Committee of national NOW, Kathy organized challenges to license renewals in twenty-five states, winning agreements for hiring women and reducing sexist program content. At that time, work at NOW and NOW LDEF was interconnected.

Our hopes for continued media reform were scuttled when Ronald Reagan became president. He appointed an FCC with antifeminist commissioners. We'd been working toward FCC regulations making it easier for women to own television stations. Reagan's conservative FCC sabotaged our plans.

Kathy eventually formed a nonprofit group called the Communications Consortium Media Center, using media to help nonprofit

241

organizations. In 1985, during the International Women's Year confer-ence in Kenya, Kathy located the biggest tree in Nairobi for Betty Friedan to sit under. Unlike the previous International Women's Year conferences in Mexico City and Copenhagen, the Nairobi conference produced helpful resolutions on feminist issues, which included omit-ting the irrelevant false claim that "Zionism is racism."

Another achievement of Kathy's long career was working with Congresswoman Patricia Schroeder to pass the first Family and Medi-cal Leave Act, along with other women's rights legislation.

TRAINING THE TRAINERS

Our battle against stereotyping extended to one form of media that's sometimes overlooked—business publications. We assailed the Bureau of Business Practice for its 1969 training manual titled *Action Guide to Supervising Women*. Here's how that publication described women: "[T]hey're not as practical. They're not as objective. They don't like to discuss ideas as much as men do—they'd rather talk about people. . . . Women don't desire advancement as strongly as men. . . . Women are naturally interested in cooking, clothes, children. . . . Managers may grow a little weary of women-talk, but they should remember that for women it's as natural as conversations about the New York Jets are for men."

FLO KENNEDY SHAKES US UP

Florynce "Flo" Kennedy played a colorful role in feminism's struggle with the media. Flo and I were friends when she attended Columbia Law School and I went to Barnard (we met at the same parties). Flo was active in New York NOW, beginning with the first meeting. She and I became adversaries in several battles of 1968. In retrospect, I now appre-ciate Flo's early attacks on "sexist media," though at the time I consid-ered certain hostile actions counterproductive.

Flo was an early advocate of intersectionality. She said "niggerizing techniques that are used don't only damage black people, but they also damage women, gay people, ex-prison inmates, prostitutes, children, old people, handicapped people, Native Americans." (Randolph 2015, p.158)

In the spring of 1968, Flo was the lawyer for Valeria Solanas, who had shot artist Andy Warhol, extolling her Society for Cutting Up Men (SCUM). Flo induced our NOW chapter president Ti-Grace Atkinson to attend the trial and salute Solanas publicly as a "feminist hero."

In addition to sending Flo Kennedy a telegram telling her to "desist immediately" from linking us to Solanas, national NOW sent the press a repudiation by president Betty Friedan. Betty added, "Some 10 percent of NOW's members are men, and we vigorously oppose any 'battle of the sexes' approach to society's inequalities. Men are not an enemy, but rather fellow-victims of the current half-equality between the sexes."

At our chapter meeting on October 17, Flo supported Ti-Grace's motion to "democratize" NOW elections by choosing our officers and committee chairs by lottery and rotating them every month. When our chapter voted against the motion, Flo resigned from NOW and joined Ti-Grace in founding the October 17 Movement.

Flo was an organizer of the demonstration against the Miss America Pageant in 1968, and she attracted media attention with other actions. In a "pee-in" protesting the lack of female bathrooms at Harvard University, Flo and her followers poured jars of fake urine on the steps of Lowell Hall.

Gloria Steinem chose Flo to share some of her speaking tours, terming Flo's method "verbal karate." Gloria referred to the two of them as "the Thelma and Louise of the seventies." (Love 2006, p. 250)

Flo fought all forms of discrimination in the media as far back as 1966, when she founded the Media Workshop. In 1977, she became an associate of the Women's Institute for Freedom of the Press (WIFP), to promote women-based media. Her books and personal appearances (wearing a cowboy hat and boots) became feminist legend. Her targets included the Catholic Church. Flo once wrote, "It's interesting to speculate how it developed that in two of the most anti-feminist institutions, the church and the law court, the men are wearing the dresses." (Seering, Freedom from Religion Foundation)

18

RADICAL FEMINISTS, WOMEN'S LIBERATION

SUSAN BROWNMILLER REFERRED to NOW members as "clubwomen." Her allies say NOW's legal gains will prove to be only "piecemeal" solutions until women can overturn the entire systemic power of the patriarchy.

This book focuses primarily on NOW and the ACLU and our pragmatic contingent of law-changers. The movement that seeks more fundamental change calls itself "women's liberation" in most parts of the country. In the New York area, they're radical feminists.

Actually, we all agree that we must fight on *all* fronts for women to end the age-old power of "That's how it's always been." Feminists must transform laws and practices during our lifetime, while other activists work to unseat the deeply held beliefs that undergird patriarchy. The two approaches serve each other.

Feminists share the same ultimate goals, but our differences are a matter of *emphasis*. I personally share Betty Friedan's strategy: "The gut issues of this revolution involve employment, education and new social institutions." (Turk 2023, p. 99; Shteir 2023, p. 3)

With deep gratitude, I devote this chapter to women's liberation and radical feminists. Their activists produced mind-changing protests, consciousness-raising revelations, books, articles, and educational materials, while our NOW troops attacked specific laws and regulations. We worked together when large demonstrations were needed.

In the days before cell phones and the internet, women's liberation-ists were unable and unwilling to combine their forces into one national organization. Each group had its own ideology; they quarreled fiercely. You'll see below that Shulamith Firestone cofounded numerous groups, each one disagreeing with the dogma of its predecessors. Although the various liberation groups succeeded in enlightening the minds of many thousands of women and men, "they lacked national coordination, goals, an accepted leadership, and . . . an effective fundraising mecha-nism." (Carabillo, Meuli, and Csida 1993, p. vii)

Here's a brief rundown of the most effective groups: One of the ear-liest, New York Radical Women, was founded early in 1967 by Shulamith Firestone, Robin Morgan, Carol Hanisch, and Chude Pamela Allen. At Hanisch's suggestion, they led the renowned protest of one hundred women against the Miss America Pageant in Atlantic City on Septem-ber 7, 1968. Though the media were incorrect in using the term *bra burn-ing*, the radicals did dump bras, curlers, cosmetics, and other symbols of the beauty industry into a large trash can, but there was *no* burning. Protesters also crowned a live sheep. As you read previously, NYRW played a leading role, with other women's organizations, in the famous eleven-hour sit-in at the headquarters of *Ladies' Home Journal* on March 18, 1970. NYRW also introduced a radical psychology program that taught members how to be more assertive.

Consciousness-raising, introduced by liberationists, revolutionized the entire movement. The term was probably invented by Anne Forer. Women gathered together in small groups to talk about their personal oppression in their homes and workplaces and the world at large. The first known consciousness-raising group was founded in November 1967 by New York Radical Women members Kathie Sarachild, Shulamith Firestone, Anne Koedt, and Carol Hanisch.

I remember the first time consciousness-raising was introduced, though not by that name, at a NOW chapter meeting in 1969. Prince-ton psychologist Dan Sullivan had been invited to speak. In discussing our oppression by sex discrimination, he exhorted us: "I'm not inter-ested in abstractions. Talk about how you feel." (Fox 1991) I was impa-tient with Sullivan's approach, and I tried to steer the meeting back to

246

talk of protests and lawsuits. Other NOW members in the room got the consciousness-raising message sooner than I did. Within a short time, consciousness-raising groups became a feature of NOW chapter meetings throughout the country.

A group with slightly different doctrines from NYRW, New York Radical Feminists, was founded in 1969 by Shulamith Firestone and Anne Koedt. Their January 1971 speak-out against rape informed the public that rape is a tool for maintaining patriarchal control.

In Chicago, the Westside Group, founded in 1967 by Jo Freeman and Shulamith Firestone, created *Voice of the Women's Liberation Movement*, the movement's first newsletter, in 1968. That publication gave the women's liberation movement its name. They met weekly in Jo Freeman's apartment.

Chicago Women's Liberation Union (CWLU) was founded in 1969 by Heather Booth, Naomi Weisstein, Vivian Rothstein, Amy Kesselman, and Ruth Surgal, among others. Many of their accomplishments were generated by my good friend Heather Booth, whom we'll discuss below.

Apart from abortion actions to be described when we focus on Heather, here's a partial rundown of CWLU activities: Their Liberation School for Women, created in 1970, taught women practical and technical skills. Their Prison Project helped improve local prison conditions for women. For instance, they obtained a nursery room for inmates' children. They published popular newsletters and a 1972 pamphlet titled *Socialist Feminism: A Strategy for the Women's Movement.*

Collaborating with NOW and other groups, CWLU won a major sex discrimination wage lawsuit against the city of Chicago. They created an Anti-Rape Movement with a rape crisis hotline. They helped launch a women's studies program at the University of Chicago in 1972 to "make knowledge by, about, and for women in all fields accessible to students." They worked with the Committee to End Sterilization Abuse to end unnecessary sterilizations and sterilization without consent among women of color living in poverty.

CWLU also promoted feminism in music and the arts. The Chicago Women's Liberation Rock Band is still making rhythmic waves; I enjoyed the band's performance at the conference celebrating NOW's fiftieth anniversary in 2016.

Despite those historic achievements, CWLU disbanded in April 1977, only eight years after it began. The reason was all too familiar a one for progressive organizations. Members fell into destructive disputes with one another.

Other productive women's liberation groups arose in Berkeley, California, as well as in Ohio, Florida, Michigan, and Massachusetts. The Boston Women's Health Book Collective created *Our Bodies, Ourselves.*

In the New York area, the most visible and influential radical group was Redstockings, founded in January 1969 by Ellen Willis and the ever-active Shulamith Firestone, among others. Their uptown and downtown groups disagreed on ideology. Both groups played a key role in promoting consciousness-raising nationwide. Redstockings members stormed a New York State government hearing on abortion law, which amazingly comprised fourteen men and one nun. Their March 1969 speak-out on women's true-life abortion experiences energized public demand for abortion law reform. The Redstockings Manifesto protested against men's exploitation of women as "sex objects, breeders, domestic servants, and cheap labor."

Unfortunately, Redstockings suffered from trashing—personal attacks on prominent feminists. Their tirades against celebrities were especially brutal to Gloria Steinem. Jo Freeman's 1976 article about trashing generated more letters to *Ms.* magazine than any article it ever published. Jo charged: "Like a cancer, the attacks spread from those who had reputations to those who were merely strong; from those who were active to those who merely had ideas; from those who stood out as individuals to those who failed to conform rapidly enough to the twists and turns of the changing line." (Faludi 2013, p. 52) That damaging behavior was all too common in 1970s feminism.

Redstockings published several attacks on NOW for promoting institutional reform "while ignoring the interpersonal power of men over women." Reflecting the homophobia of some members, they accused gay men of "misogynistic rejection of women."

The organization disbanded in 1970. Shulamith Firestone and Anne Koedt had left in 1969 to cofound New York Radical Feminists.

NOW found it increasingly difficult to attract press attention for important feminist issues. We were yesterday's news. The media preferred to publicize the movement's internal battles—or colorful, offbeat groups, however small.

One organization received publicity disproportionate to its small size. In fact, publicity was one of its main goals. The Women's International Terrorist Conspiracy from Hell, better known as WITCH, was founded by Robin Morgan, Florika, Peggy Dobbins, Judy Duffett, Cynthia Funk, Naomi Jaffe, and several socialist feminists. In their first action on Halloween, 1968, WITCH members, dressed as witches, put a "hex" on Wall Street. The Dow Jones average dropped sharply the next day! In February 1969, they protested a bridal fair by letting loose a gaggle of white mice. They demonstrated against Bell Telephone Company and other corporations, as well as the inauguration of President Richard Nixon.

Heather Booth is a hybrid feminist who deserves a special place in history. She has advanced the feminist cause over five decades through a broad spectrum of doctrines—socialism, women's liberation, NOW activism, Democratic Party politics. These days, Heather helps the Democratic Party win important campaigns. Yes, a mainstream political party. I said previously that I'd nominate Gloria Steinem and Heather for feminist sainthood. They are both exceptionally kind and generous, apart from their savvy organizing skills. Heather is the most considerate person I've ever known. She praises and encourages contentious colleagues, and never forgets a birthday.

In the aftermath of America's 2008 financial crisis, Heather campaigned successfully to help enact the Dodd-Frank Wall Street Reform and Consumer Protection Act of 2010. This enabled the Bureau of Consumer Financial Protection to make sure women are treated fairly by banks and other financial institutions. Heather heads outreach to progressives and seniors for the Democrats in national elections. She's the subject of a moving documentary titled *Heather Booth: Changing the World.*

In 1965, as a student in the University of Chicago, Heather founded the now famous Jane Collective. Their members personally performed or arranged for some eleven thousand abortions in the

Heather Booth
Photographer K. K. Otteson
Photograph courtesy of Heather Booth

days before the *Roe v. Wade* decision. In 1965, she also started a campus women's group called Women's Radical Action Project (WRAP). They introduced consciousness-raising long before it became a national phenomenon.

In 1973, Heather reinvested the money she'd won in a labor dispute to establish the esteemed Midwest Academy, a training organization that teaches nonprofit activists how to organize for social change. The Midwest Academy expands on techniques developed by the legendary Saul Alinsky. Numerous leaders of NOW, among other organizers, have been trained there.

When Heather and I discussed our movement, she urged me to add this: "The joy of the early years—finding other wonderful and caring women, finding ourselves and our own voices, building real sisterhood. The later years did have conflicts, but the sisterhood should not be lost when recounting the history and why it was so powerful and attracted so many."

OTHER RADICAL FEMINISTS

Jo Freeman is another "hybrid" who combined radical feminism with NOW activism. She still serves the movement as a writer, photographer, lawyer, organizer, and political scientist. Jo cofounded the Chicago chapter of NOW in 1969, then moved east and became active in our New York chapter, then moved to D.C. and became treasurer of the chapter there. She was the first official photographer for Veteran Feminists of America.

Jo's *Women: A Feminist Perspective* (1975) has been a valued text for women's studies courses. Her articles "The BITCH Manifesto" (1970), "The Tyranny of Structurelessness" (1972), and "Trashing: The Dark Side of Sisterhood" (1976) aroused heated debate.

After her stormy relationship with NOW, Ti-Grace Atkinson still remains an intellectual force in radical feminist activities and writings. Despite our arguments through the years, we are good friends today. I recall the night that Betty Friedan introduced us to this tall, beautiful socialite. She was twenty-nine years old then, and a doctoral candidate at Columbia University. We figured she'd add "acceptability" to our public image. In 1968, we elected her president of the New York chapter.

I also remember one evening when Ti-Grace brought financier John Loeb to my apartment for dinner. She kept hinting that he should donate financial support to our chapter, but John was uninterested in discussing policy. He clearly had romantic designs on Ti-Grace. The evening ended as a failure for everyone.

In 1968, Ti-Grace attracted wide publicity to our New York chapter, but not the kind that pleased us. In fact, we were furious. In a *New York Times Magazine* article, she was quoted saying "Marriage is slavery. The institution of marriage must be abolished." She also argued for communal upbringing of children. (Lear 1968)

At our March 21 chapter meeting after that article appeared, half the people in the room were unconventionally dressed strangers. Professor Gerda Lerner, on her way to fame as a feminist historian, whispered to me, "Who *are* those people?" None of the new recruits attended later meetings; we probably disappointed them with our serious, conventional attitudes.

Later that spring, Ti-Grace hailed "a new feminist hero"—Valerie Solanas, who had shot artist Andy Warhol on behalf of her Society for Cutting Up Men. The executive committee of NOW's New York chapter issued a decree insisting that officers should not make public statements without the committee's approval, but Ti-Grace kept defying us.

The conflict would come to a head on October 17, when the New York chapter voted on a new set of "non-hierarchal" bylaws proposed by Ti-Grace and a small group of other members to make the chapter more democratic. They proposed that officers and committee chairs should be chosen by lottery and should rotate every month. As I've said previously, Mary Eastwood surprised us by praising Ti-Grace's proposal at a national board meeting.

We all took to our phones to recruit votes for the October 17 meeting. Ti-Grace's group objected to my living room as the chapter's usual meeting place—"too prejudicial." So we met in a church on the West Side of Manhattan.

To nobody's surprise, the new bylaws were overwhelmingly defeated. Ti-Grace resigned from NOW, joined by Flo Kennedy and a few others. Ti-Grace and Flo cofounded the October 17 Movement, which observed those controversial bylaws.

In early 1970, the group renamed itself The Feminists, stipulating that only one-third of its members could be married or in a relationship with a man. (Redstockings of the Women's Liberation Movement 1975, p. 165) A year later, Ti-Grace resigned because members were trashing her, resenting her numerous speaking engagements.

In Ti-Grace's authorized biography in *Feminists Who Changed America,*" she is described as "frustrated" by NOW's "resistance to taking on abortion as an issue." (Love 2006, p. 21) This is not accurate. NOW supported abortion rights earlier than other national organizations, beginning at our national conference in November 1967.

Ti-Grace remains a fiery feminist theorist. On March 10, 1971, she accused Catholic University of "incitement to rape." She wrote to the university president: "Motherfuckers: We have heard your answer to my appeal for reason at Notre Dame. . . . The struggle between the liberation of women and the Catholic Church is a struggle to the death." (Gloria Steinem Papers, Smith College)

Ti-Grace wrote the book *Amazon Odyssey* in 1974. She later resigned from the Sagaris collective because they accepted ten thousand dollars from Gloria Steinem's Ms. Foundation, which Redstockings had attacked.

In Chicago, feminist organizations with Shulamith Firestone as a founding member included the Westside Group and the National Conference for New Politics. She was a major influence in progressive feminist thinking, blending it with the theories of Sigmund Freud, Frederick Engels, Wilhelm Reich, Karl Marx, and Simone de Beauvoir. Her 1970 book, *The Dialectic of Sex: The Case for Feminist Revolution,* showed how feminism related to modern technology.

After helping to organize the Miss America Pageant protest, Shulamith staged a mock funeral called "The Burial of Traditional Womanhood" at Arlington National Cemetery in 1968. Feminists buried a dummy dressed as the "common housewife." Shulamith also organized the first abortion speak-out in March 1969.

Sadly, Shulamith's later years were shaded by her struggle with paranoid schizophrenia. She died in reclusive poverty at the age of sixty-seven, in August 2012, perhaps dying of starvation. No food was found in her apartment.

Several radical feminists wrote well-received books. An early member of Redstockings, Alix Kates Shulman, told the feminist story through persuasive fiction. Her *Memoirs of an Ex–Prom Queen* sold over a million copies, and four other novels found a welcoming readership. Alix helped me connect with the publisher of this book, even though she doesn't completely agree with my emphasis on NOW's preeminence. Alix insists I should give more credit to consciousness-raising for the success of our revolution.

Women's liberationists still communicate with one another every day. I'm part of an email group involving two dozen early feminists—mostly radicals but also including a few women from the NOW side. We emailers still argue passionately and share dreams for the future.

19

WE WERE INFILTRATED

AS EARLY AS 1969, J. Edgar Hoover's FBI assigned secret agents to observe and influence what he called "WLM." Hoover wrote to his agents: "It is absolutely essential that we conduct sufficient investigation to clearly establish subversive ramifications of the WLM and to determine the potential for violence presented by the various groups connected with this movement as well as any possible threat they may represent to the internal security of the United States." One FBI report in the early 1970s said that "the so-called Women's Liberation Movement had its origins in Soviet Russia." Years later, when *Ms.* magazine requested the FBI's WLM file under the Freedom of Information Act, that file was found to be nearly fourteen hundred pages long. (I requested my own file; it contained only one newspaper clipping.)

I wrote to Hoover in 1970, urging him to hire women agents in the FBI; he replied with a letter saying this was impossible. (I don't recall his reasoning; I've lost his letter. He probably relied on some version of "That's how it's always been.") Ironically, the FBI paid a price for not hiring women agents until 1972. They had to rely on less-informed freelancers.

In 1975, Barbara Seaman got word from a friend in government that the FBI and CIA were pursuing Operation Chaos (a CIA term) to disrupt the women's movement.

Many of us had suspicions about who might be an FBI infiltrator. We based these on the combative behavior of certain women, and the disruption they inflicted on our movement. I will not mention names because there's no way of knowing for sure. I recall that the treasurer of New York City NOW in the 1980s absconded with all our money. Was this due to greed or to the FBI? Or to the Socialist Workers Party?

A possible example of infiltration took place in July 1975, in a feminist conclave at Sagaris, an experimental feminist summer school in the tiny village of Lyndonville, Vermont. A third of the attendees marched out in protest because the Sagaris event had received financial support from the Ms. Foundation. Several women seemed to be acting as "agent provocateurs" in stirring up controversy. Lucinda Franks wrote in *The New York Times,* "The women under suspicion were finally confronted and accused of acting destructively, of spreading misinformation, of manipulating people, and of slipping silently back and forth between the two sides." (Franks 1975) Those women denied the charges, but many feminists viewed their behavior as typical infiltration.

Whereas FBI infiltrators clearly intended to undermine our movement, a group of socialist feminists tried to *influence* our ideology. A third group of infiltrators tried to *replace* existing organizations, such as NOW chapters, with their own entities. During the 1970s, we exchanged warnings about try-to-replace groups affiliated with the Socialist Workers Party (SWP) and its ally, the Young Socialists Alliance (YSA). At the national YSA convention in December 1969, delegates openly talked of "intervening with" and "helping to broaden" feminist organizations. (Davis 1991, p. 139)

Here's how the Socialist Workers Party (SWP) describes itself on its website: "Originally a group in the Communist Party USA that supported Leon Trotsky against Soviet leader Joseph Stalin, it places a priority on 'solidarity work' to aid strikes and is strongly supportive of Cuba."

In the 1970s, some activists favored cooperation with the socialist movement. Calling themselves "socialist feminists," they were loyal to our basic organizations. On the other hand, SWP members aimed to take us over completely. A question often circulated in our meetings was, "Could she be an infiltrator?"

YSA scored a damaging hit in the fall of 1970 by taking over the politics, treasury, and mailing list of the radical feminist Cell 16 in Boston. They seized complete control of Cell 16's bank account. Original members fled in dismay. According to *Moving the Mountain*, by Flora Davis, feminists had written proof that the Trotskyites were planning to infiltrate the National Abortion Action League next. (Davis 1991, p. 141) They did not succeed.

Heather Booth, a leader of the Chicago Women's Liberation Union, says both SWP and the Progressive Labor Party tried to take over CWLU, but without success. "They were well organized, but they were small."

Even more than with SWP, we were swept by paranoia because of WONAAC, the Women's National Abortion Action Campaign. Formed by SWP in the spring of 1971, WONAAC organized large pro-abortion rights marches in Washington, D.C., and San Francisco on November 20, 1971. Despite our interest in supporting abortion rights, Betty Friedan warned in September against joining the WONAAC marches: "We are going to be infiltrated." After much discussion, NOW leaders decided not to participate in the marches. Leaders of the National Women's Political Caucus, which had previously endorsed the demonstration, also canceled their support.

Some feminists claimed that WONAAC secretly wanted abortion repeal to fail. Or they wanted to arouse public resentment against NOW and NWPC, in order to woo supporters to SWP. Those were fear-ridden times. Another reason for our reluctance to associate with WONAAC was its refusal to endorse lesbian rights. In late 1971, the NOW national board passed a resolution "to condemn the actions of groups and organizations that act to divide and exploit the feminist movement for their own goals and purposes." The resolution named WONAAC specifically.

I have no doubt that organized entities continue today in their attempts to infiltrate, co-opt, and influence the women's movement. Our national and local groups remain vigilant.

20

YEARS OF TRIUMPH AND TENSION

"GOOD NEWS AND BAD NEWS" describes our feminist situation in the year 1974. The Department of Labor, the EEOC, and other government agencies were beginning to make a difference *for us* by enforcing antidiscrimination statutes in the business world. Women were beginning to obtain credit cards in their own name. "Help Wanted" ads were desexigrated. Title IX began to outlaw sex discrimination in education. And, the Senate had passed the Equal Rights Amendment on March 22, 1972, pending ratification by thirty-eight states. (The House had passed it in October 1971.) Energetic NOW chapters sprang up in towns and on campuses, attacking injustices in their own localities. Consciousness-raising groups blossomed everywhere. While many marriages ended in divorce, other marriages morphed to stronger partnership between equals.

However, the media paid less attention to our outreach. Pointing to millions of women pouring into new jobs and graduate schools, journalists seemed to believe our revolution was over. Instead of covering important feminist issues, they were more interested in covering our internal squabbles. Unfortunately, they found lots of squabbles to cover.

Because women had held little power through the centuries, we were inexperienced in coping with the power struggles that intensified in 1974. Feminist groups accused one another of heresy. Celebrity feminists were trashed by their sisters. And national NOW suffered from a damaging rift between the old and the new. The split at our national conference in Houston in February 1974 seemed almost generational. Karen DeCrow attacked the slogan Betty Friedan had written in NOW's "Statement of Purpose," "to bring women into full participation in the mainstream of American society." Karen's campaign slogan was "Out of the mainstream and into the revolution." I found it ironic that NOW founders were suddenly called "conservative" after we'd overcome barriers that had oppressed women for thousands of years.

Because of my busy professional and family life, I decided not to run for reelection after one term as chair of NOW. Despite increasingly divisive attacks between NOW's competing factions, I had managed to keep our thirty-five-member board meetings focused on major issues. All joined together in applauding me when the weekend meetings ended on Sunday evenings. Judy Lightfoot, my successor as chair after the Houston conference, was unable to cope with the intensifying squabbles. Members describe 1974–1975 as "a year of Hell."

Half the new board's members in 1974 were supporters of Mary Jean Collins, who had lost the presidential election to Karen DeCrow by a narrow forty votes out of some fifteen hundred. The other half supported Karen in a new faction calling itself the Majority Caucus. Eleanor Smeal was its leader and Aileen Hernandez, popular second president of NOW, an active participant. The group repeatedly excoriated NOW's new executive director, Jane Plitt, whom the board had hired in 1973. Every issue ignited a battle. At a board meeting in New Orleans, the entire Majority Caucus group walked out in protest against chair Judy Lightfoot. I didn't attend that meeting, so I don't know if the issue was major or minor.

The Majority Caucus accused NOW's devoted treasurer, Bonnie Howard, of malfeasance. The board hired Price Waterhouse to audit NOW books for financial irregularities. The auditors, after investigation, announced that everything was fine. Several board members insisted, "Something's wrong. Go back again." Price Waterhouse reviewed the books again in greater detail, and still found no irregularities. (Bonnie

Howard moved over to the NOW Legal Defense and Education Fund, where we appreciated her work as our treasurer.)

The factional battle grew even more intense at our next national conference, held in Philadelphia in October 1975. This was a time of rampant antiprofessionalism. Esther Kaw announced her candidacy for NOW Public Relations vice president although she had no communications experience. Gerry Kenyan ran for Legal vice president, though not a lawyer. Nada Chandler ran for treasurer despite a lack of financial expertise.

Tightly contested voting lasted all night, disrupted by a false fire alarm that caused a need for recredentialing and revoting. Karen DeCrow was reelected president. The new NOW board voted against continuing our action against Sears, Roebuck; Majority Caucus leaders called the Sears campaign "socialistic."

ELEANOR SMEAL SAVES THE DAY

Under Karen DeCrow and our inexperienced treasurer, Nada Chandler, NOW fell into serious financial difficulties. We were rescued by our next president, Eleanor Smeal.

When Ellie was elected in 1977, the media hailed her as NOW's first homemaker president. She held an M.A. in political science and administration, and had served on the board of the League of Women Voters. Ellie had never held a paid job. Despite her graduate degree, she prides herself on working-class roots. She's a strong, persuasive speaker.

Ellie hired the fund-raising firm of Roger Craver to conduct NOW's first direct mail campaigns. These appeals, focused on the Equal Rights Amendment, were wonderfully successful.

Ellie professionalized our leadership. Until then, all officers were volunteers; we'd paid all expenses out of our own pockets. Since that time, NOW officers have received a salary, plus expenses. They're now required to move to D.C. At first, all officers earned the same salary, a modest thirteen thousand dollars a year. By 1985, the president's salary had been raised to $55,000.

Eleanor Smeal
Photograph courtesy of the Feminist Majority Foundation

Eleanor Smeal led strenuous campaigns on two major issues: trying to ratify the Equal Rights Amendment and making abortion widely available. After the Senate voted for the ERA in 1972, it was ratified quickly by twenty-two states. But Congress had set a deadline of March 22, 1979 for full ratification. If thirty-eight states had not ratified by that date, the ERA would fail. When the time came, only thirty-five states had ratified it.

Ellie led an aggressive fight to win extension of the ratification date to June 30, 1982. NOW staged demonstrations across the country. Our July 1978 march for extension drew 100,000 activists to D.C.

Apart from our founding president, Betty Friedan, most of us consider Eleanor Smeal our most effective NOW president. By the end of Ellie's second term in 1982, NOW had 220,000 members and a healthy annual budget of thirteen million dollars. Our fund-raising appeals continued to focus on the ERA. National NOW and its chapters also campaigned for Social Security reform, lesbian and gay rights, and other issues. Ellie organized a big National March for Lesbian and Gay Rights in 1979.

Ellie held grudges against people she perceived as enemies. She didn't get along with Mary Jean Tully, the wealthy socialite who presided over NOW LDEF in the early days of Ellie's presidency. In 1976, Mary Jean organized a faction called Womansurge. Whatever its stated purpose, the real goal was to counterbalance the Majority Caucus. Patricia Burnett was an active member. They never gained any influence and quietly faded away. Though I was a close friend of Mary Jean's, I never joined the organization.

In the years before NOW LDEF cut its ties to NOW, bylaws called for NOW's top officers to serve on the NOW LDEF board, and vice versa. I recall one NOW LDEF board meeting held at my home. Ellie Smeal attended. My VCR machine, which was located behind Ellie's chair, suddenly turned on automatically to record a movie I'd preprogrammed. Ellie reacted suspiciously. She thought NOW LDEF was spying on her and recording what she said. I'm not sure I ever fully convinced her of our innocence.

Our bylaws prevented NOW presidents from serving more than two successive terms. At our 1982 national conference, Ellie supported Judy Goldsmith, a likable Wisconsin professor, for election as her successor. Judy labored hard during her presidency to increase the political power of American women, regarding this as the only way to achieve social justice. Ronald Reagan's presidency, begun in 1981, was wreaking havoc with feminist goals. Under Reagan, government agencies declined to confront businesses guilty of sex discrimination if the proof was supported by statistics alone. They required proof of *intent to discriminate.* To make matters worse for us, affirmative action was weakened by the Supreme Court's Bakke and Weber decisions.

Judy Goldsmith led NOW in a campaign to persuade Walter Mondale, who ran against Reagan in 1984, to choose a woman as his candidate for vice president. At all our meetings, Judy led us in an anthem with the refrain "Run with a woman." Feminist pressure succeeded in persuading Mondale to add Geraldine Ferraro to his ticket. Alas, Reagan was reelected.

Ellie Smeal, Judy Goldsmith's previous mentor, decided to run again for NOW's presidency at the 1985 national conference in New

Orleans. Once again, we endured a bruising NOW election battle. *The Washington Post* quoted an Ellie Smeal supporter: "If you're coming to New Orleans, wear your bulletproof vest. These elections aren't known for their niceties." (Peterson 1985)

At first, we thought Judy was running ahead in potential votes. But she damaged her campaign with an abrasive final speech. She accused Ellie of "duplicity, character assassination, and a ward-boss political mentality."

A sample ballot distributed by Ellie's followers was found to be faulty. This led the elections committee to throw out the first 505 votes and start over again. Judy complained, "It's not a mistake that would be easily made. . . . That gave them several more hours to lobby." Ellie defeated Judy by 839 to 703. Ellie reported spending eighteen thousand dollars on the campaign; Judy spent fourteen thousand. To those of us who remembered the days when every dollar was hard to find, those amounts were breathtaking.

In the years following the election, I tried to broker a peace between the two women, but Ellie refused. She continued to criticize Judy publicly.

In her third term, from 1985 to 1987, Ellie concentrated on bringing back the ERA and abortion rights. To stand up for reproductive freedom, NOW's 1986 March for Women's Lives drew 150,000 marchers in D.C. and Los Angeles.

In 1980, Ellie published *How and Why Women Will Elect the Next President*. She coined the term *gender gap*, reflecting how women's votes differ from men's votes on key issues. The gender gap remains a factor in today's political elections.

Throughout the 1990s, Eleanor Smeal fought to win approval in the United States for mifepristone, a drug then known as RU-486, to induce nonsurgical abortions. It had been used effectively and safely in France since 1988. In numerous states today, after the overturn of *Roe v. Wade* in the Supreme Court, we've relied on the drug to rescue women from unwanted pregnancies. Combined with a second medication, misoprostol, it causes contractions in the uterus to expel an embryo.

RU-486 was developed in France by Rousell-Uclaf, but its German parent company, Hoechst AG, bowed to pressure from antiabortion groups and refused to market the drug in the United States. Feminists exerted their own pressure, and the Population Council obtained patent rights in this country. Finally, on September 28, 2000, the FDA approved mifepristone as a safe and effective medication. Today it's strenuously attacked by antiabortion forces.

At the end of her term, Eleanor Smeal continued to advance her goals through her close friend Molly Yard, who served as NOW president from 1987 to 1991.

Ellie still maintains close ties to NOW leadership, and attends executive sessions as a member of the Advisory Council. In 1987, she created a sister organization, the Feminist Majority Foundation (FMF), with financial backing from Peg Yorkin, after Peg won a huge divorce settlement from movie producer Bud Yorkin. Other cofounders were Gloria Steinem, Kathy Spillar, Judy Meuli, and Toni Carabillo. In 2001, when *Ms.* magazine was foundering financially, FMF stepped in and took over publication as a nonprofit service to feminists. The Feminist Majority does trailblazing work these days to ratify ERA, protect abortion rights, and advance other crucial causes.

Eleanor Smeal has been prescient in identifying and addressing the problems and attitudes of American women. She demonstrates special compassion for women at lower-income levels. Our movement benefits greatly from her strategic wisdom and toughness. Some women have learned that it's dangerous to cross her. In Betty Friedan's *Second Stage,* Betty quotes Ellie as saying "You can't count on any woman, once she gets some power, not to sell other women out." (Friedan 1981, p. 25) Ellie and Betty opposed each other on several occasions, though they worked well together most of the time.

I recall the huge 2004 March for Women's Lives that Ellie's team organized in D.C. During the preceding week, Betty antagonized NOW staff with rude insults on the telephone. At that Sunday's March, Betty rode in a special bus with elderly and disabled women. I ran up to Ellie's deputy, Alice Cohan, to suggest that Betty should speak at the podium. They refused to call on Betty because "she mistreated our staff."

When my term ended as president of NOW LDEF, Ellie led a NOW tribute, saying, "It has been Muriel's love for the organization that has made possible so much of what we have done."

Through the years, NOW has suffered from fierce disagreements among its leaders. I compare these to sibling rivalry—or to power struggles that seem to have plagued all do-gooders as far back as the French Revolution. True, we never cut off the heads of opponents. In recent years, each president of NOW has fought bitterly with her predecessor and with her successor. These counterproductive struggles distress me. Today's president of NOW, the dynamic Black leader Christian Nunes, gained the office after charging president Toni Van Pelt with insensitivity to racial issues. When Toni resigned in midterm, she cited health reasons. Christian was reelected to a second term by a large majority. Christian and I work well together.

TISH SOMMERS HELPS US THINK DIFFERENTLY

In the 1970s, Leticia Sommers led us into history with four feminist initiatives. She is a hero whom history should not forget.

Like Ellie Smeal, Tish was a homemaker who did unpaid volunteer work. When she was divorced in 1972, after twenty-three years of marriage, she immediately lost her medical insurance, which was attached to her husband's job. She lost her credit cards, all in her husband's name. When she applied for jobs, employers ignored her volunteer experience in the civil rights movement.

Tish joined NOW and made invaluable contributions in four areas:

1. Volunteerism
2. Displaced homemakers
3. Older women
4. Women's centers

Tish Sommers created and chaired our NOW committee on volunteerism. In those days, nearly all volunteers in U.S. nonprofit

Tish Sommers
Photograph courtesy of the Schlesinger
Library at Harvard University

organizations were women—except for male executives in the highest ranks. Tish awakened us to a new way of thinking. Women volunteers should not be exploited as free labor, competing with workers who would otherwise be paid for that labor. Under Tish's leadership, our 1971 NOW conference passed a resolution setting revolutionary new guidelines for volunteers: Women should volunteer only for "change-directed activities that lead to more active participation in the decision-making process." Instead of working as unpaid helpers to men at the top, we should use our "volunteer power" to overcome policies that are harmful to women.

Tish's resolutions provoked an angry backlash. Since our work for NOW was unpaid, was it hypocritical for NOW to go on record against volunteerism? In the biography she approved for *Feminists Who Changed America*, Tish did not include her work on volunteerism. I've never encountered a mention of volunteerism in her other biographies. But Tish was right! She led us to think hard about women's role in the nonprofit world.

When I was president of NOW LDEF, I organized a 1981 event called the Convocation on New Leadership in the Public Interest. Prominent figures in civic organizations discussed new ideas for public service. Part of my motive for the event was to win friends for feminism among civic leaders. Another motive was to dispel accusations that NOW opposed volunteer work. Our stress was on creating *change*, rather than *service* alone.

Today the situation has changed. As women move up in the *paid* workforce, fewer women donate time to menial volunteer tasks. And nearly all nonprofit organizations have elevated women to top decision-making positions.

In 1973, Tish Sommers created a NOW Task Force on Older Women. In 1974, she and her friend Laurie Shields took this further and founded the Alliance of Displaced Homemakers. They succeeded in passing state laws to assist homemakers in need of financial aid and job training after divorce. Maryland, Florida, and Massachusetts led the way in passing those laws.

Tish and Laurie set up a women's service center in Oakland, funded by the state of California, to train displaced homemakers and help them find jobs. It was one of the first women's centers in the country. They lobbied for similar havens across the country, to be funded by states and the federal government. Their project attracted the attention of Phyllis Schlafly, of anti-ERA fame. Did Schlafly's Eagle Forum newsletter (*The Phyllis Schlafly Report*) welcome these centers to assist homemakers? No. Schlafly urged her readers to write letters to Congress opposing them as "feminist indoctrination centers."

Tish campaigned for reevaluating the work of full-time homemakers in case of divorce. She stated that marriage is an economic partnership. A woman's work in homemaking and child-raising advances her husband's career; this should entitle her to an equal share of the marital assets. As NOW kept insisting, "Every mother is a working mother."

Tish led NOW's lobbying campaign, which Ellie Smeal later advanced, for Social Security reform to help homemakers. After divorce, unless a couple had been married more than twenty years, the wife could not collect benefits based on the Social Security taxes she and her ex-husband had paid for years. In 1979, feminists got the marriage duration reduced to ten years.

Building on the work of her NOW Task Force on Older Women, Tish Sommers also founded the Older Women's League (OWL) with Laurie Shields in 1980. They pointed out that two out of five older women in the United States were poor or near poor. OWL lobbied for financial security, health, and long-term quality of life.

I've often declared that "NOW is the trunk of the tree." OWL and the Alliance for Displaced Homemakers were among its many branches, along with WEAL, NWPC, NARAL, Legal Momentum, and other feminist organizations.

Although OWL's national organization disbanded in 2017, many of its 120 chapters are still active. The group's victories include a law that allows widows to continue using their spouse's health insurance. And the Retirement Equity Act of 1984 specifically benefits women workers. It allows women to begin vesting for pensions at the age of twenty-one, and it protects the retirement benefits of women who take maternity leave.

Tish Sommers looked at feminist issues with fresh eyes. Her insights produced results for millions of women.

21

SO MUCH UNFINISHED BUSINESS!

HAVE WE WON THE WOMEN'S REVOLUTION? Not yet. We've failed to enact the ERA and universal child care, and abortion rights have been taken away. Too many women in this country live in poverty. Women of color are especially disadvantaged. Nevertheless, we deserve to celebrate. Despite sad setbacks, feminists have changed the world enough to boast about a permanent, irreversible transformation. We've created opportunities and new respect that benefit women of all races, all classes, all sexual identities.

This was not a minor victory affecting only the middle-class. All women are better off because of what we did. After thousands of years, we've ended the age-old social contract that gave men absolute authority over women. Today's new contract, while far from perfect, would have thrilled suffrage leader Elizabeth Cady Stanton when she daydreamed in 1871 that a change in the contract would require "a social revolution greater than any political or religious revolution that the world has ever seen, because it goes deep down to the very foundations of society." (Schneir 2021, p. 257)

Our revolution is still incomplete. Women are still treated unfairly in our homes, our workplaces, our society. But now we have laws that help us, and governments must enforce the laws. Women play active roles in the world. We can participate. We can compete. It's fair to say

"Yes, we did it!" And since our revolution of the twentieth century, we've continued to build on its ideals with intersectional gains in the twenty-first century. The links between gender injustice and racial injustice are better understood than ever before. The #MeToo Movement has brought sexual harassment into public consciousness. And speaking of consciousness, *Ms.* magazine is still going strong.

IT'S ALL ABOUT POLITICS

Although the feminist movement has accomplished miracles, so many wrongs must still be set right! Future success depends upon one achievement above everything else: Somehow, we must wrest *control of government* from the patriarchy that rules politics. We must find ways to empower new leaders, both in governments and institutions large and small.

Our leaders can be women or men, as long as they believe in feminist ideals. Not all women are good guys. Humane, people-friendly policies will triumph only if we elect true feminists to public office.

If we win power in U.S. government, two goals that were within our grasp for a brief time can be readdressed and finalized: the Equal Rights Amendment and the reassurance of a woman's control over her own reproductive rights.

I'm confident the Equal Rights Amendment can be ratified in the near future. How will we do it? Congress might vote to reverse its 1972 appendage of a seven-year deadline for ratification by thirty-eight states. The ERA was the only amendment that failed to be ratified because of a congressional deadline (Suk 2020, p. 4) in contract to other amendments. The deadline for the ERA is not included in the constitutional text of the amendment itself. Activists say Congress has the power to remove the appended deadline.

Congress could recognize the fact that thirty-eight states have now voted for ratification. (True, a few states rescinded their ratification, but the Constitution does not permit rescission.) If we don't succeed with that scenario, we'll need to pass the ERA through Congress once again, and ratify it again in state legislatures. It can be done—if we win political power.

A recent poll says that 85 percent of the U.S. population supports the principles of the ERA, with its stipulation that "equality of rights under the law shall not be denied or abridged by the United States or by any state on account of sex." (Baker 2023, p. 12) When legislatures in failed states voted against ratification, our loss did not reflect popular opinion. We lost because a handful of politicians in those states were under the control of corporations—especially insurance companies that profit from discriminatory rates in health and auto policies. Phyllis Schlafly and other anti-ERA campaigners were merely a front for those lobbyists. We must organize to win control of the state legislatures that we lost in the past.

In reestablishing abortion rights, it's again, of course, a matter of political strength. We need power in Congress to reconstitute a favorable majority in the Supreme Court. Congress might revise the number of justices in the Court, or create new Court procedures. We'd also need power to reconstitute federal and state courts. Judicial realignment would guarantee other feminist rights with regard to contraception, sex education, same-sex marriage, trans rights, and reproductive justice.

When we fight for reproductive justice, we include maternal health and intersectional priorities. A woman's control over her body involves the right to determine her own gender(s), marry or divorce according to her own choices, obtain birth control, choose and access abortion if necessary, and give birth in safety.

How can feminists revolutionize our country's politics? All agree on the need to organize strategically. We must build coalitions with groups that share our goals. (Some of NOW's most important victories have been won through coalitions.) We must strengthen the resources of activists working to get out the vote. We must find better ways to utilize *communications.* Our opposition, the capitalist patriarchy, has grown increasingly sophisticated in manipulating control of what people are told and what they believe. Soon, with artificial intelligence, our opponents will own technology that spreads untruths more effectively than ever. We will never have as much money or power as our enemies, but we have talents and skills. Our talents can produce our own techniques for communicating truth to the public.

If you read NOW's "Statement of Purpose" and see that women held little political voice at all in 1966, you realize how much progress we've made. We've elected hundreds of women (most of them feminists) as governors, mayors, state legislators, school board officials, and to other positions of power. We still need to elect our first woman president (thirty-one other countries have a woman head of government or head of state today). I say we should rejoice in the near victory of Hillary Clinton, who never hesitated to proclaim feminist values.

You may be surprised to hear one excuse politicians used in the old days when they refused to support women for state and local government: They mansplained that it was because statehouses and city halls did not have enough bathrooms for women. (In D.C., there was no bathroom for women senators until 1992.) I once remarked that NOW's board of directors should include a plumber.

OVERCOME INEQUALITY AND STRENGTHEN UNIONS

It's a fact that most people living in poverty in the United States are women and their dependent children. Females still earn far less than males. In the early days, we wore a green button with the figure "59¢," reminding the public that women earned only fifty-nine cents for every dollar earned by men. Today, this ratio has improved somewhat. In 2022, women earned an average of 87 percent of what men earned, according to a Pew Research Center report on median hourly earnings. Sadly, the pay gap has hardly improved at all in recent years. In 2002, women earned 80 percent as much as men (Pew Research Center 2023). We advanced only two cents in twenty years. Even more outrageously, Black women in 2023 earned only sixty-seven cents for every dollar earned by white men (Noerdlinger 2023).

Our movement must work for progressive tax reforms that reduce inequality, and for antipoverty benefits such as the earned income tax credit, child welfare payments, more liberal food stamp payments, and student debt relief.

I believe we must fight for regulations that make it easier for workers to join labor unions. Nearly all economists agree that inequality in the United States began to climb when President Ronald Reagan vanquished the Professional Air Traffic Controllers Organization and fired their strikers. Reagan gave businesses a green light to crush attempts at unionization. Union power has declined sharply ever since. Today, federal and state governments have begun to respond somewhat more favorably to attempts at union recruitment. Union demographics are changing to include more women, people of color, and young people.

A promising recruitment aid for unions these days is the influx of women into service professions. Service employment now surpasses manufacturing employment. But many service jobs pay the lowest wages. We need to push for decent wages in service jobs.

In the early days, it's true that some unions opposed our feminist movement. Their leaders fought against moving women into "men's jobs." But most, though not all, unions have come around. Today, many union officers are women. We need to show the public that viable labor unions are essential for preserving the middle class. Since the decline of union power in this country, millions of workers have descended from comfortable security into poverty. Millions of working families can no longer count on two cars, a yearly vacation, and a college education for their children. Within corporations, the salary gap between top management and workers grew from a ratio of 20:1 in 1965 to 399:1 in 2021. As for CEOs, the outrageous ratio between CEOs and workers was 670:1 (Rushe 2022).

LET'S FIGHT FOR COMPARABLE WORTH

I want our feminist movement to keep supporting the principle of comparable worth, or pay equity, as it's called today. Too often, female-dominated jobs pay less than male positions requiring equivalent skill. Because of traditions in the job market, a child-care worker earns less than a janitor.

That tradition is prevalent across the entire world. Anthropologist Margaret Mead, after comparing several hundred tribes, concluded that when an activity is performed by women—pottery making, food gathering, planting, etc.—society values it less than the same activity performed by men.

Sociologist Rosabeth Kanter remarked in 2001, "If women ran this world, running the world would not be a valued occupation."

Jobs should be reevaluated to reward employees for comparable skills and responsibilities, regardless of sex. Twenty states have made a start by introducing comparable worth evaluation for civil service workers.

Comparable worth is rightly considered a feminist issue. When the state of California passed a comparable worth act in 1981, it specifically instructed salary reviewers to compare the work of women employees with work done by men, with a goal of "improving and equalizing" pay for women.

CHILD CARE ABOVE ALL ELSE

A top priority for our movement must be universal, high-quality child care. Women cannot achieve equality in the U.S. workplace until our nation provides the service that is taken for granted in most other countries. We rank at the bottom (behind Zimbabwe) in all aspects of child care. And we're the only developed country with no paid maternity leave. Bella Abzug lamented, "Without adequate, low-cost day care facilities, women are doomed to occupy low-paying, low-prestige jobs; without day care, women must remain economic serfs." (*Congressional Record—House* 1975, p. 8581)

President Obama stressed that early childhood education benefits children as well as their mothers. Research shows that early education promotes cognitive skills, attentiveness, motivation, sociability, and self-control.

The United States has come close several times to enacting legislation to improve child care. In 1971, NOW and sister organizations lobbied successfully for the Comprehensive Child Development Act to pass through Congress. But President Nixon vetoed the bill. His veto message, written by Pat Buchanan, called it "the most radical piece of legislation to emerge from the 92nd Congress" and said it would lead to "the Sovietization of American children." (*Congressional Digest*, 1972)

In 2022, a Democratic-led Congress featured a generous child-care program in its proposed package of infrastructure reforms. But in the bill that finally passed, we lost out to bridges and tunnels and other projects whose proponents had stronger lobbying clout than American families.

Instead of waiting for the federal government, numerous cities have introduced their own programs for preschool child care. Unfortunately, these programs can be decimated if budgets have to be tightened. My great-grandson attended a preschool in Brooklyn. But when conservative Eric Adams became mayor of New York City, he decreed that half the programs would be cut back, and a lottery decided which children could attend a preschool in their neighborhood.

Feminists need a program like the $700 billion federal child-care bill introduced by Senator Elizabeth Warren in 2021. It includes provision for paid parental leave, so fathers can share the responsibilities and rewards of raising children.

LET US NOT FORGET . . .

Much more unfinished business lies ahead for feminists today and tomorrow. Violence against women has greatly decreased since VAWA arrived, but it's still a reality. Rates of homicide against women are as high as ever. Maltreatment of incarcerated women must be ended. Can we resolve disagreement among feminist groups on laws concerning sex work and pornography? Can we prevent artificial intelligence from imposing huge job losses in the professions where women have begun to make headway?

As a high priority, we must change the way boys and men are indoctrinated in U.S. society. This calls for vast reforms in education and media. Our culture must reprogram mothers, as well as fathers, to raise nonsexist boys. We need new models for manly behavior. In fact, we need new models for *human* behavior, unrestricted by labels of male or female.

Binary modeling has blocked us from reaching our full potential. We've begun to work out answers to a new question raised by the feminist revolution: What does it mean to be male or female? Or a nonbinary person? We must find ways to disentangle today's counterproductive conflicts between straight and LGBTQ feminists. Society must ensure fairness and respect for everyone.

Another target for our feminist revolution might be termed *connectedness*. We should advocate for greater reliance on women's ways of connecting. This means moving away from patriarchal, androcentric models of human behavior and mental health. Society must learn to value a tend and befriend response to stressful situations, rather than fight or flight. Psychiatrist Jean Baker Miller says supportive relationships are a central human necessity (Miller 1976). Human beings would benefit from developing higher amounts of an essential hormone, oxytocin, which is increased when there's bonding, trust, and conflict resolution.

Technological advances in birth and fertility have presented new opportunities and new questions for feminists. Will men be less essential for women if they're less needed for sperm or sexual fulfillment? Will women be less essential if embryos are grown in artificial wombs?

ARTS, RELIGION, SPORTS

The feminist movement has created amazing progress for women in the arts since 1966. But, we still have far to go. Today women benefit from innovations in the process of selection. For instance, major orchestras place a screen in front of auditioning musicians to avoid gender bias. And some museums follow long-overdue affirmative action in choosing works of art. Art historians are now bringing "lost" works by women into public awareness.

The multifaceted world of religion is definitely unfinished business for the feminist movement. The descriptive word today is *polarization*. Since 1966, most religions have overturned previous barriers against women's appointment as pastors and executives. Some religions are leading the way as public champions of gender justice. On the other hand, extremely orthodox religions have doubled down in bias. Suppression of women remains a basic tenet of their doctrines and policies. In 2023, the Southern Baptists convention voted to expel churches (some of them large and prominent) that employ women pastors, specifying "only men as any kind of pastor or elder as qualified by Scripture." (Graham & Dias 2023)

In sports, Title IX has promoted much greater participation for women and girls. The Women's Sports Foundation, which was founded by tennis star Billie Jean King in 1974, reports that high schools today offer girls three million more sports opportunities than they offered before Title IX. More than 44 percent of all college athletes are women, compared to only 15 percent before Title IX (Tumin 2022). Nevertheless, school budgets still tilt heavily to sports dominated by males. In college sports, the Women's Sports Foundation says men still have nearly 60,000 more opportunities than women (Tumin 2022). There's a new dilemma in sports: conflicting views on the role of transgender women.

THE WORLD NEEDS YOU

This book has focused on women in the United States, where the modern feminist revolution came to life in 1966. Since then, feminists have created change in every land, everywhere. Some countries have made even more progress than the United States. But women still face so much unfinished business in so many parts of the world! Although women comprise half of the world's population, they still do two-thirds of the world's work. We earn only a fraction of the world's income, and we possess only a tiny share of its property.

We can rejoice that much has changed in a very short time, after many thousand years of injustice. How can we maintain the momentum that began in October 1966? Since you're reading this book, I hope it's an expression of your interest. I hope we might count on you to carry on the progress set in motion by the feminists you've read about here. There's much more work to be done, and we depend on you. Thank you!

APPENDIX

SCAN OF INVITATION TO FIRST PRESS CONFERENCE

CARL BYOIR & ASSOCIATES, INC.
800 SECOND AVENUE
NEW YORK 17, N.Y.
—
YUkon 6-6100

MURIEL FOX ARONSON
VICE PRESIDENT

Dear Editor:

Through the years I've used a lot of adjectives to describe press conferences, but this is the first time I'd presume to use the word "historic." Here's hoping you'll agree on November 21 that history has indeed been made.

You are cordially invited to a press conference Monday morning, November 21, at 10:30 a.m. in the home of Mrs. Betty Friedan at 1 West 72nd Street, New York City. Apartment 55.

At that time the men and women heading a new action organization, NOW, will reveal their immediate targets and tactics toward the NOW goal of "full equality for all women in America . . . in truly equal partnership with men."

A story about the membership and purposes of NOW is enclosed. The story to be released on November 21 will unveil specific projects and plans of action.

The officers and board of NOW look forward to answering your questions on November 21. We hope you'll have reason to tell your grandchildren one day, "Yes, I was there when it all started."

Very best wishes,

Muriel Fox

P.S. NOW has no connection to any Byoir clients. I'm helping with the publicity because I believe in NOW's goals.

SCAN OF FIRST PRESS RELEASE

This press release launched the modern Women's Movement.
Best Wishes from
Both of Us —
Betty Friedan
Muriel Fox

From: NOW
   Suite 500, 1629 K Street, N. W.
   Washington, D. C. 20006

FOR IMMEDIATE RELEASE

     Press Contacts: Muriel Fox, 212-986-6110
             Betty Friedan, 212-724-7711

More than 300 men and women have formed a new action organization called National Organization for Women (NOW), to work for "true equality for all women in America" and "a fully equal partnership of the sexes, as part of the world-wide revolution of himan rights."

Meeting in Washington the weekend of October 29, NOW members elected educator Dr. Kathryn Clarenbach chairman of the board, and author Betty Friedan president. Dr. Clarenbach is Director of Continuing Education at the University of Wisconsin and Chairman of the Wisconsin Governor's Commission on the Status of Women. Mrs. Friedan is a writer, lecturer and social critic, author of the best-selling "The Feminine Mystique."

The conference named Aileen Hernandez, former Senior Commissioner of the Equal Employment Opportunity Commission, as executive vice president, subject to her consent.

The conference elected Dr. Anna Arnold Hedgeman of New York City, author and special events coordinator of the Commission on religion and race of the National Council of Churches as temporary acting executive vice president. Richard Graham, director of the National Teacher Corps and former Equal Employment Opportunity Commissioner, was elected vice president. Secretary-treasurer is Caroline Davis, Director of the Women's Department of the United Auto Workers, AFL-CIO, who served with the President's Commission on the Status of Women.

NOW's 300 charter members include men and women of all religious and ethnic and economic groups, a number of married couples, Catholic nuns, and an age range

varying from a student leader just out of her teens to a veteran of the battle to win the

vote for women half a century ago. Most members are in the 25-to-45 age range.

The Statement of Purpose of the new organization says, "There is no civil

rights movement to speak for women, as there has been for Negroes and other victims

of discrimination."

It pledges aid for all women, factory workers as well as executives, "to break

through the silken curtain of prejudice and discrimination against women in

government, industry, the professions, the churches, the political parties, the

judiciary, the labor unions, in education, science, medicine, law, religion and every

other field of importance in American society."

NOW has vowed to press for enforcement of laws which prohibit discrimination

on the basis of sex, especially Title VII of the Civil Rights Act of 1964, charging that

"Although nearly one-third of the cases brought before the Equal Employment

Opportunity Commission during its first year dealt with sex discrimination and the

proportion is increasing dramatically, the Commission has not made clear its

intention to enforce the law with the same seriousness on behalf of women as of other

victims of discrimination."

The statement rejects "the current assumptions that a man must carry the sole

burden of supporting himself, his wife and family, and that a woman is automatically

entitled to lifelong support by a man upon her marriage . . . a true partnership

between the sexes demands an equitable sharing of the responsibilities of home and

children and of the economic burdens of their support." NOW states it will work for

re-examination of marriage and divorce laws which "discriminate against both men and women alike" and cause "much unnecessary hostility between the sexes."

NOW calls for a nationwide network of child-care centers and other social innovations to enable more women to work while raising a family, as well as national retraining programs for women who join the work force after their children have grown.

It attacks "the traditional assumption that a woman has to choose between marriage and motherhood on the one hand and serious participation in industry or the professions on the other."

"We do not accept," says the statement, "the token appointment of a few women to high-level positions in government and industry as a substitute for a serious continuing effort to recruit and advance women according to their individual abilities." In the 1950's and '60's, it continues, the position of American women has been "declining to an alarming degree." It sees working women "increasingly concentrated on the bottom of the job ladder."

"Although 46.4 per cent of all American women between the ages of 18 and 65 now work outside of the home, the overwhelming majority--75 per cent--are in routine clerical, sales or factory jobs; or they are household workers, cleaning women, hospital attendants."

NOW laments lack of implementation of "the excellent reports of the President's Commission on the Status of Women and of the State Commission . . . Such Commissions have power only to advise. They have no power to enforce their recommendations; nor have they the freedom to organize American women and men to press for action on them."

It urges women to work for equality "not in pleas for special privilege, nor in enmity toward men, who are also victims of the current half-equality between the sexes, but in self-respecting partnership with men. "

Political action is pledged well beyond today's "separate-and-not-equal ladies auxiliaries in the political parties. " NOW promises to mobilize ballot power to prevent election or appointment of officials who betray or ignor" women's drive for equality.

Elected to the NOW board of directors were Collen Boland of Chicago, leader of the Airline Stewardesses' fight against forced retirement at marriage or at age 32 (the NOW Board passed a resolution supporting the Stewardesses' cause under the Title VII prohibition against sex discrimination); Professor Carl Degler, Chairman of the Department of History at Vassar College; Dr. Elizabeth Drews, psychologist and professor of education at Portland State College in Oregon; Jane Hart, wife of the Senator from Michigan, mother of 8 children, and professional pilot who campaigned for admission of women into the NASA astronauts program; Reverend Dean Lewis, Secretary of the Office of Social Education and Evangelism, United Presbyterian Church in the U.S.A.; Betty Furness, CBS network commentator and former movie star; Sister Mary Joel Read, Chairman of the Department of History of Alverno College, Milwaukee; Sister Mary Austin Doherty, Chicago psychologist, and author; Dorothy Haener, assistant director of the United Auto Workers Women's Department; Professor Alice S. Rossi, sociologist, of the Committee on Human Development and the National Opinion Research Center of the University of Chicago; Charlotte Roe, National Affairs Project Director for the United States Youth Council; Muriel Fox of New York City, vice president of Carl Byoir and Associates, Inc.,;

Inka O'Hanrahan, biologist, Public Affairs Chairman of the Soroptomist Federation

of the Americas, and vice-chairman of the California Governor's Commission on the

Status of Women; Dr. Patricia Plante, first woman to head a Jesuit college, the Dean

of Thomas More College of Fordham University, New York City; Phineas Indritz,

attorney, Government Operations Committee, U. S. House of Representatives; Dr.

Vera Schletzer, head of the Program for Continuing Education for Women at the

University of Minnesota; Inez Cassiano, administrator in Puerto Rican community

projects and poverty projects in New York City; Edna Schwartz of St. Paul, Minnesota,

office manager, National Electrical Contractors Association and first woman member

of the Minnesota Civil Service Commission; Catherine Conroy, midwest regional

representative, Communications Workers of America; Herbert Wright, New York

City attorney, Director of the Community Resources Corporation; Grace Olivarez, a

leader of the poverty program and of the Mexican-American community in the

southwest; Eva Purvis, head of the women's division of the Indiana AFL-CIO and a

member of the Governor's Commission on the Status of Women; Dr. Gretchen Squires,

a practicing physician in Florida, and Mary Finnan, leader of the Nurses Association.

-0-

ACKNOWLEDGMENTS

THIS BOOK WAS MADE POSSIBLE by hundreds of thousands of women (and some men) who *lived* our second-wave feminist movement. My files contain letters, clippings, and scraps of paper with information about their courageous struggles and achievements.

Until the spring of 2022, I disregarded entreaties from family and feminist friends to write a book about my second-wave experiences. (My son, Eric, pressed me strenuously through the years.) In addition to being busy with other activities, I knew that my scraps of paper did not have academic citations. I recommended books like Gail Collins's informative *When Everything Changed.*

I changed my mind a year ago because I was furious. The women's movement had lost hard-won gains. And I encountered educated young people who said they'd never heard of Betty Friedan. Some had never heard of NOW. How could Americans not know how we changed their lives? I urgently wanted to spread the word about pioneers whom history seemed to be forgetting—great heroes like Mary Eastwood, Ann Scott, Phineas Indritz, Holly Knox, and Pat Reuss. Happily, Pauli Murray and Heather Booth are acclaimed in recent documentaries about their lives, but other pioneers must be recognized, too. I narrowed my number down to twenty-nine women, plus Phineas. I especially wanted their stories to inspire students in colleges and high schools.

My first draft of this book featured long sections on each of those thirty people, including birth and death dates, education, and referral to their archives. But sagacious agent Alice Martell advised me to condense the biographical information, incorporating their stories into my narrative about the movement. (I hope *you* will take time to research more intensively the individual heroes who interest you the most.)

Once I'd started writing this book about our revolution, I began to acknowledge my own role in changing the world. Although my public relations training had taught me to remain in the background, I decided to describe my contributions without false modesty. The women's movement teaches this!

I take some credit for one valuable resource that helped me compile this book. I was senior editor of *Feminists Who Changed America,* the University of Illinois book edited by the late Barbara Love. It's available through Kindle and through the VFA website. Barbara deserves accolades for her ten-year labors in compiling the book, with biographies of 2,200 U.S. feminist leaders. (Yes, all were leaders, who produced trailblazing results in their community or organization or profession.) Barbara thanked me publicly for nagging her to plow ahead at times when the job seemed too arduous. Veteran Feminists of America recruited feminists to round up hundreds of biographies, and Barbara insisted on fact-checking with all living subjects for approval of their stories. I proofread every entry.

Veteran Feminists of America was my other major resource for this book. VFA, whose members are pioneers of the modern women's movement, is the foremost source of information about this country's second-wave feminism for historians, educators, writers, and civic leaders. It seeks to educate and motivate young people through the example of feminist victories and sacrifices. I frequently consulted VFA's Pioneer Histories Project and its more than six hundred oral histories.

Once I'd decided to write this book, my advanced age (then ninety-four) pressured me to finish promptly. I worked on the book day and night, forgoing most leisure activities. I fact-checked carefully with the few veterans who are still alive, and with many other sources.

My daughter, Lisa Aronson Fontes, Ph.D., has read every word and helped me tremendously. Lisa has written four books and numerous articles on interpersonal violence and culture. A progressive, she challenged me often. I could not have produced this book without her.

I also showed the chapters to Marjorie Miller, Ph.D., former chair of the Philosophy Department at Purchase College, State University of New York. Marjorie made perceptive suggestions.

I especially acknowledge the resourcefulness of my author friend Alix Kates Shulman, who suggested that this book would be a good match for New Village Press. When we learned more about each other, NVP director Lynne Elizabeth and I responded enthusiastically to Alix's suggestion.

I did spend two years writing a novel about our movement, after my retirement from Carl Byoir. The title was "Penny and Fran." A lightly disguised roman à clef, it depicted characters based on real-life figures in the founding of NOW. Penny was an executive much like me. Fran was my unsinkable secretary, a survivor of unfair abuses in the business world. The Betty Friedan character was named Cynthia, and an unkind male chauvinist in the book used the expression "ugly as Cyn." I had dreams of selling my novel to the movies. But alas, two prominent editors gave me the same evaluation: "You write well, but this isn't best-selling fiction. The plot isn't compelling, and the characters aren't full-bodied." Sadly, I retired the manuscript to my storage closet. I'm not a good writer of fiction. My specialty has always been journalistic nonfiction.

After my disappointment with fiction, I decided to become a resource for *other* people's books. I've organized numerous feminist events and written articles. I chair the board of Veteran Feminists of America. Thanks to VFA president Eleanor Pam, VFA remains strong and meaningful. We've been supported by my good friend Marcy Syms, whose devoted crusades include ratification of the Equal Rights Amendment. With Marcy's encouragement, the Sy Syms Foundation has made it possible for VFA's Pioneer Histories Project to produce hundreds of oral histories that will educate and inspire people for generations to come. Kathy Rand and Mary Jean Collins, two movement veterans from the early days, supervise the project astutely. We've been fortunate to have expert assistance from Kristina Joukhadar and Jodi Moran.

If any of my readers plan to write their own book, with photographs, they should learn from my experience that it's an arduous task. Many photos in my files failed to meet the requirements for clarity and high resolution. I spent weeks researching archives for pictures of the heroic women I salute in this book. Kristina Joukhadar was invaluable in assembling and scanning photos, as was photo editor Megan Waldau Chang.

I offer special thanks to the talented feminist photographer Dori Jacobson-Wenzel, a member of VFA's board of directors. Dori donated some of the most memorable portraits in this book. Other wonderful photos came from Jo Freeman, whose activism I salute in the book, and from Diana Henry. Lois Herr, a hero of the AT&T campaigns, donated photos.

I also appreciate the assistance of NOW's inspiring president, Christian Nunes, and of Laura Gross, who was prompt and efficient in researching feminist history.

Alix Shulman insists that the radical feminist side of the movement, with special emphasis on consciousness-raising, contributed even more to changing the world than our NOW side. I have a different viewpoint. But we do concur in our gratitude to *all* the activists who worked tirelessly to create our feminist revolution. We agree, happily and proudly, that WE DID IT ALL TOGETHER!

I say in the book that I didn't have optional time to spend with girlfriends during my hardest-working years. However, I've made up for that since retiring. In late-adult life I've finally been able to enjoy the blessing that has sustained women through the centuries: the sisterhood of women. Yes, it is powerful! Wise, caring women help me feel less sad about setbacks, and keep me informed about opportunities. I am grateful for the support of such inspiring friends as Gloria Steinem, Heather Booth, Georgette Bennett, Letty Cottin Pogrebin, Lynn Schafran, Gail Collins, Lynn Povich, Lynn Sherr, Nancy Kaufman, Katha Pollitt, Joyce Antler, Gina Gantz, Marilyn Webb, Lilly Rivlin, Blu Greenberg, and Jurate Kazickas. I've had dinner at our home, Kendal on Hudson, with one group of comrades every Thursday night for the past eight years: Annette and Eleanor Leyden, Roberta Poupon, Barbara Rachlin, Mary Alice Walker, Gisa Indenbaum. Roberta comes to my aid promptly whenever I have a computer problem.

In the book I mention that life in this senior community of Kendal on Hudson has given me the impetus for remaining active and relevant in my tenth decade of life. It has also given me the security of feeling "taken care of." Ellen Ottstadt and Briana Giuliano at Kendal make our active and secure lifestyle possible. Briana also facilitated this book by scanning photos you see here. I received invaluable information technology assistance from Anthony Bradford.

I'm proud and grateful that my adult progeny, without exception, are working to create a better world. They are Eric Aronson, Lisa Aronson Fontes, and AnaLua, Marlena, and Gabriel Fontes. My very young great-grandchildren, Ignacio and Oceana Gonzales Fontes, share a family heritage that helps me feel confident optimism for the future.

REFERENCES

Baker, Carrie N. "ERA Centennial Convention in Seneca Falls: Intergenerational, Diverse and Determined." *Ms.,* July 26, 2023.

Barrer, Myra E., ed. *Journal of Reprints of Documents Affecting Women,* vol. 1-1. Washington, D.C.: Today Publications, 1976.

Blackstone, William. *Commentaries on the Laws of England.* Oxford: Clarendon Press, 1765.

Brooks, David. "The Crisis of Men and Boys." *New York Times,* September 30, 2022.

Carabillo, Toni, Judith Meuli, and June Bundy Csida. *Feminist Chronicles 1953–1993.* Los Angeles: Women's Graphics, 1993.

Clark, Heather. *Red Comet: The Short Life and Blazing Art of Sylvia Plath.* New York: Alfred A. Knopf, 2020.

Cohen, Marcia. *The Sisterhood.* New York: Fawcett Columbine, 1988.

Collins, Gail. *When Everything Changed.* New York: Little, Brown, 2009.

Combahee River Collective. "Combahee River Collective Statement." https://www.blackpast.org/african-american=history/combahee-river-collective-statement-1977.

Congressional Digest. May 1972, Vol. 51, No. 5, pp. 138–9

Congressional Record—House. June 20, 1966.

Congressional Record—House. March 25, 1975.

Davis, Flora. *Moving the Mountain.* New York: Simon & Schuster, 1991.

Degler, Carl N. "American Women in Social and Political Affairs—Change and Challenge." Paper presented at Southern Methodist University, Dallas, Texas, January 27, 1966.

Dominus, Susan. "A Vicious Cycle." *New York Times Magazine,* February 5, 2023.

Evans, Sara. *Born for Liberty.* New York: Free Press, 1991.

Faludi, Susan. "Death of a Revolutionary." *The New Yorker,* April 15, 2013.

Family Law Quarterly 4, no. 1 (March 1970): 6–12.

Fox, Muriel. Interview by Jacqueline Michot Ceballos, 1991. Tully-Crenshaw Feminist Oral History Project Records, Schlesinger Library, Harvard.

Franks, Lucinda. "Dissension Among Feminists: The Rift Widens." *New York Times,* August 29, 1975.

Friedan, Betty. *The Feminine Mystique.* New York: W. W. Norton, 1963.

———. "How NOW Began." NOW document, 1967.

Friedan, Betty. *The Second Stage.* New York: Summit Books, 1981.

———. *Life So Far.* New York: Simon & Schuster, 2000.

Graham, Ruth, and Elizabeth Dias. "Southern Baptists Vote to Further Expand Restrictions on Women as Leaders." *New York Times,* June 14, 2023.

Green, Penelope, "Barbara Love, Who Fought for Lesbians to Have a Voice, Dies at 85." *New York Times,* December 6, 2022.

Guy-Sheftall, Beverly, "History Is Incomplete Without Black Women." *Ms.,* July 24, 2023.

Hammel, Lisa. "The Grandmother of Women's Liberation." *New York Times,* November 19, 1971.

Hathaway, William Maine. Testimony to Labor Subcommittee of the House of Representatives, September 1965.

Heilbrun, Carolyn. *The Education of a Woman: The Life of Gloria Steinem.* New York: Dial Press, 1996.

Hill, Latoya. "Racial Disparities in Maternal and Infant Health." Kaiser Family Foundation, November 1, 2022.

Hole, Judith, and Ellen Levine. *Rebirth of Feminism.* New York: Quadrangle Books, 1971.

Jackson, Harold. "Martha Griffiths." *Guardian,* April 28, 2003.

Lear, Martha Weinman. "The Second Feminist Wave." *New York Times Magazine,* March 10, 1968.

Levine, Bettijane. "The Tireless Warrior." *Los Angeles Times,* April 28, 1993.

Liptak, Adam. "Another Factor Said to Sway Judges to Rule for Women's Rights: A Daughter." *New York Times,* June 16, 2014.

Lithwick, Dahlia. *Lady Justice.* New York: Penguin, 2022.

Love, Barbara J. *Feminists Who Changed America.* Urbana: University of Illinois Press, 2006.

Miller, Jean Baker. *Toward a New Psychology of Women.* Boston: Beacon Press, 1976.

Millett, Kate. "Token Learning: A Study of Women's Higher Education in America." New York: National Organization for Women, 1968.

Morgan, Kendall K. "What Is Reproductive Justice?" *Web*MD, August 4, 2022. https://www.webmd.com/women/reproductive-justice-what-is-it.

Mosher, Steven. "Abortion for All: How the International Planned Parenthood Federation Promotes Abortion Around the World." Lifeissues.net, December 28, 2001. https://www.lifeissues.net/writers/mos/pri_03abortionforall1.html.

Murray, Pauli, and Mary O. Eastwood. "Jane Crow and the Law: Sex Discrimination and Title VII." *The George Washington Law Review,* December 1965.

National Women's Hall of Fame. "Martha Wright Griffiths." https://www.womenofthehall.org/inductee/martha-wright-griffiths/.

Noerdlinger, Rachel. "Why Black Women Must Work Harder: Overcoming Sexism, Racism and Still Succeeding." Women's eNews, July 26, 2023.

NOW Bill of Rights for Women. November 1967.

O'Connell, Pat. "When Women Reach the Top." *Redbook,* November–December 1983.

Paterson, Judith. *Be Somebody: A Biography of Marguerite Rawalt.* Austin, TX: Eakin Press, 1986.

Peterson, Bill. "NOW's Time of Choice." *Washington Post,* July 14, 1985.

Pew Research Center. "The Enduring Grip of the Gender Gap." March 1, 2023.

Randolph, Sherie. *Florynce "Flo" Kennedy: The Life of a Radical Black Feminist.* Chapel Hill: University of North Carolina Press, 2015.

Redstockings. *Feminist Revolution.* New York: Random House, 1978.

Roberts, Sam. "Roxcy Bolton: Feminist Crusader for Equality, Including in Naming Hurricanes, Dies at 90." *New York Times,* May 21, 2017.

———. "Sophie Freud, Critic of Her Grandfather's Gospel, Dies at 97." *New York Times,* June 3, 2022.

Rosenberg, Rosalind. *Jane Crow: The Life of Pauli Murray.* New York: Oxford University Press, 2017.

Rushe, Dominic. "Wage Gap Between CEOs and U.S. Workers Jumped to 670-to-1 Last Year, Study Finds." *Guardian,* June 7, 2022.

Sabin, Janice A. "How We Fail Black Patients in Pain." *Association of American Medical Colleges Newsletter,* January 6, 2020.

Sanday, Peggy. "The Burden of Proof." *Hackensack (NJ) Sunday Record,* February 7, 1993.

Sandler, Bernice Resnick, Lisa A. Silverberg, and Roberta M. Hall. "Chilly Classroom Climate: A Guide to Improve the Education of Women." Washington, D.C.: National Association of Women in Education, 1982.

Schneir, Miriam. *Before Feminism: The History of an Idea Without a Name.* Montclair, NJ: Mews Books, 2021.

Seering, Lauryn. "Flo Kennedy." Freedom from Religion Foundation.

Self, Robert O. *All in the Family: The Realignment of American Democracy Since the 1960s.* New York: Hill and Wang, 2012.

Shahalimi, Nahid. "Afghan Women Reflect on the Anniversary of the U.S. Withdrawal." *New York Times,* August 13, 2022.

Shanahan, Eileen. "Women's Group Vows Poverty Fight." *New York Times,* February 20, 1973.

Shteir, Rachel. *Betty Friedan: Magnificent Disrupter.* New Haven: Yale University Press, 2023.

Smeal, Eleanor, and Gloria Steinem. "Steinem and Smeal: Why 'Mrs. America' Is Bad for American Women." *Los Angeles Times,* July 30, 2020.

South Florida Sun Sentinel, December 8, 1994.

Steinem, Gloria. Gloria Steinem Papers, Sophia Smith Library, Smith College, Northampton, Massachusetts.

Suk, Julie C. *We the Women: The Unstoppable Mothers of the Equal Rights Amendment.* New York: Skyhorse Publishing, 2020.

Tumin, Remy. "Despite Critics, Title IX Proves Durable and Far-Reaching." *New York Times,* June 26, 2022.

Turk, Katherine. The Women of NOW: How Feminists Built an Organization That Transformed America. New York: Farrar, Straus and Giroux, 2023.

U.S. Department of Veterans Affairs. Sexual Assault: Females—PTSD: National Center for PTSD. https://www.ptsd.va.gov/understand/types/sexual_trauma_female.asp.

U.S. Equal Employment Opportunity Commission. https://www.eeoc.gov/meetings /meeting-january-14-2015-workplace-harassment/graves.

Wall Street Journal, June 22, 1965

Witchel, Alex. "AT HOME WITH—Betty Friedan; Beyond Mystique, A Frank Memoir." *New York Times,* May 11, 2000.

"Who Was Your Mentor?" *Cosmopolitan,* August 1979.

"Women Workers Get Until June to Wed; Kansas City Power Company Says That After That Date They May Not Marry and Keep Jobs." *New York Times,* December 29, 1932.

Women's Forum Inc. New York 1974–2009: A Brief History Celebrating Our 35th Anniversary. New York: Women's Forum Incorporated, 2009.

INDEX